SOCIOLOGICAL REVIEW

CW00540539

Picturing Power: Visual Depiction and Social Relations

The Sociological Review

Managing Editors: John Eggleston, Ronald Frankenberg,
Gordon Fyfe

University of Keele

SOCIOLOGICAL REVIEW MONOGRAPH 35

PICTURING POWER: VISUAL DEPICTION AND SOCIAL RELATIONS

Edited by Gordon Fyfe and John Law

Routledge
London and New York

First published in 1988 by
Routledge
11 New Fetter Lane, London EC4P 4EE

Set in Times
by Hope Services, Abingdon
and printed in Great Britain
by Butler & Tanner Ltd., Frome

British Library Cataloguing in Publication Data

Picturing power: visual depiction and social
  relations. — (Sociological review monographs; 35)
  1. Visual arts. Sociological perspectives
  I. Fyfe, Gordon   II. Law, John, 1946–
  306.'47

0–415–03144–3

Contents

List of Illustrations

List of Illustrations

Chapter 4

Gordon Fyfe, Art and Its Objects: William Ivins and the Reproduction of Art

Chapter 5

Belinda Loftus, Northern Ireland 1968–1988: Enter an Art Historian in Search of a Useful Theory

Chapter 8

Michael Lynch and Samuel Y. Edgerton Jr, Aesthetics and Digital Image Processing: Representational Craft in Contemporary Astronomy

Chapter 9

Geof Bowker, Pictures from the Subsoil, 1939

Contributors

Stephen Bann read history at Cambridge, and completed a Ph.D. on historiography under Herbert Butterfield in 1967, before joining the staff of the University of Kent, where he is presently Reader in Modern Cultural Studies. He has published widely on the history and theory of modern art. His work on the representation of history in the nineteenth century resulted in the writing of *The Clothing of Clio* (Cambridge University Press, 1984), and he is compiling a collection of more recently published essays which extend the inquiry back into the eighteenth and forward into the twentieth centuries.

Geof Bowker works at le Centre de Sociologie de l'Innovation, Ecole Nationale Supcrieure des Mines de Paris. His doctorate was on the relation between the social and scientific perceptions of time. He maintains this interest, but is currently working on the history of the Schlumberger geophysical company, and the introduction of research laboratories into industry, and the history of the artificial intelligence language, LISP.

Robert Bud is Deputy head of Physical Sciences at the Science Museum, and is responsible for coordinating research within collections management. Trained as an historian and sociologist of science at the University of Pennsylvania, he has worked on the development of chemistry, and is co-author of *Science versus Practice: Chemistry in Victorian Britain* (Manchester University Press, 1984) and *Chemistry in America 1876–1976: Historical Indicators* (Reidel, 1988). He is currently studying the progressive transformation of biotechnology in the twentieth century and the implications of our knowledge of curatorial policy, using the sociology of translation where appropriate.

Philip R.D. Corrigan is a Professor and was Chairperson in the Department of Sociology in Education, Ontario Institute for Studies in Education, Toronto, Ontario, Canada; he was previously Lecturer, Department of Sociology of Education, Institute of Education, London, 1980–3, and Head, Cultural Studies Unit, London College of Printing, 1978–9. A librarian, and library-studies lecturer, from 1960–71, he obtained his BA and Ph.D. from the University of Durham, England, and has an MA in Film and Television Studies (CNAA/Polytechnic of Central London). He writes: ' "Innocent Stupidities" quotes Guy Davenport's "Innocent Stupidity" from his essay "Ernst Mach Max Ernst" in *The Geography of the Imagination* and like him, it *is* my sense that I am always telling a story.'

Samuel Edgerton Jr. is Professor of the History of Art at Williams College, Williamstown in Massachussetts. He is the author of numerous articles on the history of scientific depiction, *The Renaissance Rediscovery of Linear Perspective* (Harper & Row (1976) and *Pictures and Punishment: Art and Criminal Prosecution during the Florentine Renaissance* (Cornell), 1985. He is currently working with Michael Lynch on the aesthetics of scientific imaging in astronomy.

Gordon Fyfe graduated from the University of Leicester in Social Sciences in 1967. He has been a Lecturer in Sociology at the University of Keele since 1971. He has undertaken extensive research on engraving, the social character of art markets, and the structure of gallery and museum displays in relation to state formation. This work has been published in a range of papers, and is currently being written up in book form.

Bruno Latour is Associate Professor at the Centre de Sociologie de l'Innovation at the Ecole Nationale Superieure des Mines de Paris, and is currently working on the anthropology of French science and technology and the iconography of the Assumption of the Virgin Mary. He is the author (jointly with Steve Woolgar) of *Laboratory Life: the Construction of Scientific Facts* (Princeton, 1986), *Science In Action: How to Follow Scientists and Engineers Through Society* (Open University Press, 1986) and *War and Peace Among the Microbes* (Harvard, 1988). His other work includes studies of the semiotics of scientific texts (jointly with Françoise Bastide) and of scientific images (*Les Vues de l'Esprit*, special issue of *Culture Technique*, 1985).

John Law is Reader in Sociology and Director of the Unit for Technology Analysis at the University of Keele. He has written widely in the sociology of science and technology, and is currently working on depictions of the science and politics of the acid rain debate (jointly with John Whittaker), on the sociotechnical development of a major aircraft project, and the sociology of power and control, particularly as this relates to machines and devices. His publications include *Science for Social Scientists* (jointly with Peter Lodge), and he is editor of *Power Action and Belief: a New Sociology of Knowledge?* and joint editor of *Mapping the Dynamics of Science and Technology: the Sociology of Science in the Real World*.

Belinda Loftus holds a BA Hons (Cantab) in Fine Art and a Ph.D. (Keele) in Sociology. She has worked in the Paul Mellon Foundation for British Art and the Art Department of the Imperial War Museum, as well as freelancing as an art critic and exhibition organiser. She is currently Arts Officer for Down District Council. Her publications include works on war posters and Irish trades union banners, and she is completing a book on traditions of political imagery in Northern Ireland.

Michael Lynch is Assistant Professor of Sociology at Boston University and is currently working on visualisation in science. He received his Ph.D. from the University of California at Irvine in 1979, and subsequently carried out post-doctoral research at the University of Toronto and at UCLA before taking his present position. In addition to writings on social studies of science, he has recently published articles on clinical diagnosis in neurology and court testimony. His publications include *Art and Artefact in Laboratory Science* (Routledge and Kegan Paul, 1985).

John Whittaker, who died tragically on August 17th, 1988, was a Lecturer in Sociology at the University of Keele from 1967 until the time of his death. Trained as a social psychologist he undertook extensive research on perceptions of social stratification. More recently he had worked on a major project on methods for summarising and depicting scientific research. He was the author of an outstandingly innovative series of computer programmes for analysing the contents of scientific literature.

Introduction: on the invisibility of the visual

Gordon Fyfe and John Law

A depiction is never just an illustration. It is the material representation, the apparently stabilised product of a process of work. And it is the site for the construction and depiction of social difference. To understand a visualisation is thus to inquire into its provenance and into the social work that it does. It is to note its principles of exclusion and inclusion, to detect the roles that it makes available, to understand the way in which they are distributed, and to decode the hierarchies and differences that it naturalises. And it is also to analyse the ways in which authorship is constructed or concealed and the sense of audience is realised.

Depictions mark the point where a process of production gives way to a range of effects. Both the character of production and the effects upon an audience are historically contingent. Indeed, to use such a term as 'audience' is already to conceal important differences, to run the danger of generalising from spectators whose subjectivity is formed through our own art reproductions, exhibitions and scientific depictions. Thus for most purposes the relationship between a patron of fine art and the painter cannot helpfully be compared with what passes between the museum curator and his or her exhibition on the one hand, and the visitor to the museum on the other. And neither can be treated as models for the interaction between the pavement artist and the pedestrian, or the astronomer and the reader of a popular scientific article. The argument, then, is that both the processes that lead to the creation of depictions, and the way in which they are subsequently used, have to be studied in their historical specificity.

Thus there is a real sense in which a sociology of visual depiction is an artificial creation: it groups heterogeneous processes and social contexts together because they happen to have something to do with the visual. Given the danger of such homogenisation, what is to be said in favour of focusing on the character and role of visual depiction in social life? The answer is that the visual has

1

been deleted from most sociologies – though not, it should be noted, anthropologies – to an extraordinary extent. To be sure, it is difficult to write about patron–client relations in the fine arts without talking about the paintings that were actually produced. However, if the sociology of art text bereft of pictures is hardly an unusual feature on the shelves of bookshops, it is also true that the sociology of the fine arts is marginal to most sociological concerns. By contrast, it is relatively easy to talk about political struggle, scientific research, or the publication of official statistics without considering the specifically visual technologies that are built into and help to reproduce them. This Monograph is not, therefore, to be treated as a manifesto for a sociology of the visual. There can be no such thing as *a* sociology of the visual. *Homo sapiens*, *homo faber*, *homo economicus* and *homo ludens* are not about to be displaced by *homo pictor*. Nor are we making a point about research methods, that evidence from surveys should be supported by photographs. Rather, we are arguing that the visual, in its specificity, should be integrated into other sociologies. There are, of course, occasional places in social life where technologies of depiction are not to be found. But such technologies are so important in most processes of production and consumption that they cannot, or should not, be ignored as they have been by most sociologists.[1] Depiction, picturing and seeing are ubiquitous features of the process by which most human beings come to know the world as it really *is* for them. The point is not that social life is guaranteed by some shared visual culture, neither is it that visual ideologies are imposed on individuals. Rather, it is that *social change is at once a change in the regime of re-presentation* (see Latour and Fyfe in this volume). Once this is understood, a range of questions pose themselves. Thus, there is the problem, explored by Loftus, of the way in which the different aesthetics help to reproduce, and are in turn reproduced by, social conflict. And there is the question, posed by Corrigan, of the way in which dominant authorised depictions, related as to different ways of picturing, are socially and historically constructed. The argument here is that what can be seen is in part a question of what visual languages allow us to see. This was one of the things that Ivins (1953) taught us about art reproduction. As a curator of the Metropolitan Museum of Art he was in the business of evicting an aesthetic from the museum. His account of curatorial practice is an admission that curators, along with the rest of us, have *learned* to see art photographically. It is also the story of the visual tricks that he played on those who saw pictures differently. In effect he was saying: how could you be so stupid as to see things otherwise?

But why is the visual marginalised in sociology? Why do we write papers and books which neither use technologies of visualisation themselves, nor discuss the way in which these are *used* in our topics of study? There is a superficially attractive answer to these questions which is that it is difficult if not impossible to persuade sociological journals to reproduce pictures and diagrams: reasons of cost and paper quality are offered as justifications for exclusively verbal presentations. But in fact, this answer is no answer at all. There are whole categories of publications which are built around visualisations – ranging from newspapers and magazines, through books about the arts to standard scientific journals. Both art reproduction and scientific depiction are significant in the present context: the pages of *Nature* depend upon depictions; and, as Berger (1972) effectively argued, art reproductions are not mere illustrations of the texts they accompany but are in themselves *arguments* about the originals – albeit arguments that vary in the adequacy of their formulation and the extent to which they are open to doubt and uncertainty. Again, the pages of a scientific journal such as *Nature* depend upon depictions: tables, graphs, scattergrams, maps, sketches and photographs – all of these and more are to be found in the articles that it publishes. The science that it reproduces would be impossible without visualisation: depictions are *constitutive* of scientific production.

But if the visual is marginalised in sociology, it is not entirely absent. First, the language of sociology is built around a set of visual metaphors: structure, superstructure, base, iron cage, network, field, framework, survey, perspective – there are many that come readily to mind. Second, diagrams are to be found as modes of explanation in textbooks and scholarly articles, and appear to be common features in our didactic blackboard work. Perhaps sociologists are picturing animals despite themselves? At least one introductory textbook uses diagrams as a mode of theoretical critique and argument (Elias, 1978a), and today we are beginning to remember the pioneering photographic work in the *American Journal of Sociology* (Henny, 1986b). Third, there has been recognition by some sociologists – that is taken up by some contributors to this volume – that the making of the twentieth century world has had a distinctively visual aspect, that modernisation has involved the eye (Simmel, 1950; Bell, 1976). However, despite both this and the exceptions mentioned above, it appears that depictions do not form part of the tool-kit of most sociologists and neither – as several contributors to the volume suggest – is there any systematic recognition of the role of picturing as a medium for social interaction.

If the absence of the visual cannot be blamed on the publishers then why are so many branches of science built around the pictorial while sociology remains so obstinately verbal both in its methods and its subject-matter? There are, we think, three parts to an answer to this question. The first is that the legitimacy of technologies of summarisation is unquestioned in most areas of scientific inquiry. What counts as an object is usually relatively uncontroversial, and it is possible to quantify features of that object and simplify them using the normal technologies of statistical manipulation. The product of the latter is often a visual display – a table, or a graph. We do not need to take our own view on the character of quantification in sociology to observe that the use of quantitative methods is fundamentally controversial – though it is somewhat ironical that the disappearance of photographs from the *American Journal of Sociology* followed the take-over of the journal by behaviourists. Sociology does not have and has never possessed a generally agreed set of methods for identifying, discriminating and counting what it takes to be significant objects of study, and it may be that the meaning and lack of significance assigned to the visual reflect paradigmatic struggle within the discipline.

But this is only the first part of an answer: it explains, at least in part, why visual depictions of *summary* data might not be universal in sociology. But what of depictions of *individual* empirical elements? There are, after all, a number of branches of natural science in which drawings and photographs rather than graphs and scattergrams predominate. The article by Lynch and Edgerton considers one such case – the production of computer graphics in astronomy – but photographs, sketches and maps are also extremely common in a range of areas of geology, biology and physics. Thus Lynch (1982) has shown elsewhere that in neuro-anatomy the production of publishable electron micrographs is a matter of abiding concern to research scientists. The inference that we draw from this and similar cases is that in many of the natural sciences *seeing is believing*, whereas belief arises from quite other sources in sociology.

We do not wish to consider the philosophical implications of this distinction in any depth here. We would, however, suggest that the hermeneutic character of sociology is only a partial explanation for its relative indifference to visual evidence. Thus it is possible to gloss interpretative data visually – think, for instance, of political cartoons, or maps that indicate the patterns of world trade. Again, the absence of (say) photographs or plans from most ethnographies, though less true in social anthropology, is a possibly disabling convention. Thus one of the present authors recently published a paper on laboratory work (Law, 1986a) where photographs of the experiment and of the laboratory as a whole, though in fact absent, would have materially contributed to argument of the article. We would like to say that in this (and many analogous) instances seeing would have been believing – but the conventions of evidence in sociology are so verbally oriented we are not certain that this would have been the case.

In case it be thought that sociological subject matters are non-visual by their nature, while such subject matters as art history and natural science lend themselves readily to visual depiction, it is worth noting that there is nothing 'natural' about the visual depictions deployed in these. Freitag (1979) and Fawcett (1982) have shown how the emergence of the discipline of art history was attended by disputes about the meaning of photographic art reproductions. Moreover anxieties and uncertainties still surround reflections on the use of art reproductions. In the case of science, depictions are constitutively conventional in character, and the way in which such visual languages have developed in science has been traced in a number of different areas (Tufte, 1986; Rudwick, 1976). Again, Shapin (1984) has described the way in which 'virtual witnessing' – that is, the notion that an experiment in science might be properly observed via the agency of literary and illustrative publication rather than by being physically present – came into being in the particular circumstances surrounding the birth of the Royal Society. In this way a space for a visual language in natural science was created – a space that has not yet been generated in sociology.

It may be that the double hermeneutic character of sociological argument is partially responsible for the lack of visualisation in sociology. However, the theoretical fragmentation of the discipline is surely more important. Thus, as we have suggested, most of the time most scientists are able to agree about what it is that should be observed, the appropriate technology with which this should be done, and the proper way in which the findings so generated

5

should be laid out graphically. Disputes about visualisation tend to be rather specific and do not undermine the general legitimacy of virtual witnessing. However, in sociology the general position is quite different. The centre of gravity of sociology, lying close, as it does, to the expression and articulation of general philosophical differences, neither lends itself well, nor allocates much priority to differences that might be resolved by recourse to visual depictions of its subject-matter. This, then, is the second reason we believe that the visual has been marginalised in sociology.

A third possible reason for visual marginalisation may, we believe, be drawn from Turner's (1984) analysis of the way in which the body was deleted from mainstream classic social theory. The disappearance of the body was, suggests Turner, an outcome of the well-known process in which social theory was constructed in an anti-reductionist mode as part of a hostile dialogue with both biology and psychology. Though Durkheim's search for social facts *sui generis* may not have been directed by indifference to the body *per se*, the effect was to remove bodies from mainstream social theory for many decades. Indeed, it is only in the last ten or fifteen years, with the writing of Foucault, that an interest in the body has been reintegrated with the concerns of broader social theory – though there have, of course, been a handful of distinguished but possibly marginalised sociologists (one thinks of Elias and Goffman) who have consistently attended to the body, its expressions, and its depictions despite the indifference of social theory. However, Turner's argument also helps to explain the marginalisation of the visual. Thus, when the body was deleted from social theory, so, too, was the eye. The analysis of perception and representation disappeared into psychology, biology, art history or, indeed, into anthropology – which, with its different intellectual struggles, was never led to deny the physical and the biological. And most sociologists were blinded to the visual, and the social character of perception and reproduction.[2]

We cannot, and neither do we necessarily wish to, reform sociology so that it uses the technologies of visual depiction more centrally in its own projects. What we do believe, however, is that in its aversion to visual argument it should not act as if the visual were absent in, or simply peripheral to, its objects of study. The present Monograph, then, is a plea for the visual to be taken seriously in sociologies of subject-matters that are not necessarily at first sight explicitly visual. Taken as a whole, the papers consider a range of different circumstances in which representations have been generated and deployed, and they consider the relationship between these circumstances and the different technologies of visual production. The individual case studies, and the theoretical concerns of the authors, vary considerably – as indeed we might expect if we take the view, as we have argued above, that there can be no such thing as *a* sociology of visualisation.

The papers in the Monograph fall naturally into three categories. First, there are those that chart the way in which particular technologies of visualisation have responded to, and in turn reproduced social and natural similarities and differences. Four papers fall within this broad historical perspective: those by Bruno Latour, Stephen Bann, Gordon Fyfe and Belinda Loftus.

Bruno Latour charts the visual transition that takes us from Memling's Veronica to the scientific picturing of Holbein's anamorphic portrait of the Ambassadors. His argument is that the turn of the fifteenth and sixteenth centuries sees a shift between two regimes in religious painting. Religious painting was once confident: it represented the Virgin again and again, suitably transformed so that she could speak to each new audience, re-present the story of Jesus to each new viewer as if for the first time. However, after about 1500 the notion of representation starts to change its significance in painting. It is no longer a question of preserving an essential meaning via a chain of locally valid reinterpretations. Rather it becomes necessary to preserve the internal relations of objects as they are re-presented in different media from different perspectives. *The Ambassadors* portrays a world different from Memling's, for Christ is in a different place: '(t)he event of the Passion is not represented anew as if it was happening again and was contemporaneous with the Ambassadors; it is replaced by a crucifix that alludes to a past and closed event which is not depicted'.

The skies have displaced the heavens and a division has appeared between the supernatural and the mundane worlds – a division that Durkheim taught us to see as a social construction. We will now, bizarrely, picture religion as *above* the sky. The social change that is this displacement *is* change in the repertoires of the visual imagination. Latour asks the question: how can the divide be painted? Le Bault's painting of St Luke indicates that the attempt cannot be wholly successful. Holbein's portrait maps the new world 'while maintaining a trace, a scar of the other' but the relationship between the two worlds is truly a puzzle. That, as Latour says, is the drama that Holbein presents to us.

7

How is the past visualised? What does it mean to say that we *view* the past. Stephen Bann suggests that to view the past is to do something different from seeing the past: it is less neutral, and more cultural. He argues that Riegl's early twentieth century sense of 'age-value' as a view of the past is an historical phenomenon. Whilst detected and theorised by Riegl and Nietzsche, this sense of the past has its origins in the eighteenth- and nineteenth-century exhibitions of antiquarians. Bann's object is to reveal these embryonic stages of a mature late nineteenth century mode of 'viewing the past'. Thus Henry James, in finding a scene 'very sketchable', makes a by then commonplace connection between dusk, mould and dilapidation. Had narrative appropriated a view of the past that was first revealed through visual representation? In answering this question, the author shows the way in which changes in the relationship between visual and narrative modes have mediated a sense of what it means to view the past.

Thus exhibitions and displays are arguments about the things that they contain. Bann shows that antiquarians did more than store up collectable objects; they cherished, accumulated and ordered them through the medium of the museum. The arrangements of Lenoir and du Sommerard involved a persuasion of the spectator that was ocular but which also involved other senses. In the case of Du Sommerard's museum, an act of representation and of power set the viewer in motion through the space in which objects were displayed. Again, Lenoir's museum was closed down and dispersed by the Bourbons on the grounds that no French national art existed before the Renaissance. If museums are arguments about objects then there are voices that may be silenced. The creation of the modern museum is related to the process of state formation, but Bann offers us a salutary reminder that museums and art collections may also be destroyed – or suffered to decay.

Gordon Fyfe uses the puzzle posed by two *trompe l'oeil* paintings of about 1800, to re-exmaine Ivins's analysis of the theory and social history of art reproduction. Ivins's *Prints and Visual Communication* (1953) is a classic account of the effects that photography had on art reproduction. Yet some of its implications for a sociology of art – and in particular what it means for the social construction of authorship – has not yet been explored.

Fyfe argues that our understanding of the normalizing effects of the camera on art is enhanced by a critical reading of Ivins's account of its significance for pre-photographic methods of art reproduction. Ivins's contribution was in his recovery of the meaning of photographic reproductions as they related to the handicraft reproductions which they displaced at the end of the last century. The construction of a photographic way of seeing was social in character. It involved a change in the rules for knowing art. It allowed art lovers to see the difference between art and mere pictures of things, between art and illustration. It publicised art objects altogether differently from those of the old connoisseurship. However, Ivins bases his discussion of art reproduction on a contrast between the subjectivity of older methods and the objectivity of the camera. Fyfe argues that the illustrated argument presented in Ivins's own book challenges the basis of such a contrast and unconsciously proposes that all art reproduction may be seen as exegesis.

Belinda Loftus brings us to a contemporary case-study. Elsewhere, in an extended study of a wide range of visual images, she has argued that conflict in Ulster is not only between people who hold very different political and religious viewpoints, but also between people whose very modes of seeing and therefore comprehending political, religious and other aspects of their lives is distinctive (Loftus, 1983). Depiction is an aspect of conflict in Ulster: 'wearing the wrong tattoo or ignoring the territorial claim of the wall painting can lead to injury or death'. But little has been done to enhance our understanding of the social functions of such images and such work as there is has obscured the relationship between visual depiction and social processes.

Thus Loftus shows how analyses of such visual images and the troubles have usually abstracted them from their contexts, treating them either as illustrations of political events or as autonomous artistic creations. Correspondingly, exhibitions of visual imagery have tended to offer spectators the same way of seeing images: either as reflections of, or as inspired interpretations of, Ulster's politics. The curatorial separations and abstractions, associated with a museum's re-presentation of images-in-conflict, fail to grasp the lived relationship between visual depiction and politics. How can such an approach which compartmentalises and divides such images without reference to their functions possibly come to terms with their meanings? The danger is that we elide the relationship between image and conflict because we focus too readily on image *or* conflict, on depiction *or* society.

If the first section of the Monograph is concerned with the way in which particular technologies of visualisation have responded to, and in turn reproduced social and natural similarities, and proposes methodologies for gaining leverage on patron/producer relationships, then the second section focuses on the processes which lead to the production of specific visual depictions. Though, as it happens, these are all relevant in one way to science and technology, this is coincidental: there are wide differences between the technologies of visualisation described, though some of the case studies point to methods of visual domestication that may be quite general.

Robert Bud offers us an insider's account of the way in which an important new gallery in the Science Museum in London was conceived, designed, and brought into being. Using the theory of translation developed by Michel Callon (1986) and others, he meticulously describes the way in which the Museum brought together actors with a range of different interests and acted as a broker in a successful attempt to realign those interests and reach agreement about the message, the content and the physical structure of the gallery. In this process the role of the gallery as a producer of myth – that is as the context in which an authentic and unmediated experience of the sacred is available to the visitor – was gradually restructured by a set of practical concerns which ranged from ideas about the content of specific messages to architectural and engineering preoccupations with the physical safety and efficiency of the gallery. Writing, as we have noted, as an insider, Bud not only offers us an important theoretical contribution to the theory of translation, but also provides us with a most unusual insight into the negotiations that shape an important class of visualisations, that of museum displays.

The paper by John Law and John Whittaker is also written from the standpoint of the sociology of translation and, like Bud, they are concerned with depictions of science by non-scientists – in this case with popular writing, and policy-relevant depictions of research on 'acid rain'. Their focus is on the way in which what they call 'technologies of representation' are deployed by writers about science to build persuasive accounts about the structure of the natural and social worlds. Thus in the central section of their paper they outline the processes of negotiation and decision-making which led to a set of policy-relevant depictions of research on acid rain and in a subsequent section they consider the way in which such technologies were deployed to generate illustrations in an important popular book on acidification. Their argument is that technologies of representation suppress what it is that they purport to represent, and create novel objects which stand in the place of what has been silenced and speak on its behalf. The analogies between this process and that of political representation are explored, but though both rest for their legitimacy upon the silence of those who are represented and thus constitute techniques of power, the authors argue that the specificity of technologies of visual representation deserves study in its own right and should not be reduced to politics as this is conventionally understood.

Michael Lynch and Samuel Edgerton offer a preliminary account of work in an astronomy laboratory. Their focus is on the digital image processing that leads to conventional representations of astronomical objects, and in particular they are concerned with the way in which aesthetic criteria drawn from art are mobilised in order to make decisions about the block size and false colours used in such depictions. Could there, they wonder, be any connection between such conventions and expressionist and related forms of art? Or could it be that scientists 'package' their findings in fashionable formats and colour schemes in order to attract readers? In fact, Lynch and Edgerton do not find much evidence of direct biographical or cultural links between science and art. Rather, they observe that scientists distinguish between 'science' on the one hand and 'pretty pictures' for popular use on the other – but they also find that when scientists are asked about their aesthetic criteria these turn out to relate strongly to astrophysics: 'Rather than expressing something *other* than an aesthetic under-standing of a picture, such narrative explications . . . reveal an intimate association between science and a *particular* version of aesthetics emphasizing the simplicity, "graphical elegance", and representational utility of compositional detail'. Furthermore, the work that leads to preparation of images reflects one of the traditional objects of art – that of perfecting nature by removing imperfection and obscurity.

Geof Bowker's paper is another skilful attempt to look at the way in which actors themselves conceive of and use their visualisations. He describes a pre-war patent infringement hearing between two geophysical companies. The court case turned around the use of geophysical techniques, and in particular, around the evidence of the 'logs' – the graphs – produced by these techniques which purportedly registered important (for instance oil-bearing) features of subterranean rocks. In the course of the court hearing there was debate about the logs – were they or were they not representations of nature? Were they, or were they not, the product of human intervention? Were they or were they not dependent on context for interpretation? Was this log 'the same' as that? Settling these issues was difficult, both because they were, in any case, endlessly negotiable, and also because the plaintiff, Schlumberger, sought to conceal details of its methods for commercial reasons.

In an analysis of courtroom argument Bowker shows that the logs were perceived quite differently by different relevant groups. Thus for the oil companies who purchased them as a diagnostic tool they appeared as a finished but mysteriously generated product. However, for Schlumberger itself, their meaning was often quite unclear, and the field was used as a laboratory within which they could be interpreted. The company thus walked a tightrope, maintaining the multi-interpretability of the logs, and thereby attempting to reconcile a range of different and conflicting interests, and so domesticate and control both nature and society.

The third and concluding section of the Monograph addresses the issue of visualisation and power touched on by a number of other authors. Its single paper, by Phillip Corrigan, represents a remorseless challenge to all reifications of social relations. It is also a penetrating account of how dominant, authorised, depictions make the world obvious and (sometimes exotically) picturable. Corrigan's challenge to the reifying impulse which is present in so much cultural history reaches into his account of the very cultural apparatus itself. There is no room here for that *thing* photography which is technologically imposed on what may be depicted and seen. Rather, we must acknowledge photogrammar – socially contingent and historically situated rules of depiction.

Corrigan reminds us of Foucault's concept of pastoral power. But, as he puts it, he 'bends the light a little, just a little, toward' picturesque power(s). Picturing is an aspect of a symbolic-cultural constitution of the world so that 'That is the way the world has to be'. If we are to address the question of those depictions that are dominant then we need to recover their invention, their social construction as inventions that embody authority as systematised, standardised and normalised. Here the question concerns which 'subjectivities are encouraged, invited, or harmfully imaged' through picturing, rather than what is done to individuals in the name of power. Bann notes how Henry James found a cloister 'sketchable' and Corrigan provides an important amplification of what this means. What is also at stake here is the declaring of difference that is not measured against some norm.

Corrigan sketches one particular historical-social construction, the picturesque and more specifically the picturesque depiction of Imperial India. Following Cohn he notes how the exotic becomes real: 'how even an Indian of great importance who came to talk with an English (imperialist) official' finds the identity of the visitor endorsed by pictures on the wall. We have a depiction of India and Indians that is no mere illustration, that is more than the social made evident. It is an imperialisation of India: a 'creation and sustaining of distance through . . . depiction' that is also a decontextualisation of Indians who are depicted in terms of the services rendered to sahibs and memsahibs.[3]

Notes

1 There are, of course, a number of distinguished exceptions. Among classical sociologists Simmel (1950) was unusual in his concern for the visual. Again, several contemporary or near contemporary writers – Becker (1974), Goffman (1976), Foucault (1976), Bourdieu (1984) and Elias (1987b) – have revealed a sustained concern with depiction. We will return to this concern below. Finally, there is some sign of a recent increase in interest for the visual (Henny, 1986a), perhaps particularly in the sociology of science (Latour and de Noblet, 1985; Lynch and Woolgar, 1988).

2 An analogous process has occurred in the social analysis of science. For many years philosophers and historians preferred to emphasise the head at the expense of the hand: as scientists conjectured and then refuted they were turned into disembodied reasoners whose study was the province of epistemologists. In recent years, in part under the impetus of the work of Thomas Kuhn, the craft character of science has been reclaimed, and with it a concern with practice including the practice of perception.

3 It is worth noting how one topographical artist of the Near East, David Roberts (1796–1864), 'orientalised' his pictures with foreground figures (Llewellyn, 1986). Roberts was astonished by the 'picturesque population' of Cairo. He was also sickened and horrified by the squalor and misery that he encountered: '(b)ut these were the natural reactions of a compassionate man and a pious Presbyterian, and they do not intrude into his pictures' (Llewellyn, 1986: 81).

References

Becker, Howard S. (1974), 'Photography and Sociology', *Studies in the Anthropology of Visual Communication*, 1: 3–26.

Bell, Daniel (1976), *The Cultural Contradictions of Capitalism*, New York, Basic Books.

Berger, John (1972), *Ways of Seeing*, Harmondsworth, Penguin.

Bourdieu, Pierre (1984, *Distinction: A Social Critique of the Judgement of Taste*, London, Routledge and Kegan Paul.

Callon, Michel (1986), 'Some Elements of a Sociology of Translation: Domestication of the Scallops and the Fisherman of St. Brieuc Bay', pp. 196–233 in Law (1986b).

Elias, Norbert (1978a), *What is Sociology?*, London, Hutchinson.

Elias, Norbert (1978b), *The History of Manners (The Civilizing Process)*, Vol. 1, Oxford, Blackwell.

Elias, Norbert (1987), *Involvement and Detachment*, Oxford, Blackwell.

Fawcett, T. (1982), 'On Reproductions', *Art Libraries Journal*, 7, 1: 9–16.

Foucault, Michel (1979), *Discipline and Punish: the Birth of the Prison*, Harmondsworth, Penguin.

Freitag, W.M. (1979), 'Early Uses of Photography in the History of Art', *Art Journal*, 39, 2: 117–23.

Goffman, Erving (1976), *Gender Advertisements*, London and Basingstoke, Macmillan.

Guiterman, G. and Llewellyn, B. (eds) (1986), *David Roberts*, London, Phaidon Press and Barbican.

Henny, Leonard M. (ed.) (1986a), *Theory and Practice of Visual Sociology*, *Current Sociology*, 34, 2.

Henny, Leonard M. (1986b), 'A Short History of Visual Sociology', pp. 1–4 in Henny (1986b).

Ivins, William M. (1953), *Prints and Visual Communication*, London, Routledge and Kegan Paul.

Latour, Bruno and de Noblet, Jocelyn (eds) (1985), *Les 'Vues' de l'Esprit, Culture Technique*, 14.

Law, John (1986a), 'On Power and its Tactics: a View from the Sociology of Science', *The Sociological Review*, 34: 1–37.

Law, John (ed.), (1986b), *Power, Action and Belief: a New Sociology of Knowledge*, Sociological Review Monograph 27, London, Routledge and Kegan Paul.

Loftus, Belinda (1983), *Images in Conflict*, Keele, Keele University Ph.D. thesis.

Llewellyn, B. (1986), 'Robert's Pictures in the near East', pp. 69–85 in Guiterman and Llewellyn (1986).

Lynch, Michael (1982), 'Technical .Work and Critical Inquiry: Investigations in a Scientific Laboratory', *Social Studies of Science*, 12: 499–533.

Lynch, Michael and Woolgar, Steve (eds) (1988), *Representation in Scientific Work*, *Human Studies*, 11.

Rudwick, Martin (1976), 'The Emergence of a Visual Language for Geological Science, 1760–1840', *History of Science*, 14: 149–95.

Shapin, Stephen (1984), 'Pump and Circumstance: Robert Boyle's Literary Technology', *Social Studies of Science*, 14: 481–521.

Simmel, Georg (1950), 'The Metropolis and Mental Life', pp. 409–24 in Wolff (1950).

Tufte, Edward R. (1986), *The Visual Display of Quantitative Information*, Cheshire, Connecticut, Graphics Press.

Turner, Bryan S. (1984), *The Body and Society*, Oxford, Basil Blackwell.

Wolff, Kurt H. (ed.) (1950), *The Sociology of George Simmel*, New York, Free Press.

VISUALISATION AND SOCIAL REPRODUCTION

Opening one eye while closing the other . . . a note on some religious paintings

Bruno Latour

Abstract

Religious paintings offer an excellent testing ground to compare the various kinds of displacements or translations. The paper focuses on two such displacements: the repetition of the message of Jesus versus the movement of immutable mobiles allowed by perspective. These two regimes offer completely different definitions of what it is to 'represent' something: to the re-*present*ation of the Presence is opposed the accurate representation of distant places and times. In between 1450 and 1520 these two regimes of displacement first merge, then collide, and later go their separate ways. Religion on the one hand, and Science on the other ignore each other. Going to *Heaven*, and going through the *Sky* are two different movements of representation that generate different space-times.

Introduction

The most humble of us lives surrounded by a princely retinue of delegates and representatives. Every night, on television, our representatives in Parliament talk on our behalf. We have delegated to hundreds of non-human lieutenants the task of disciplining, making, and moving other humans or other non-humans – lifts, cars, trains, machines. Hundreds of scientific disciplines and instruments constantly bring far away places, objects and times to us which are thus represented – that is presented *again* – for our inspection. In dozens of books, movies, plays and paintings, human and non-human characters represent us with our violence and our fears, populating our world with crowds of friends and enemies. Elusive and rare, angels bring cryptic messages offering us a chance to live again in the presence of He who is ever present, while immense populations of objects trace the intricate networks of empires and emporiums which make their presence felt in the daily lives of billions of people. Spokespeople, machines, instruments, characters, angels, manufactured objects, these are the names of some of the representatives which are crowding our lives. If we are in society it is because we live among those delegates, very few of which look like fellow humans. If sociology is the study of society it has to take full account of those crowds of non-humans mingled with humans.[1]

To take full account of this retinue of delegates, sociologists have to look carefully at their conflicts over who is the most representative. In this paper I want to study one such conflict, that between angels and instruments, or, to say it with older words, between religion and science. But instead of studying this conflict of two different definitions of representation through theology or history, I have chosen to do it through the medium of paintings at the very time, between 1450 and 1550, when the representation of *Heaven* becomes that of *Sky*.[2]

1 Holbein's anamorphosis

If you look straight at *The Ambassadors* painted by Holbein you will notice a strange, elongated, brownish shape near their feet right in the middle of the picture.[3] If the attendants at the National Gallery of London allow you to kneel down at the painting's left side, your face as if touching the varnished pigment, this unidentified flying object will appear to be a skull – the accepted symbol of the many *memento mori* painted at the time. But then, how will the fiery Ambassadors appear? As a grotesque and distorted medley of bright and meaningless shapes. If the Ambassadors are straightened up, the skull is skewed. If the skull is rectified, the two Frenchmen are slanted, fleeing away like flying saucers.

Geometers and historians of perspective call 'anamorphosis' a projective technique that gives a distorted image of a scene when seen from the usual viewpoint, but so executed that if seen from a particular angle, or reflected in a curved mirror, the distortion disappears, and the image in the picture appears normal. For more than a century, painters and decorators delighted in offering

Plate 1 Hans Holbein, *The Ambassadors*
The National Gallery, London

puzzling and disorderly shapes that suddenly fell into place when, for instance, a cylindric or a conic mirror was put in their middle.[4] Discover the right angle of view, the right polished surface and from the utmost disorder a familiar order will emerge.

What unsettles us so much in this work by Holbein, is that we do not know for sure what is the normal plane of projection. Is it the skull that is out of place, or the Ambassadors? Jean de Dinteville, lord of Polisy, obsessed by death, and Georges de Selve, Bishop of Lavour, terrified by the raging wars of religion, do not seem to be too sure of the answer. This picture, that is often taken as the triumph of representation (Berger, 1972), is a double and reversible anamorphosis. You can reverse at will the definition of what is oblique and unnatural. Besides, were you to draw the heavy curtain open you would find yourself in the middle of Westminster Abbey whose rich and rare paving is reproduced in exact perspective under the Ambassadors' feet. What are they doing in a mausoleum, these Renaissance men so proud of their science, of their account books and of their scientific or musical instruments?

The answer is as uncertain as the quaint position of the most ubiquitous Christian symbol. Half-hidden by the heavy curtain, a crucifix is nailed on the left uppermost part of the painting. The French Ambassador and the Catholic Bishop are not kneeling on both sides of a crucifixion looking piously at the Passion as so many donors in so many pictures of the past did; they look at us. The event of the Passion is not represented anew as if it was happening again and was contemporaneous with the Ambassadors; it is replaced by a crucifix that alludes to a past and closed event which is not depicted. What was at the centre of all religious pictures, is now at the periphery. What was at the periphery – humble and kneeling donors of whom the spectator saw only the back or the profile – is now at the centre, standing and looking back at us. Here too, there is an anamorphosis. Place yourself in front of the crucifix; push the curtain back; replace the ivory object by the bleeding flesh of Jesus; replace the wall by a painted scene of Golgotha, and you won't even notice the slanted presence of the two men. They would be in the wings, in another plane of projection, as invisible or as distorted as the ghostly skull in the normal presentation at the National Gallery. Focus back on the two geographers and the religious scene will again veer away, will disappear as a mirage. There is no Golgotha, no Passion, no bleeding flesh, no presence of Jesus, but a decorative ivory crucifix. The *real presence* of the Ambassadors has replaced that of Christ.

Such is the drama of Holbein's painting. There exists no plane on which both the visible and the invisible worlds could be projected so as to be seen *from the same viewpoint*. Either you see one and render the other invisible, or you see the other, and the first becomes a ghost.

After 1533 there will be many other paintings either representing religious subjects or representing scientific objects, but none, to my knowledge, will be so anxious to map the new world while maintaining a trace, a scar of the other, as a navel marks the ancient nourishing womb. Holbein pushes the new realist rendering of shapes, spaces, noblemen and matters to its extreme but he keeps the former regime of representation *anamorphosed* into the first one. The two men he portrays are as uncertain and as anxious as their painter in the face of dual loyalty. The Catholic Bishop is seen standing by Luther's 'Shortened version of the Ten Commandments' and the Ambassador by a terrestrial globe on which one could follow not only Magellan's circumnavigation but also point out the place of Polisy castle. Under the globe is an arithmetic book for merchants.[5] What is religion going to become while geography, astronomy, mercantile capitalism and the Reformation are all expanding? How is an *iconophile* such as Holbein, trained by his father to paint religious icon after religious icon, going to get by with the *iconoclastic* movement sweeping all Protestant countries? Who is more iconophile than Holbein, who is able to render fur, silk and brown parchment with nothing but pigments and varnishes? Compared to the miracle of this rendering of fabrics, fleshes and shapes out of an empty flat and white surface, does it really matter that the miracles of Jesus are not represented? On the other hand who are more iconophile than geographers, geometers, and scientists obsessed with instruments, inscriptions, representations and rendering of shapes? In the seventy years on both sides of 1500 a new quarrel of images takes place that has given its present shape to our *vision* of science and of religion.

2 Veronica's representation of Jesus

Veronica holds in her hands the veil on which is inscribed, painted, collected, depicted and reproduced, the Sacred Face.[6] She is squatting on the parched earth fusing the folded veil with her folded garment. She has come a long way along the narrow meandering road behind her. She keeps her eyes modestly focused on the veil she holds open for us, but the Christ depicted, carried by the humble Veronica through space and time, looks straight at us. Has the face of the Crucified, like the imprint of a body on the shroud of Turin, travelled intact and unadulterated all the way from Jerusalem in the year 30, to the Flemish Low Country? Of course not. Has Veronica herself, now about fifteen hundred years old, survived all the way to Memling's workshop in order to be once again represented? Of course not. Veronica is a young woman of Memling's time, dressed in the favoured folded clothes of the Flemish, in a landscape of Memling's country. As to the Sacred Face, it is not the negative two-dimensional inscription of a sweating and bleeding man carrying his cross up Golgotha, the head girded in a crown of thorns, but the positive three-dimensional painting of a glorious resurrected Jesus.[7] The face has not been transferred to a veil and brought to us unmodified. It is painted anew.

In Memling's painting, Veronica is holding *another* painting. The same artist painted the delicate landscape on a wooden surface, the saint – herself nothing but veils, fabrics and delicate linen – and the face of Jesus floating out of the white background; but Memling chose to attribute the quality of the second painting not to his craft but to that of Veronica, not to brushes and paint but to the direct meeting with Jesus' face. The first painting is what any skilled artisan should be able to achieve. The second one is achieved only if a saint equipped with a veil meets Jesus in person. Memling offers a very indirect and mediated way indeed of pointing to an unmediated face to face with God. The first miracle – how could any three dimensional shape and any matter be obtained out of pigments on wood? – is used to point to the second miracle: how can the Son of God be inscribed on this earth? The relation of the world out there to the surface of the painting is the same as that of the sacred world to this one. The first one is a complex projection of three dimensions on two; the second is a complex *incarnation* of other dimensions in two.

This representation in a work of art of religious representation, is as instructive as Holbein's *Ambassadors*, which pictured the beginning of scientific picturing, because they both work at cross purposes. In a religious painting, the prefix 're' of re-presentation means presenting *again and anew*. Veronica is presented again and anew to Memling's pious patrons, and what she holds inscribed on her veil – on Memling's white varnished surface – is a new chance to be presented again with an ever present Jesus. This insistence on *presence* explains why there is no effort at historical reproduction. It is not in the past that Veronica has met Jesus. It is now that we, through the painter's mediation, meet Him again. The event is contemporaneous. Memling is not staging a scientific proof that someone called Veronica really held an authentic negative stain of a tortured Jewish prophet. The kerchief of Veronica's legend is not a photographic plate. Memling is not engaging us in one of these rationalist debates about the authenticity of the shroud of Turin or of the Virgin's girdle. But then, why is Veronica holding a veil? Why not, for instance, as in so many other paintings presenting us with Christ's face, frame the picture in a smaller square that holds just the face? Because Jesus is never the object of an unmediated presentation, but always the subject of a re-presentation. You have access to the face of Jesus through Veronica, and to Veronica through Memling's art, and to both through the theology on images, and to all others through the piety and wealth of active religious orders, and to all the others through the complex mediation of the Church's teaching. If you try to shortcut one of these mediators, what is left? Nothing. A religious painting never offers direct access to the sacred. It is a renewed commemoration of what other people – usually apostles or saints – said and saw. Were you to use this very painting to obtain information on 'how did the historical Christ look' you would be very disappointed.[8] And yet, this is an exact re-presentation of Christ, of the legendary trace Veronica gathered, and of the incarnation. For any Flemish viewer, this picture is meant to be used for prayer. We might have forgotten what it is to live in the presence, and under the sight of Jesus, but faced with the Sacred Face brought to us before our very eyes by a long chain of legends, dozens of Saint Veronicas, dozens of crafted painters, myriads of rich patrons and uninterrupted chains of Bishops and preachers, we kneel down and reenact *hic et nunc* what it was that people contemporaneous with Jesus saw and heard.

No one, not even a romantic aesthete, would kneel in front of Holbein's Ambassadors and nobody, not even a very naive Christian believer, would start to pray by the half-hidden crucifix, that does not re-present a crucifixion as if re-enacted now.[9] As to the half-hidden slanted and distorted skull it only suggests that something might be wrong with the rest of the picture, but it does not present the viewer with anything more to renew his piety. The instruments gathered in between the two men are not like the instruments of the Passion so often painted to remind believers and to induce them to reenact sacred events.[10] Apart from the viola, they are geographical and mathematical instruments. To be sure the beautiful terrestrial globe on the lower shelf does also *represent* the earth, but what it means to represent has been deeply modified. The globe *stands in the place of the absent and large earth*, but it offers a reduced, manageable and readable model of it. If you read off the globe that the distance between the castle of Polisy and the city of London is so many inches, you can deduce that, were you to undertake the travel on the surface of the 'scale one' earth, you would have to ride for so many leagues and cross a sea of so many nautical miles. Were you to measure up the size of Jesus' face on Veronica's veil in Memling's picture, nothing would ensue about the real, 'scale one', historical Jesus. Dominating the scaled-down globe tells you things about far away places and allows you to brace yourself for travel. Kneeling by the altar piece allows you to be dominated by the Sacred Face and brace yourself for meeting Jesus *again*. The terrestrial globe represents the earth, Veronica re-presents Jesus, but what viewers can do with the two representations is entirely different.

3 Conflicts of representation

What has been kept intact from the Polisy–London journey all the way to the inscription onto the curved surface of the globe and then again through the careful projection by Holbein of the spherical globe onto the painting? The relative distance between the two points compared, for instance, to the distance Polisy–Paris, or Polisy–Rome (angles have been distorted again in the movement from the scaled down globe to the painting of the globe). What has been kept intact from Jesus' ascent of Golgotha all the way to Memling's workshop? A legend about Veronica's keeping a trace of Jesus' face on her kerchief, hundreds of sermons, arguments, metaphors, similes and interpretations about what it is to live facing Jesus, what it is to paint and to capture again the Sacred Face onto a thin veil of pigment and cloth. In both cases, something has been kept intact, something has been transported and deposited onto the flat picture, but what matters for the two *regimes of re-presentation* is vastly different.

For a religious scene to be exact and faithful what matters above all is that, along its travel through space and time, every viewer

gets the feeling that the story of Jesus is presented anew to him or
to her, right here, *as if for the first time, but in keeping with* all the
other scenes, all the other viewers, all the other interpretations of
the 'same' scene. The word same is to be put in quotation marks,
because the very definition of what it is to be 'the same as' in such a
regime is very different from what it will be later in the other
regime. For instance, the legend of Veronica is a very late one, but
it does not matter much, because it is a very faithful one since it
reenacts what it is to inscribe the face of Jesus. The dozens, the
hundreds of monks, painters, and preachers who embroidered and
rendered the legend are all faithful if, in doing so, they produced
through the legend, the meeting of Jesus and of one abandoned
and dispirited soul. The re-presentation is faithful if it is a
repetition of the first scene, repetition meaning not the exact
imitation of the first, but, on the contrary, a very different
presentation that re-captures the same essential meaning:[11] we are
in the presence, not in the absence of Jesus. The very word 'Jesus'
means this renewed presence – I understand it now, for the first
time, and I also understand what the other interpreters, my elders
and brothers in the Faith, understood by the same words 'Jesus' or
'Grace of God' etc.[12]

How is the other regime of representation going to evaluate this
religious one? As a tissue of lies and it is very true from their own
perspective, since the Legend of Veronica has been made up, since
none of the features of Memling's painting could be used to
establish any connection with any other historical scene involving
the scale one real Jesus.[13] To be sure they established connections
but repetitive ones that required to be modified all along so that
every viewer could be converted on the way. The new connections
established by Magellan's travels, by cartographers, by astronomers, by account books, by Ambassadors, are not of that sort.
Their definition of exactness and faithfulness looks askance at the
other from the same bizarre angle as the anamorphosed skull in
Holbein's painting. In this regime, what is meant by faithful is the
ability to maintain through all the transformations of scale, and all
the various places and times, some inscriptions, some traces, that
allow those who hold them and look at them, to return to the
original setting with a *prior* acquaintance of the scene.[14] Someone
who had looked at Memling's picture and who had been
transported by a time machine to the ascent of Golgotha would not
have the slightest familiarity with the scene no matter how many
Crucifixions they had looked at – indeed there might be no scene

at all, or a scene so unlike the one they had anticipated that they would be entirely lost and in despair.[15] On the other hand, someone who had collected all the maps of Europe, all the recent globes and descriptions of France, even if they were often inaccurate and incomplete, would be able to tell a lot of things about Polisy's castle and how to get there from Paris, Rome or London. Even if they were discouraged by the discrepancies between the guides, the maps and the landscapes they visited, they would still be so much embedded in the new regime that they would try to amend the guides, correct the maps, and improve the fit between the representation and what is being represented. In this new regime, the prefix 're-' of re-presentation means that whatever is out there has already been inscribed, mapped and drawn. The prefix 're-' is there to point out a two-way metonymic relation between the scale-model and the scale one phenomena.[16] It is not the ever-present that is presented anew, as in the old regime, but the realm of *absent*, distant, inaccessible and unmanageable things that have already been mastered and dominated by sight *here*. The absent is made present. The distant is brought here. The big is scaled down. The small is scaled up. Places that one has never visited can be visited. We become familiar with the world once absent through the manipulation of its representatives and substitutes.[17]

There is a huge difference between a visual display that solves the problem of renewing in the heart the ever present God, and a visual display that solves the problem of the absence of distant things. God is not far and absent – He is only going to become so once the new regime of representation has won over – but His presence is constantly forgotten by us, poor sinners. What the religious painting does for the iconophiles is to cancel out this forgetting by repeating and renewing for the viewer the presence of God.[18] On the other hand, Africa, flora, fauna, satellites of Jupiter, Jerusalem in the year 30, are far away places and times. This distance and this absence did not matter too much before, compared to the huge problem of putting oneself in the presence of God. It is going to matter now. Some vehicle has to be invented to *move* the scenes *through* space and time. What the scientific visual display is going to do for the new iconophiles is to displace those scenes and to do so in some recognizable shape. Small wonder that Holbein has some difficulty in reconciling the *movement* of geography, geographers, and economies with the *movement* of the faith in the same optically coherent space. Small wonder if the Bishop of Lavour is thwarted as in Dinteville in their common efforts to avoid a schism with the reformers and to offer to the faiths a *communion*.[19]

4 Generating different space-times

Space and time are not, contrary to Kant's demonstrations, the *a priori* categories of our sensibility. Gods, angels, spheres, doves, planets, steam engines, are not *in* space and do not age *in* time. On the contrary, spaces and times are traced by reversible or irreversible displacements of many various types of mobiles. They are generated by the movement of mobiles, they do not frame those movements. Tell me what is on the move and what transformation it undergoes through these moves, and I will tell you what sort of space and what sort of time has been thus *designed*. Consequently, since each regime of representation defines differently what should be maintained intact through displacements, each regime defines space-time differently.

What can be carried through space and time without distortion and adulteration for the first regime? Nothing but the very movement of re-invention, re-petition, re-interpretation of what the Sacred Deposit of the Scriptures means. Every displacement has to be paid for by a re-formulation. Who is going to evaluate if a given re-formulation is a betrayal or a translation of this hidden meaning? Long chains of mediators inside the Church. Who is going to decide if each mediator is faithful or corrupt? Another long chain of mediators inside the Church. This is how the Church was able to adapt and to adjust, from an Aramean sect somewhere around the reign of Tiberius, all the way to the European quattrocento.

What can be carried through space and time without distortion and adulteration in the second regime? Everything, provided there are means to maintain the internal relations of the objects through the transportation, and through the variations of scales and projections on various mediums. Each displacement is going to be paid for not by a reformulation but by the reinscription of the same shape on a different medium. Who is going to evaluate if a given representation is an exact rendering of the original scene or a distorted view? Anyone who is in a position to compare, feature after feature, the original scene, the movable version of it and its present rendering. Who is going to decide if someone – anyone – is in a position to confirm the faithful superimposition of the various scenes thus aligned? Again, anybody faced with a series of superimposable traces. This is how the new Ambassadors, merchants, cartographers are beginning to progress from lowly insignificance to hegemony.

As Ivins pointed out years ago, here lies the true importance of perspective.

> Perspective may be regarded as a practical means for securing a rigorous two-way, or reciprocal, metrical relationship between shapes of objects as definitely located in space and their pictorial representations. Important as this is to picturemaking in the narrowest sense, it is doubtless even more important to general thought, because the premises on which it is based are implicit in every statement made with its aid. Either the exterior relations of objects, such as their forms for visual awareness, change with their shift in locations, or else their interior relations do. If the latter were the case there could be neither homogeneity of space nor uniformity of nature, and science and technology as now conceived would necessarily cease to exist. Thus, perspective, because of its logical recognition of internal invariances through all the transformations produced by changes in spatial location, may be regarded as the application to pictorial purposes of the two basic assumptions underlying all the great scientific generalizations, or laws of nature. (Ivins, 1938: 9–10)

Controversies on the importance of perspective for the development of science, technology and religion are raging now[20] but they often miss the earlier point made by Ivins. What is at stake are not the *visual* characteristics of a painting, of a drawing, of a map, of a diagram, but the regime of re-presentation of which the visual implementation is but a consequence. The key question is not about degrees of 'realism' but about the articulation to be made between mobility and immutability. Is it possible to move a scene from one medium to another and keep its characteristics or is it necessary to retranslate its meaning for each different viewer and listener along the way?

Religious icons that do not build a three dimensional space are not less 'realist' than those which do. It is simply impossible for the viewer to anticipate a predictable movement of the Virgin on her throne, of the throne, of the angels and still more impossible to imagine himself moving in a predictable way through the space created by the painting. Faced with Cimabue's *Virgin and Child on the Throne* (in the Louvre), the viewer cannot answer questions like these: were I to come to the throne from below how would I see the now hidden face of the throne? If the top left angel were to fly away from me through the golden space how would I see it? If I want to come closer to the Virgin or to move behind her, how would I do it? If the angel is holding the throne what force is he/ she exerting? In other words, no movement of the characters of the picture or of the viewer are thinkable that would not completely *transform* the characters or *transform* the motives and internal state of the viewer. Moving the Virgin and the angels would mean painting another picture. Moving the viewer would mean a transformed, converted or corrupted viewer. Religious characters before perspectives are mobiles but they are mutable, constantly transformed and renewed in an *ad hoc* space-time that surrounds them differently each time and that makes up their 'niche' in front of which a different individualised believer confronts again the mysteries of the Presence of God *hic et nunc*.

A perfected point perspective space like that of Holbein's Ambassadors induces a completely different relationship between mobility and immutability. The viewer can walk on the paving of Westminster Abbey – which allegedly was meant to be a *trompe l'oeil* in Polisy's Castle.[21] He can turn around the scene and redraw it from there without any difficulty. He can re-draw it from five feet farther or from a 10 per cent narrower angle. He can pull the curtain open or take off the Ambassadors' clothes one by one, modify the readings of each of the instruments, turn the terrestrial globe slightly and make the celestial sphere point at a different constellation. For him, the painting is like a computer aided design screen: one possible version of a series of reversible and combinable displacements that do not entail any transformation of the characters or of himself. Each element of the scene is movable but since their internal relations are maintained through this movement they remain in effect immutable. With one given picture you can make thousands of others which are like so many projections of the first. The old Greek geometrical question: what can be maintained intact through a series of transformations, is now applied to the three-dimensional artificial space of the painting. Mobiles that are becoming immutable – painted scenes, planets, account books, anatomical plates, printed books, etched plates – are tracing a new space that has the strange characteristic of establishing new continuous links with each of these discrete and heterogeneous novelties. Of course, neither perspective, nor printing, nor etching, nor Copernican astronomy, nor double entry book keeping, are enough to explain any of the others. Serious historians can always point out the gap between those discontinuous innovations – and they are right. What they miss, however, is that each of these inventions, of more immutable more mobile elements is creating a new specific type of space that allows them to *merge with the other* in a specific homogenising way. The question of their obvious differences is thus less pertinent than that of their ability to tie in with one another.

5 The contagion of immutable mobiles

Still, in the religious regime of representation too, something is maintained through a series of transformations, the meaning of the Gospel as interpreted by the Church. Yes, but the very meanings of 'something', of 'maintain' and of 'transformation' are, in turn, deeply transformed. They sound the same, they slowly appear to be entirely divergent. The theological principle – what is re-peated through translations– becomes, by contagion with the other regime, a topological principle: what is kept constant through deformations.[22]

What is so fascinating in the history of the space created by various styles of religious painting, is that it took approximately seventy years to realise this deep discrepancy of meaning – this at least is my falsifiable hypothesis. In religious painting perspective was welcomed at first as the perfect medium to inscribe the sacred. Apostles, Virgins, Christs, angels themselves could appear for the first time not in their hieratic pose in front of a golden background, but in a perfect geometrised space that was the very imitation of God's own light and vision. Neither Antonello da Messina, nor Masaccio, nor Piero della Francesca, nor Bellini, nor Mantegna, saw perspective as a realistic anti-religious instrument. On the contrary, for them, geometry, science, theology of vision, and piety, merged again as never before in the Middle Ages.

Antonello da Messina's *St Jerome in his Study* (National Gallery of London) does not need a golden halo to provide us with a deep respect for his sanctity, no golden surface is necessary to tell us that we are in earthly heaven – openings in the far away skies are enough.[23] The re-presentation of the sacred is obtained here by one *fusion*, in one 'optically coherent space' (Ivins's terms), of religious characters (the Saint, his symbolic Lion), of natural actors (landscape, birds), and of artificial objects (books, pots,

Plate 2 Antonello da Messina, *St Jerome in his Study*
The National Gallery, London

furniture), the meeting place of all these various realms being provided by a man-made and yet religious space: the beautiful Church inside which the scholarly saint is reading the scriptures.[24] As Edgerton pointed out, what counts here is the possibility for all these foreign elements now brought together in a common medium to *exchange their properties*:[25] heraldic animals take on the appearance of African lions; saints take on the appearance of present day cardinals; lowly objects and landscape immersed in this calculated space take on the aspect of sacred objects. Moreover the Church and the painting exchange their properties too: the first one houses all those Eucharistic transformations of one nature into another and is in turn housed by the two dimensional painting which becomes the sacred place where Incarnation is re-presented. This work, painted around 1470 is no less perfect than Holbein's 1533 Ambassadors, as far as perspective and the rendering of material and fabrics is concerned. Still, it manifests none of the religious doubts of the other. Through the mediation of perspective, of the Church, and of the painter's craft, the mystery of Incarnation is presented again to the viewer in a painting which is unambiguously sacred. If there was a time when the *Real Presence* could be accurately and happily painted it was in between 1450 and 1520 while the regime of re-*present*ation and the means of *real*ising it were not yet in opposition.

Thereafter religious art will never be the same, will never be so radiant and self-confident. Something has happened: the very regime of repetition and representation that defined religion is replaced by another. Religious subjects will still be painted – at least in Catholic countries – but they will have to fight for a breathing *space*. Everything happens as if people were discovering that the two-way avenue through space, this mobility without mutability, was much better still for going from the original to the representant, that is for reaching distant things. Instead of re-presenting the Presence of God the same vehicle appears to be much more convenient for reaching away from one centre to all other peripheral places. What is maintained incorrupted in Holbein's painting is not the Presence of God – dispersed along in an anamorphosed plane – but the presence of maps, of accounts, and of human Ambassadors. It is like building a machine to reach heaven, and to realise en route that it is a neat way to reach the sky. The iconography of the Assumption of the Virgin Mary is a marvellous indicator of this shift: she was brought up into Heaven; now she flies overhead like a rocket through the sky.

Sky has invaded Heaven. The net effect on the viewer is dramatically different: instead of praying by a painting whose beauty, richness and style add up to the series of mediators that are represented in the picture – the saints, Jesus and Mary – the viewer now dominates a landscape of distant things brought to him by a series of mediations that *can be annihilated.* The same immaterial three-dimensional rendering of space falls on religious subjects one by one, but instead of providing them with the oxygen that in the late 1400 gives them the brilliance of the St Jerome, it kills them after 1520 as if it had become carbon dioxide. As if to avoid asphyxia, the painters will have to maintain or reinvent the sacred by breaking up the three-dimensional space with eddies and bank of clouds (Baroque) or by chiaroscuro (Rembrandt, Caravaggio). In the meantime the painting, mapping, collecting, surveying, classifying of the new world of objects will follow its increasingly separate path, that of Empires and of Emporia which I call, more generally 'centres of calculation'.[26] Science and religion have become literally *worlds* apart. The bizarre idea then appears that religion has to do with 'another world beyond this one', that is, somewhere above the blue skies so magnificently painted and rendered. More absurdly, while religion used to create spaces and times through its *own* regime of re-presentation, it is now turned into a rump: what is beyond space-time. The regime of Presence has been turned into that of Absence. An irreversible partition has been made: to humanity, to its sciences and to its technical dominion, this world is offered; to God, the other. How can you *paint* such a divide?

You cannot, and the worst is when painters, borrowing from the new regime of representation, imagine that they can still paint as if in the other. No work is more rationalistic than a seventeenth-century painting by Le Bault now in Dijon Museum. The painter has painted himself as St Luke, his back toward us so that we can look over his shoulder directly at his easel. On St Luke's canvas is a Virgin Mary with Child. If Le Bault had painted only this scene we could still imagine ourselves in the old regime of re-presentation, very close indeed to Memling's Veronica, the indirect imprinting of Jesus' Face being replaced here by the indirect brushes and colours of St Luke. But in the middle of the seventeenth century, the very idea of this regime is fading away. We are in the midst of Foucault's Age Classique. Le Bault cannot think of a religious painting as anything other than the representation of a model. But what could the *original* model of a Virgin

31

Plate 3 Claude Le Bault, *St Luke Painting a Portrait of the Virgin Mary*
Musée des Beaux-Arts de Dijon (with permission)

with Child be? In former times, this question could have received an indefinite number of mediated answers, none of them being an exactly similar Virgin with Child – indeed the Child himself is an indefinite series of mediators of that sort and so is the Virgin, mediatrix *par excellence*. In this new time, however, there is only one possible answer. The original model of the representation has to be an *exact replica* of what is represented. Thus, Le Bault, without hesitation, paints behind the easel *another* Virgin with Child, this time as if appearing to St Luke in a bank of clouds. The poor St Luke – the patron of painters – is turned into a retired Sunday landscape artist who paints what he sees *d'après nature*; had he seen a cow or carriage he would have painted it all the same.[27]

The exactness of Le Bault's rendering of the Virgin is supposed to be authorised by the superimposition of St Luke's portrait with the glorious model appearing in the sky. We are to *subscribe* to this work as if it were a scientific proof.[28] This is exactly what Memling's Veronica avoided. There was no hint that you could subscribe to the proof by comparing the painted face, with the Sacred Face of Jesus. Now it is the comparison, the superimposition, the underwriting that is supposed to give credit to the representation. To be sure, Le Bault is not entirely taken in by the rationalisation since there are slight discrepancies between the model and the picture, and since he needs no less than one angel and one cherub to make him able to interpret what he sees. Even then, the angels in this painting play one of their saddest roles in their millennia old history. Instead of being the indispensable mediator of any translation of one meaning of God into another, they are transformed into mere go-betweens who establish two way correspondence between features of a model by aiding the slow hand of a human. The poor fellows are like telephone lines fighting against noise or like the arms of a mechanical plotter. The world of representation is not a place fit for angels. Theirs is that of re-presentation, almost entirely absent from Le Bault's painting.[29]

Conclusion

While one Western eye is opened, the other blinks a bit and then closes. As implied by the anamorphosis in Holbein's work, there seems to be no point from which angels and instruments can be represented together in an optically coherent space. Immutable mobiles chase away saints, mediators and angels. Centres of

Bruno Latour

calculation lay waste to all other delegates but *factotums*. The representation of Presence that was repeated over the millenia has
been pushed aside into the exotic realm of transcendence, into the
depth of the inner individual soul, or, worse, into some obscure
spiritual or ethical dimensionless 'dimension'. Hence this bizarre
definition of the modern world as an a-religious or a secular one
that makes it apart from all the others.

Now that the modernity of our world is coming to a close,[30] we
understand that it was no more secular than any other. The super-
human delegates are as present as ever among the other human
and non-human delegates, but askance and distorted like Holbein's
skull seen from the view point of Jean de Dinteville and Georges
de Selve. We are still surrounded by a long retinue of delegates.
We never left the old anthropological matrix. The queer sociology
that is emerging from the careful study of instruments, lieutenants,
representatives, objects, angels and characters – to name but a few
of the delegates with whom we build our daily life – will hopefully
create this optically coherent space in which we will be able to
represent at once all our different regimes of representation.
Then, we will realise, I wager, that we are not *that* Western. A new
fraternity might emerge with the rest of the world that will have
nothing to do with the expansion of immutable mobiles, but with
the relative distribution of our regimes of delegations.

Notes

This article owes a lot to many conversations with Protestant semiotician and
nevertheless friend Françoise Bastide. I am also deeply indebted to Antoine
Hennion for his long meditation on mediators. I thank Geof Bowker for correcting
my English.

1 For a study of delegations in instruments see Latour (1986 and 1988a); for a
  study of delegations in non-human mechanisms see Latour (1988b). For a
  review of the literature on scientific visualisation see B. Latour and J. de Noblet
  (1985). For the most sophisticated case study on the relations between political,
  scientific and religious delegations see S. Shapin and S. Schaffer (1985). For the
  most articulate distinction between techniques (namely the bridge over the
  Firth of Forth) and art (namely Picasso's portraits) see Baxandall (1985).
2 The empirical material for this paper is extracted from an ongoing project
  'From Heaven to Sky' about the iconography of the Assumption of the Virgin
  Mary.
3 For a precise description of the picture see Mary Hervey (1900). Describing this
  painting is a topos of art history. For one well known commentary see Berger
  (1972).
4 See Jurgis Baltrusaitis (1984) for the most complete study on the science, art
  and magic of anamorphosis.
5 The title of the German book reads 'A New and well grounded instruction in all

34

merchant's arithmetic in three books compiled by Peter Apian of Leisnig, Astronomer in Ordinary at Ingolstadt' (cited in Harvey, 1900: 224). See also M. Ruskill and C. Harbison (1987).

6 Memling, National Gallery of Washington.

7 In an older St Veronica portrait by the Master of St Veronique's school in the National Gallery, London, there is so little effort at 'realism' that the face of Jesus is about three times that of Veronica and the face is complete with its golden halo! At the other extreme, there is, in Washington National Gallery, a more 'rationalised' portrait of the Sacred Face. Veronica is absent, and the *trompe l'oeil* kerchief is nailed onto the picture representing a brown Golgotha Face. Zurbaran's Veronique's veil from 1658 now in the Valladolid National Museum of Culture is as close as one can get to a photographic rationalised *negative* image: Véronique is absent, but the face itself is barely visible; see Baticle (1988).

8 Even the rationalised dispute over the shroud of Turin is still showing some remnants of this ancient paradigm of Presence. The Catholic Church cannot really treat the shroud as a scientific trace submitted to laboratory trials. It wavers and recently limited access to samples of the shroud (Ian Anderson, *New Scientist*, 21 March 1988: 22). Funnily, the article is illustrated with a picture of the negative face of the Shroud with the following legend: 'Is this the face of Christ? Fudging by the Vatican could hide the truth'. However, what is the truth, what it is to hide it or to show it, and what is to 'fudge' are entirely different in the two regimes. What is extraordinary is not that the Catholic Church limits the laboratory inquiry but that it accepts it at all. In the old paradigm of Presence, it is *as unthinkable* to submit the shroud of Turin to carbon datation techniques as it would be to take a sample of Memling's red pigment in order to do a blood analysis of Jesus.

9 A proof that the modern definition of art has not completely won over is offered in the British Museum in London by troops of Christians equipped not with a tourist guide but with a Bible led not by historians of art but by preachers and who visit the Egyptian and Babylonian rooms to reenact what is written in the Bible.

10 In a popular northern iconographic theme 'St Jerome's mass' the painting was used to double the real presence of Jesus in the mass. In the midst of the Eucharist St Jerome was seeing the bleeding Christ appear straight above the altar surrounded by all the instruments of the Passion.

11 Of course, as Foucault pointed out although in a very different context in *Words and Things*, the very meaning of each of these words – repetition, exact, imitation, different, same, essential, and also 'meaning' – is going to be deeply altered when going from the Prose of the World to Classical Age. On repetition the best book remains Gille Deleuze's thesis (1968) and the deepest meditation Charles Péguy (1914).

12 The word Jesus itself is a mediator's term that stands for thousands of other actions of re-presentation. This result is well known in Biblical exegesis, as for instance, when the Jesus who announced the Kingdom of God was turned, by his disciples, as the one whose venue should be announced. The word Jesus – and later in Paul's work – the word Christ, no more than the word Kingdom of God, or indeed the word God itself, is about represented things out there. Those words have no significance, which does not mean, as will be understood by a later scientistic age that they have no meaning, but simply that they are signifiers. On this exegetic point see Bultmann (1971).

13 In shifting to this regime the reader should of course retranslate the meaning of words like 'made up' 'historical' and 'real'.

14 On the definition of the key notion of 'immutable and combinable mobiles' see Latour (1986; 1987; 1988a).

15 This is exactly what happened to so many Biblical exegets of the nineteenth century, who used archaeology and history to reach what Jesus said and what really happened there at the time. Many felt so disappointed by the little facts they could maintain that they had to consider the whole story as a myth. The very idea of another regime of faithfulness, description, transcription and interpretation had become so foreign to them in their scientistic century, that they could not even imagine it.

16 Arbib and Hesse (1986) make the comparison between metonymic scientific translation with metaphoric religious ones. In the metonymic regime of representation the part counts for the whole (that is, the theory for the data, the scale-model for scale one, the laboratory for the field) whereas in the metaphoric regime of representation it is possible to go from one meaning to the next without ever getting closer to a literal meaning.

17 For a careful distinction between two modes of representation that have different relations to time and to pictorial matters, the Glance and the Gaze, see Bryson (1983).

18 Byzantine and Protestant Iconoclasm, although largely different, were opposed by Orthodox and Catholic preaching with the same line of argument: if Jesus is not God incarnated then it is wrong to represent Jesus' life and miracles, but if Jesus is God incarnated then the re-presentation of the scenes in the Word of the Gospel or in the Images of frescoes and painting is the same movement.

19 No book has more beautifully studied how the same movement generated on the one hand more science and on the other more religious conflicts as Elizabeth Eisenstein (1979).

20 Ivins is the pioneer (1953; 1973). See Edgerton (1976) and for one of the many critiques of Edgerton see Kemp (1978).

21 '*Trompe l'oeil*' is a fascinating play on absence and presence which, in a way, is anathema both for the religious and for the scientific regime of representations (although both made use of it) (Milman, 1982). When Mary is ascended to Heaven she is not supposed to take off through the Sky in such a way that viewers could see her from beneath as happens in many Baroque *trompe l'oeils* of the Assumption. When scientific instruments, doors or books, are displayed in a *trompe l'oeil* scene they are not scaled and transformed to be made more knowable and manageable; they resemble too much the distant scale one.

22 This very presentation will itself be forgotten when positive or rationalist theology takes over and will try to understand in topological terms what is the minimum dogma that should be kept through all the adulterations and embroidery. When theology itself started to raise this question it became as deeply scientificised as any other discipline. From Descartes to Renan the rationalist effort of philosophers will be to extract the grain of *intangible* truth hidden in the confusion of naive and transitory similes and figures. The very notion of the religious movement is for them simply *un-understandable*.

23 The theme of St Jerome is itself the epitome of this merging of knowledge and faith, see Daniel Russo (1987).

24 For a complete description see Fiorella Sricchia Santoro (1986).

25 See Edgerton (1976).

26 No book has done more to map this separate path that Svetlana Alpers (1983). An Imperium is created once a locus becomes a centre of calculation that extends, through the gathering of many representants, to many other loci thus transformed into periphery. For an Imperium to exist, means of gathering, representing, stocking, combining and reexporting are essential. It does not matter too much if part of this work is done through painting, through theory of visions, through mapping, through legal constraints or through war. The key thing is how one locus can be made a whole. It is, in effect, a metonymic transportation of the Earth.

A note on some religious paintings

27 In Van der Weyden's *St Luke's painting the Virgin Mary* (now in Bruges) St Luke, to be sure, is seen with the Virgin but he is made, by the artist, a contemporary of the real Virgin and his lead drawing does not resemble the model in any way.
28 For the notion of subscription or underwritten referent see Latour (1988a). The presence of an underwritten referent is the key feature of scientific texts.
29 After Le Bault, religious subjects are heading for worse as even a brief visit – a long one is unbearable – at the Vatican's Museum of Modern Religious Art will be enough to show. Apart from a few painters like Chagall the deeply sacred destiny of painting is not to be found in works that are *officially* religious. I decided to undertake this project after visiting the Frari in Venice where the breathtaking Titian's *Assumption of the Virgin* was supplemented by a horrible picture (a *croûte*) of a saint newly canonised by the Church. How did the same oil medium become unable to re-peat, to re-present, to re-enact what it did for so many centuries?
30 In my view, no work is more important for modifying our definition of what it is to be post-modern (should I say pre-modern?) than Shapin and Schaffer's book (1985) on the invention of the modern way of distributing rôles between constituencies of humans (Hobbes) and constituencies of non-human witnesses (Boyle). They get us much further than this disappointed form of very modern rationalism that pretends to be 'post-modern'.

References

Alpers, Svetlana (1983), *The Art of Describing Dutch Art in the Seventeenth Century*, Chicago, University of Chicago Press.
Arbib, Michael and Hesse, Mary (1986), *The Construction of Reality*, Cambridge, Cambridge University Press.
Baltrusaitis, Jurgis (1984), *Anamorphoses*, Paris, Flammarion.
Baticle, Jeannine (ed.) (1988), *Zurbaran*, Catalogue de l'Exposition des Musées Nationaux, Paris, Editions de la Reunion des Musées Nationaux.
Baxandall, Michael (1985), *Patterns of Invention: On the Historical Explanation of Pictures*, New Haven, Yale University Press.
Berger, John (1972), *Ways of Seeing*, Harmondsworth, BBC & Penguin Books.
Bryson, Norman (1983), *Vision and Painting: The Logic of the Gaze*, New Haven, Yale University Press.
Bultmann, Rudolf (1963), *History of the Synoptic Tradition*, New York, Harper & Row.
Deleuze, Gilles (1968), *Différence et Répétition*, Paris, PUF.
Edgerton, Samuel (1976), *The Renaissance Discovery of Linear Perspective*, New York, Harper & Row.
Eisenstein, Elizabeth (1979), *The Printing Press as an Agent of Change*, (two volumes), Cambridge, Cambridge University Press.
Foucault, Michel (1973), *Words and Things: An Archaeology of the Human Sciences*, New York, Random House.
Hervey, Mary (1900), *Holbein's Ambassadors, the Picture and the Men: An Historical Study*, London, George Bell & Sons.
Ivins, William M. Jr. (1969), *Prints and Visual Communication*, Cambridge, Mass. and London, The M.I.T. Press.
Ivins, William M. Jr. (1938), 'On the Rationalization of Sight', *Papers*, no 8, New York, The Metropolitan Museum of Art.
Kemp, Martin (1978), 'Science, Non-Science and Non-Sense: the Interpretation of Brunelleschi's Perspective', *Art History*, 1, 2: 134–62.
Kemp, Martin (1984), 'Geometrical Description from Brunelleschi to Desargues:

A Pictorial Means or an Intellectual End?', *Proceedings of the British Academy*, 70: 89–132.

Latour, Bruno (1986), 'Visualisation and Cognition' in H. Kuclick (ed.) *Sociology of Knowledge Studies in the Sociology of Culture Past and Present*, 6: 1–40.

Latour, Bruno (1987), *Science in Action*, Milton Keynes, Open University Press.

Latour, Bruno (1988a), 'A Relativistic Account of Einstein's Relativity', *Social Studies of Science*, 18: 3–44.

Latour, Bruno (1988b), 'Mixing Humans and Non-Humans together: Sociology of a Door Closer', *Social Problems* 35: 298–310.

Latour, Bruno and De Noblet, Jocelyn (1985), 'Les Vues De L'Esprit: Visualisation et Connaissance Scientifique', *Cultural Technique*, Numero special 14.

Milman, Miriam (1982), *The Illusions of Reality: Trompe l'Oeil Painting*, Geneva, New York, Skira, Rizzoli.

Péguy, Charles (1914), *Clio*, Paris, Gallimard.

Ruskill, M. and Harbison, C. (1987), 'On the Nature of Holbein's Portraits', *Word and Image*, 3: 1–26.

Russo, Daniel (1987), *St Jérome en Italie*, Paris and Rome, La Découverte-Ecole Française de Rom.

Santro, Fiorella Sricchia (1986), *Antonello e l'Europe*, Paris and Milan, Jaca Books.

Shapin, Steven and Schaffer, Simon (1985), *Leviathan and the Air Pump*, Princeton, Princeton University Press.

'Views of the past' – reflections on the treatment of historical objects and museums of history (1750–1850)

Stephen Bann

Abstract

It is argued that 'viewing the past' has a precise significance when this activity is interpreted within the context of the specific modes of representation which were current in the period from 1750 to 1850. Although theoretical awareness of this possibility came at a later stage, with Nietzsche's analysis of the 'antiquarian' attitude and Alois Riegl's concept of 'age-value', the antiquarians and collectors of the eighteenth century were already developing practices of installation and exhibition which gave expression to the new 'vision' of the past. The particular case of the Faussett Pavilion is examined to show how one of these antiquarians gave a strong affective character to the process of historical and archaeological retrieval. But it is also suggested that the 'antiquarian' attitude was vulnerable to ironic revision, as Scott and his fellow Romantic writers popularised the study of the Middle Ages; in Barham's *Ingoldsby Legends* (1840), the visual representation of a monument is merely the pretext for a far-fetched medieval story. It is further argued that the historical museum, essentially a product of this period, provided the most stable conditions for 'viewing the past'. Although early examples like Alexandre Lenoir's Musée des Monuments français and Sir John Soane's Museum are discussed, it is Alexandre du Sommerard's Musée de Cluny (opening in the early 1830s) which is shown to have fulfilled these conditions to greatest effect.

The title for this article is borrowed from a recent exhibition at the British Museum. On the poster which advertises it, there is a reproduction of a watercolour of Bramber Castle, Sussex, dated 1782. Two diminutive figures are observing the venerable pile, and one of them evidently sketching, in this work by the topographical artist James Lambert, which was commissioned by the local antiquary Sir William Burrell, as an illustration for his projected

Stephen Bann

History of Sussex.[1] But the title of the exhibition, as applied to this watercolour, might be accused of begging the question. In what sense, if any, are these two figures – the artist and his companion – 'viewing the past'? Is there any sense at all in claiming that these attentive observers (and the late eighteenth-century people for whom they serve as surrogates) were not simply considering a piece of architecture in its natural setting, but 'viewing' history in one of its contemporary and concrete manifestations? I shall take it for granted here that the question is not nonsensical, and that (this example apart) there is a sense in which modes of visual representation, from the later eighteenth century onwards, became increasingly inflected with what might reasonably be termed the vision of the past. But I shall not take this as a self-evident truth. Rather, it is a notion that must be sustained and defended with reference to the particular modes of representation which were being developed and refined at that historical juncture.

Of course there is nothing specially adventurous about the argument that 'viewing' (which gives a distinct cultural connotation to the more neutral activity of 'seeing') is a practice which is historically conditioned and determined. From Riegl to Foucault, art historians and cultural historians have been willing to recognise the particular kinds of investment which Western man has made in the notion of 'visibility', at least from the time of the Renaissance. In one of his early writings, Panofsky began a debate about 'perspective as a symbolic form' which has persisted (though sometimes in a subterranean fashion) for more than half a century, and is still far from having lost its interest.[2] The implication that perspective established a regime of strictly determined visibility, and so facilitated the creation of discourses of power over bodies and classes of objects, has been advanced and tested in many different contexts. Among recent examples of this type of argument encountered almost at random, I would cite the discussion of the visual term of 'conspectus' or 'theatre' as a mode of scientific classification in the seventeenth century, and that of the 'panorama' as the dominant paradigm of landscape gardening in the century following.[3] The notion of visibility as applied to landscape has moreover attained a special prominence in the close study of the realities of power and the modes of representation in the eighteenth century which has been undertaken by John Barrell. For him, the metaphor of the 'view' has an immediate application to the attempts of political theorists and apologists to define the ideal type of the statesman:

Those who can comprehend the order of society and nature are
the observers of a prospect, in which others are merely objects.
Some comprehend, others are comprehended; some are fit to
survey the extensive panorama, some are confined within one or
other of the micro-prospects which, to the comprehensive
observer, are parts of a wider landscape, but which, to those
confined within them, are all they see. (Barrell, 1987: 23–4)

In this particular example, the 'view' is of course not solely
metaphorical. The statesman is not only figuratively possessed of a
comprehensive view, but actually (in accord with the political
rationale adopted in Pope's address to Bolingbroke) the possessor
of broad acres. It is no doubt an aspect of the pervasive change
from public to private conceptions of welfare which Barrell notes
in another recent study (Barrell, 1986), that the nineteenth-
century 'view' of landscape should not necessarily correspond to
this picture of public eminence. 'Scott's view' – a splendid prospect
of the Tweed Valley and the Eildon Hills which is still celebrated
as such by innumerable picture postcards – is not the vista of a
landed proprietor over his possessions, and hence the demonstration of a wealth which need not fear the threat of corruption. It is a
figurative taking of possession, which comprises both the picturesque aspect of the scene, and its historical and mythical
associations. Scott was, it hardly needs saying, genuinely a child of
the Borders, who resented above all else the improvidence of his
ancestors in alienating the imposing medieval ruins of Dryburgh
Abbey (just out of the field of 'Scott's View'), and built his own
surrogate medieval pile beside the Tweed at 'Abbotsford' (cf.
Bann, 1984: 93–111). But his method of doing so was by achieving
eminence and wealth as a poet and novelist, and then bankrupting
himself in the realisation of his neo-baronial ambition.

Barrell's eighteenth-century statesman is thus the possessor of
broad acres, and because of that he qualifies to be a person of
comprehensive views. Scott (if one may generalise from this
unique example) puts his signature on a view – a particular, and
potentially public vista – which becomes endowed with his own
deep feeling for the Border country, though it in no way loses its
earlier, historical connections – with the invading Romans, or the
medieval wizard Michael Scott – that are effectively subsumed in
the view. Is 'Scott's view' of the Eildon Hills then a 'view of the
past', for the public that knew his work, and made the pilgrimage
to the sites associated with him? It is impossible to answer this

41

question, or perhaps assign any meaning to it, at this stage of our argument. But what can be asserted is that a different model is operating from the one presumed in Barrell's example. For Barrell, one eye commands the view, and all the rest are seen, as objects, or at best command a 'micro-prospect'. In the case of 'Scott's view', a prospect is objectified, 'signed' by the poet, and is available to the reading public, to the extent that they have assimilated his particular ethos of the historical and the picturesque.

This implication that the notion of the 'view' has been democratised – even though it may not be strictly a political shift – fits in well with what is probably still the most illuminating of all texts concerning the 'view of the past', though it dates from the very beginning of our century: Alois Riegl's 'The Modern Cult of Monuments: Its Character and Its Origin'. Riegl is highly original in considering the 'meaning' of monuments (and their growing popular appeal) in relation to three separate criteria: their 'art-value', their 'historical value' and their 'age-value' (Riegl, 1982: 21–51). Of the first two, little need be said, except that they correspond to different ways of objectifying and distancing the 'monument', either by giving it an atemporal certificate of excellence, or by attesting its relevance to a particular sequence of past events. But 'age-value' is quite different. It is a perceptible property of the building (or object) which is hardly mediated, for Riegl, by any special knowledge of art or history. Consequently it can be registered by those who have no significant experience of high culture:

> When compared with other values, age-value has one advantage
> over all the other ideal values of the work of art in that it claims
> to address one and all and to possess universal validity. It rises
> above differences of religious persuasion and transcends
> differences in education and in understanding of art. And in
> fact, the criteria by which we recognise age-value are as a rule so
> simple that they can even be appreciated by people whose minds
> are otherwise exclusively preoccupied with the constant worries
> of material existence. The most simple-minded farmhand is able
> to distinguish an old belfry from a new one. (Riegl, 1982: 33)

Now Riegl is in no doubt that the development of 'age-value' is a comparatively recent one. He writes of the 'rise of age-value in the late nineteenth century' as having generated particular kinds of conflict (p. 44), notably the obvious one between the value attached to the visible signs of age and decay, and the functional criterion of 'newness-value'. But it is reasonable to ask whether Riegl is dating 'the rise of age-value' in accordance with the growing recognition that such a criterion needs to give due weight (his own theoretical formulation being the final stage in the process), or with some historical estimate of the stage at which people, even 'farmhands' began to observe things in this way. It is very likely that the former is the case. Riegl is completing a process of theoretical adjustment to the fact that 'age-value' – a value attributed to the visible signs of age and decay – had become a factor impossible to ignore in the course of the nineteenth century. His success in identifying and giving value to this 'third factor' is thus comparable to the achievement of Nietzsche who found an important place in his *Use and Abuse of History* for the so-called 'antiquarian' attitude, the loving attention paid by the antiquary to all that was 'small, limited, mouldy and obsolete' (1969: 27).

So we are justified in assuming that Riegl's 'age-value', like Nietzsche's antiquarian attitude, can be ascribed, as a historical phenomenon, to a period earlier than that in which it was detected and given theoretical status. But how can we proceed much further in giving more specific content to the historical genesis of such modes of 'viewing the past'? The only way, so it seems to me, is to look more rigorously at the development of forms of representation, and particularly those which were inflected, from the mid-eighteenth century onwards, with the themes of the past. We need, in other words, to try to recapture the embryonic stages of what, to the late nineteenth-century, was a fully-fledged growth. On a visit to Canterbury, Henry James took particular notice of a cloister, 'very dusky and mouldy and dilapidated, and of course very sketchable' (James, 1960: 91). By the time of James, quite evidently, the syntagm dusky/mouldy/dilapidated/sketchable is already well-established. The critic is simply repeating a series of connections which have become a commonplace. But we have to remember that these connections were originally forged in the very process of the modal shifts in the history of representation which took place from the middle of the eighteenth century onwards. The scene which is 'of course very sketchable' has been pre-constrained by innumerable similar scenes, themselves the product both of the technical history of media and of the evolving aesthetic of the picturesque.

*   *   *   *

My task is therefore to formulate a series of connected hypotheses about the possibilities of viewing the past which developed in the century from, roughly, 1750 to 1850. As good a starting point as any is the striking watercolour, by an unknown artist, of the *Interior of Letheringham Church looking west* (c. 1765), which was included in the previously mentioned exhibition, *Views of the Past*.[4] It is clear that this dilapidated Suffolk church, full to bursting with tombs that testified to its former glory, was attracting the attention of the historically minded in the mid-eighteenth century. In 1744, the Suffolk antiquary Tom Martin, impressed by the effigies of Boviles, Wingfields and Nauntons that rested there, commented that only such a great church as Westminster Abbey was 'so fully adorned with such Noble Remains of Antiquity as are to be met with here'. But it was the dilapidation of the church, as well as the richness of its contents, that also provoked attention. A decade after Martin, Horace Walpole remarked that the church was 'very ruinous, though containing such treasures'.

The anonymous watercolour which records Letheringham as it was in 1765 or thereabouts certainly conveys this message of 'treasures' amid 'ruins'. But it is quite a different matter to assume (as does the organiser of the exhibition) that this work can be classed as 'A record of decay'. This is not just a verbal quibble. The dry technique of the watercolourist, and his quirky control of perspective which includes one medieval effigy rising up out of the floor to meet us, are certainly successful in conveying the disorderly clutter of the neglected church. We can see the beams jutting jaggedly out against the sky. But 'decay' is a term that belongs to a different series of perceptions of the past – those which we have touched on in invoking Riegl's 'age-value' and the 'mouldy', as registered by Nietzsche and James. There is no mouldiness in this image of Letheringham, no sense of the actual process of deterioration which is presumably taking place. Instead, the church as a construction is undergoing a kind of extreme state of mechanical disorder, and the rhetorical force of the image is very much the same as in Walpole's comment: the catachresis of 'treasures' within 'ruins'.

I do not say that Letheringham was not perceived as an example of 'decay' – simply that this image (and these comments) do not in fact *represent* the process of decay. That it is perfectly possible to find counter-examples from the 1760s is well attested by the phenomenon of the Faussett Pavilion, a now destroyed collection of objects and inscriptions which was housed up to 1950 in the modest structure bearing that name in the grounds of Nackington Court, near Canterbury. Riegl noted the connections between age-value and 'incompleteness . . . lack of wholeness . . . tendency to dissolve form and colour' (1982: 31). The abraded and mutilated stone fragment which Faussett has rescued and installed in its niche is certainly an eloquent exemplar of those qualities, suggesting the tendency of the artefact to return, in the fullness of time to 'amorphous nature'. And Faussett has himself intervened, through the medium of the inscription, to stress the pathos of his act of historical retrieval. The figure is that of a 'bishop or abbot', truncated alas! (*proh dolor!*), and for a long period trailed from place to place, which 'Brianus Faussett' has now been able to offer an asylum of a sort (*asymum, quale quale*).[5] (Plate 1).

In the argument which is being traced here, Brian Faussett's Pavilion serves as a kind of base line for the antiquarian sensibility which (I would hold) was instrumental in revaluing and re-presenting the past in a revelatory way. Valuable recent studies have been published of individual antiquarians and of the phenomenon of antiquarianism as a whole in eighteenth and early nineteenth-century Britain (see Piggott, 1985, and Levine, 1986). But little attention has been paid to the particular issue with which we are concerned: that is, the role of antiquarians in securing not merely new interpretations of history but a novel 'view of the past'. Here the important point seems to be that the antiquarians passionately cared for the neglected and decayed objects that they were salvaging. Evidence of a psychoanalytic nature can doubtless play a part in explaining what particular mechanisms of desire were being activated in this affective process.[6] But, in the context of this argument, it is important simply to note that antiquarians like Faussett gave a strong affective character to the very process of historical and archaeological retrieval, and in so doing, no doubt contributed powerfully to the dominant myth of Romantic historiography – that the past should be 'resurrected'.

Of course, this mythic resurrection of the past was fed by a number of different currents of thought and feeling, which can hardly be detailed here. Half a century after the anonymous artist recorded the 'treasures' of Letheringham church, Thomas and Charles Alfred Stothard were well launched on their imposing collection of *Monumental Effigies*, which was a hitherto un-precedented survey of the type of medieval funerary sculpture which Letheringham had possessed in profusion. Instead of

Plate 1 Figure and inscribed tablet from the Faussett Pavilion, (1769)

46

recording them *in situ*, bunched up against one another, the Stothards carefully analysed the finer points of the monuments, displaying significant details as well as overall views. But all of this sedulous itemisation was governed by an overall programme that was epitomised in the allegorical message of their frontispiece: 'The Monumental Effigies rescued from Time'. Here a somewhat ungainly medieval effigy is being propelled into orbit by a group of *putti* attending a female figure who is presumably the Muse of History. The work as a whole, therefore, springs from a practice of careful analysis and accurate recording of historical detail. But the final aim of the two artists is to participate in the general resuscitation of past history that was so much a feature of the period that they were living through (see Bann, 1984: 64ff.).

Inevitably the image can only perform this function if it is supported by an implicit or explicit narrative. In Faussett's case (which is no doubt an exceptional one), the narrative is that of his own personal discovery and rehabilitation of the objects in question. In the case of *Monumental Effigies*, the narrative of the lives of the medieval potentates whose effigies are presented is juxtaposed with the image, supplying an abbreviated but necessary link in the chain of the historical process from which they have been removed. But beyond these partial narratives, we can imagine that the Stothards' collection depended for its full effect (as it depended for its subscribers) on the vast expansion of the historical imagination which was being effected (during the very period of their labours) by the poetic productions of an author like Sir Walter Scott.

My point is simply this. The antiquarians (and Scott clearly fell under that rubric, to a certain extent) gave value to historical objects, and it is not anachronistic to suggest that this value was of the third type later theorised by Riegl, neither artistic, nor properly speaking historical in kind, but identified with the visible signs of age and decay. But the poets, novelists and indeed historians who were tinged by the antiquarian sensibility were able to carry their intuitions further by articulating new, colourful, dramatic narratives of the hitherto neglected past. To the extent that narrative therefore took over the prime role of serving as an 'icon' of the historical process (White, 1978: 88), it tended inevitably to drain the object, and the image, of their original catalytic role. 'Viewing the past' was no longer a matter of mediation through visual representation, or not so predominantly: the reading public could conceive of a rich and colourful domain, sharply differentiated from the world of the present day, simply through the mediation of the printed word.

It needs to be emphasised, as a modification of this hypothesis, that both historical novels and histories proper were frequently supplemented with visual materials (full-page illustrations, vignettes etc.) during this period. There can be no sharp division in practice – even if one could be asserted in phenomenological terms – between the reading of narrative and the registering of images, within the published work of this period. Nonetheless, it seems valid to argue that the original stimulus offered by the image tends to be nullified by the existence of a strong narrative, which relegates it to a mere decorative role. It is fascinating to consider, from this point of view, T. Gilks's engraving of a crusader's tomb, which appears as a vignette at the end of the story 'Grey Dolphin', in Barham's *Ingoldsby Legends* (first series, 1840). The effigy depicted is indeed that of Sir Robert de Shurland, in the Abbey of Minster-in-Sheppey, which incorporates a curious horse's head by the knight's crossed feet, doubtless due to the fact that he had obtained a royal grant of the 'Wreck of the Sea' (Harper, 1906: 246). But the story, 'Grey Dolphin', is a recapitulation of a local legend which held that the aforesaid knight was killed (according to an old woman's prediction) after giving an ill-considered kick to an object found on the beach which happened to be the skull of his former charger! What Barham therefore does is to narrate, for the benefit of a popular audience, a good yarn of retribution coming to the mighty, which was obviously based (in its original legendary form) on nothing more substantial than the odd and apparently unexplained occurrence of the horse's head beside the effigy. The real effigy, in other words, serves as a mere pretext for a far-fetched legend, told anew in vivid and engaging (but wholly inauthentic) detail. Barham cannot resist underlining the irony by dealing lightly with the whole ritual of viewing, and supposedly coming to terms with, the objects of the past:

> In the abbey-church at Minster may yet be seen the tomb of a recumbent warrior, clad in the chain-mail of the 13th century. His hands are clasped in prayer; his legs, crossed in that position so prized by Templars in ancient, and tailors in modern, days, bespeak him as a soldier of the faith in Palestine. Close behind his dexter calf lies sculptured in bold relief a horse's head; and a respectable elderly lady, as she shows the monument, fails not to read her auditors a fine moral lesson on the sin of ingratitude,

Plate 2 T. Gilks, Vignette illustrating 'Grey Dolphin', from Barham's *Ingoldsby Legends* (First Series, 1840)

or to claim a sympathising tear to the memory of poor 'Grey Dolphin'! (Barham, 1843: 94)

As if to underline the irony at the expense precisely of the antiquarians who set such store by fragmentary and dismembered objects, Barham adds a note to this peroration in his second edition which is apparently mocking the pretentions of an authentic antiquarian and genealogist, John Britton (Harper, 1906: 19):

> Subsequent to the first appearance of the foregoing narrative, the tomb alluded to has been opened during the course of certain repairs which the church has undergone. Mr Simpkinson, who was present at the exhumation of the body within, and has enriched his collection with three of its grinders, says the bones of one of the great toes were wanting.

Barham's ironic text is thus a significant commentary on the modes of historical representation which he parodies. Once upon a time, he seems to imply, a modern witness might have 'seen the tomb of a recumbent warrior' and achieved an imaginative vision of the remote past. Now such a witness is so satiated with such inducements that he cannot succumb to them naively and directly, but can only be induced to participate in a game which *simulates* the process of historical reconstruction. Once upon a time, the antiquarian was a serious and respectable figure. Now he is revealed as ridiculous, and even necrophiliac, in his demeaning passion for the relics of the past.

*   *   *   *

If it were simply a question of 'objects' and 'texts' offering access to the past through visual means, we would probably have to conclude with a message of this kind: that 'viewing the past' was a fairly evanescent possibility offered by the shifting representational modes of the period, and rapidly came to seem a mere rhetorical effect, which had lost any claim to serious attention. But of course the antiquarians did not simply amass objects, and provide hints for popular story-tellers. Even Brian Faussett took care to arrange his cherished objects in the form of a Pavilion, where each relic and inscription would have contributed to an overall effect that was more than the sum of its parts. The history of 'viewing the past' in our period is therefore not simply the record of a personal investment in objects and their 'age-value'; it is also the record of a growing tendency to accumulate and order those objects in permanent installations, in other words to set up museums. Fausset failed according to this criterion, as his collection was eventually rejected by the British Museum trustees under the pretext that it was not 'high art'[7] (and even his Pavilion was finally broken up, its component elements being dispersed). But there were others who managed to give a more definitive form to their assemblages of objects, and so create distinctive types of environment in which history could be visually experienced.

Some readers may be impatient at this stage with my insistence that something new was being developed during this period. After all, there had been collections of antique sculpture, not to mention 'cabinets of curiosities', long before 1800. How can it be argued that these offered no 'view' of history, whereas their successors in the Romantic epoch did so? In part, the answer to this question lies in a simple test. To what extent were such objects brought together on historical criteria, and to what extent on purely artistic criteria? (Riegl's division of categories seems to apply here as well, even if, for the eighteenth century, it may well be that a grouping on 'historical' criteria is not yet conceptually accessible.) The other aspect to be considered is the physical and environmental aspect of the arrangement, since I would certainly claim that historical recreation implied particular attention to aspects such as the overall lighting of the space.

Robert Adam's sculpture gallery at Newby Hall in Yorkshire, built for the connoisseur William Weddell, is a useful example to take, since it was completed in the 1760s when antiquarian collections were already being set up. Recent research by Robin Middleton has brought to light the extraordinary achievement of Adam in conjuring up the 'fullness, the wholeness of classical form' through invisible contrivances of timber, lath and plaster (Middleton, 1986: 56), but the personality of his patron remains mysterious. Faced by the question of why Weddell – 'the second son of a man who had inherited a fortune, quite by chance' – chose 'to spend it on such a lavish evocation of a classical vision' (p. 59), Middleton can only hope that, as a result of some future research, 'the springs of his lifelong belief in the radiance of the classical heritage of the Mediterranean might be laid bare' (p. 60). For our purposes, it is enough to conclude that the whole vocabulary in which the achievement of Weddell, and Adam, is acclaimed points to an ahistorical criterion of excellence. The aim is to recreate the 'radiance of the classical heritage', and though this purpose may imply that a 'Mediterranean' light is being sought for, in which to set the superb classical objects brought home by Weddell, it is really a matter of transcending time and space in the realisation of an ideal vision, where history as process plays no part. Not only do the works brought together by Welland exhibit no 'age-value' (even when a repair has been made, in the eighteenth-century manner, it is delicately camouflaged in the interests of a perfect wholeness); it could fairly be concluded that their status as *historical* objects has been erased, and the smooth marble forms approximate as closely as possible to archetypes of thought.

The timeless effect of the sculpture gallery at Newby (and of many others similar to it)[8] suggests a self-enclosed visual system. Ideal temporality cancels out the visible signs of distance from the present. Indeed there are good reasons for arguing that the connoisseur of this period simply could not (or would not) see the signs of the past; in Riegl's terms, he absolutely censored the dimension of 'age-value'. When Lord Elgin performed the feat of transporting the Parthenon 'marbles' to England in 1816, a connoisseur like Richard Payne Knight bridled at the appearance of these abraded and fragmentary objects. His visual skills, formed through the study of small-scale objects like medals and statuettes, simply could not accommodate the intrusion of Elgin's epic lumps of stone.[9]

Nevertheless Payne Knight was the populariser, on another level, of the highly influential theory of the *picturesque*, which left the way open for a vision of the classical world far removed from the timeless perfection of Newby. As he proposed in his essay *On Taste* in 1805:

> Ruined buildings, with fragments of sculptured walls and broken columns, the mouldering remnants of obsolete taste and fallen magnificence, afford pleasure to every learned beholder, imperceptible to the ignorant . . . The mind is led by view of them to the most pleasing train of ideas, and the whole scenery around receives an accessory character, which we commonly call 'classical'. (Jullien, 1986: 1)

Employing the popular psychology of associationism derived from Locke, Payne Knight at least concedes that the 'learned beholder' can be transported in his thoughts, as a result of the visual stimulus. But once again, we may doubt whether any distinctively *historical* vision was involved. The tell-tale signs in the passage quoted above are no doubt the instances of *catachresis* – 'obsolete taste and fallen magnificence' – which suggest a 'pleasure' in paradox and contradiction, rather than a distinctive vision of the past. Moreover the 'train of ideas' leads ineluctably, so it would seem, to the governing concept of the 'classical', which is already overdetermined by its significance as a continuing cultural tradition. Nothing new will come out of Payne Knight's view of ruins.

The same is true, in the last resort, of the most original and influential of all early nineteenth-century collections: that contained in Sir John Soane's Museum in Lincoln's Inn Fields. Most happily, Soane's Museum still exists, whilst the French museums of which I shall speak later have been closed, or altered out of all recognition. Yet the very survival of Soane's installation, which allows us to respond vividly to the didactic and personal aspects of his work, also makes it easy to see that the vision of history was not one of his guiding themes. On the basement floor of the Museum, next to the Sepulchral Chamber which contains the Egyptian sarcophagus of Seti, we find a 'Monk's Parlour', created in 1824, which is as close as Soane gets to the mode of Gothic antiquarianism. His own description, however, makes it clear that this is a satirical inclusion. 'It may, perhaps, be asked, before leaving this part of the Museum,' he suggests, 'at what period the Monk existed whose memory is here preserved, and whether he is to be identified with any of those whose deeds have enshrined their names. The answer to these questions is furnished by Horace: *Dulce est desipere in loco*' (*A New Description*, 1986: 31–2). Of course, the monk – Padre Giovanni – is Soane himself, and the Gothic joke is pointed with a Latin tag ('it is pleasant to be nonsensical in due place').

Soane's remarkable museum is nonetheless parallel in one respect to the French museum which inaugurated the systematic classification of historical objects by their period: Alexandre Lenoir's[10] 'Musée des Monuments français'. Soane paid particular attention to the way in which stained glass, mirrors and gilded surfaces could be used to fuse individual objects into an overall visual effect.[11] Lenoir was also attentive to lighting, and to the ways in which it could be used to unify and distinguish a given space. A Scottish visitor to the Museum in 1803 described both its contents and its lighting in these revealing terms:

[. . .] we went to see The ci-devant Convent of the Augustins in
which are deposited all the tombs and monuments which
escaped the fury of the revolutionists, (they are arranged in
different cloisters and appartments) each containing the
specimens of statuary and sculpture during one century
beginning with the earliest periods of the art, and receiving light
through windows of coloured glass as nearly of the same
antiquity as possible. Some very beautiful and curious
specimens . . . are among them. (Quoted in Bann, 1984: 83)

Although this is not an exhaustive description of the contents of
Lenoir's museum, it grasps the essential principle extremely well,
and shows how clear its didactic message must have been. Lenoir
had personally intervened, during the revolutionary period, to
save significant monuments which were otherwise threatened with
destruction, and as early as 1795 he had opened – 'for the
instruction of our artists of the future' (*Le Gothique retrouvé*,
1979: 77) – the rooms of his store in the former Convent of the
Petits-Augustins, on the left bank of the Seine in Paris. Perhaps
the most significant aspect of Lenoir's pioneering work, as he
himself realised, was the fact that medieval art, from the thirteenth
century onwards, was included in the stately succession of century
rooms, which were themselves as closely adjusted to the historical
character of their contents as the original building permitted. Yet
even the most recent of the rooms, the former dining-hall of the
monks which was devoted to the seventeenth century, bore the
signs of a discreetly unified milieu, in which no intrusion from an
alien period was permitted. Hubert Robert's small oil painting of
this room of the Museum is an interesting testimony to Lenoir's
visual staging of the objects of the past, mediated though it is by
Robert's own well-defined sense of space and chiaroscuro. The
light of day which breaks into the cavernous hall reveals the
sculptural and monumental objects as having been brought
together in a provisional order (quite unlike the ideal perfection of
Newby): it illuminates their heterogeneity and their otherness,
which is redeemed only by the superior fiction of a common
historical origin.

Lenoir's Museum was closed by the Bourbon government in
1816 – significantly because the newly appointed 'intendant
général des arts et monuments publics', the classical theorist
Quatremère de Quincy, could not tolerate the notion that there
had been a 'national art' before the period of the Renaissance

Plate 3 Hubert Robert, *View of a Room in the Musée des Monuments Français*, Musée du Louvre, Paris
Photo: Réunion des Musées Nationaux

(p. 78). The collections were dispersed, with many of the objects returning to their former locations. It was nearly twenty years before Paris again had a pioneering historical museum on the Left Bank, Alexandre du Sommerard's[12] Musée de Cluny. However the pre-history of this museum extended over a long period. Du Sommerard had been largely a collector of classical and contemporary art during the years of the Empire, but with the Restoration he inaugurated his collection of medieval and Renaissance objects and progressively divested himself of the earlier acquisitions (see Bann, 1984: 79–80). A portrait by the artist Renoux, dated 1825, shows him under the guise of 'The Antiquary' (*L'Antiquaire*), with a chaotic assemblage of objects stacked around him.

It is central to the argument of this article that Du Sommerard, unlike the previous collectors and museum founders discussed in this section, had an antiquarian sensibility: that is to say, he responded to the objects of the past in an affective way which recalls Nietzsche's evocation of the 'small, limited, mouldy and obsolete'. Brian Faussett had exhumed and given asylum to antique and fragmentary objects, but his work remained a kind of strangely subversive imitation of the classical temples set up by his richer and grander contemporaries. Du Sommerard began collecting a vast range of unregarded historical materials without, at that stage, having any pre-conceived plan of how they might eventually be housed and displayed. But the chaos of 1824 was left far behind when, in 1832, he became tenant of the ancient town-house of the Abbots of Cluny. Like Lenoir, he now had a genuinely historical location in which to set out his collection. But unlike Lenoir, he would strive to achieve the maximum degree of integration of the individual object in the overall effect. His rooms would not be classed under the schematic organisation of the 'century'; they would aim to represent, through a fullness of texture and an absolute degree of integration, the reality of the lived life of the earlier periods.

In what modality, then, did the visitors who flocked to Du Sommerard's Musée de Cluny, 'view' the past? The contemporary engraving of the room dedicated to François 1er, and hence to the early sixteenth century, shows a scene which is familiar enough to the present day museum visitor, but would have been dramatically novel to his early nineteenth-century counterpart. It is not simply a matter of monumental sculpture, as in Lenoir's museum, but of the plethora of objects in domestic use: beds, coverlets, cabinets,

Plate 4 Bachelier and Godard, 'The Room of François 1er in the Musée de Cluny', reproduced from Du Sommerard, *Les Arts au Moyen Age*, 1838–1846)
Photo: British Museum.

chairs, tables and a host of other things too small to identify (but accessible to the visitor, who could peer at them and ponder over them to his heart's content). The contemporary account of the journalist Emile Deschamps gives a good impression of the overwhelming effect of the display – which is however recuperated in the end by the 'enveloping' sense of the 'chivalric times', and the narrative voice of the collector himself:

> Furnishings, hangings, stained glass, dishes, armour, utensils and jewelry – all has been miraculously recovered and preserved; you walk in the midst of a vanished civilisation; you are as if enveloped by the good old chivalric times, and the cordial hospitality of the master rounds off the illusion. (Bann, 1984: 82)

It is an important point to note that, in this description, the visual experience as such is taken for granted. Emphasis is placed on the feature of movement through space ('you walk') and on the sense of envelopment – which, as I have argued elsewhere, could well imply the invocation of the sense of smell (Bann, 1987) – not to mention the vocal contributions of the 'master', Du Sommerard. If there is a parallel with this representation of experience in the development of strictly visual strategies, it is perhaps with the history of the panorama that it should be made, rather than with the traditional pictorial mode. Du Sommerard utilises the whole space available, not offering a privileged vista or viewpoint, but surrounding the spectator with a plenum in which each individual element testifies to a greater whole – ultimately nothing less than the experiential reality of a recreated past.

Yet it is perhaps Du Sommerard's installation in the former Chapel of the Hôtel de Cluny that the achievement comes across to us most vividly, again through a contemporary reproduction. Nicolas Chapuy's lithograph, published in Du Sommerard's splendid book *Les Arts au moyen âge*, is faithful to the architectural detail of the medieval chapel, but even more so to the atmospheric effect which has been secured by the accumulation of much ecclesiastical furniture (in some cases ingeniously reconstituted from disparate fragments) and the addition of a mysterious cowled figure close to the altar. Unlike the contemporary figures tenanting Hubert Robert's painting – but like, for example, the praying monk in Bouton's picture of a ruined church from 1824[13] – the enigmatic presence serves as a

Plate 5 Nicolay Chapuy, 'The Chapel in the Musée de Cluny', reproduced from Du Sommerard, *Les Arts au Moyen Age*, (1838–1846)
Photo: British Museum.

shifter from present to past. But it would not succeed in doing so if
the rich texture of objects, and the soft, evenly diffused light, did
not prepare us to welcome this ambiguous evidence of the visibility
of the past.

*   *   *   *

I am well aware that I have been analysing not the early
nineteenth-century museum, but the museum as mediated by
different types of visual reproduction. Quite apart from the fact
that this is now our only mode of access to the visual effect of such
installations, the difference does not seem to me to matter very
greatly. The myth of the visual recreation of the past traverses
many different modes of representation in the period with which
we have been concerned, and it is not plausible to localise it in one
of them. If I have argued that the hallmark of the museum
installation lay in its 'enveloping' effect – which could not be
reproduced by conventional pictorial means – then I would hold it
no less true that a visual representation like Chapuy's lithograph
refines and concentrates a particular aspect of Du Sommerard's
programme, achieving through pictorial subterfuge an illusory
effect that could not have been achieved in any other way.

Indeed one might say that Du Sommerard's purpose was
necessarily a fragile one, dependent on a particular conjuncture of
the means of representation and the state of public awareness of
the past which could not be repeated or perpetuated. As the
present curator of the collection warns us in his official guide, Du
Sommerard made many mistakes in his attributions, let alone
engaging in questionable repairs to give his objects visual appeal.
The present Musée de Cluny is very far from Du Sommerard's
original ideal – and it cannot be said that it reflects any comparably
strong conception of what a historical museum should be. There is
a 'Room of Seigneurial Life', but it is only so called because it
houses a tapestry which illustrates features of the life of the Middle
Ages. The Chapel is an incongruous element since no one seems to
have been able to decide whether it is just another display room,
or whether it should show the enhancement, by carefully placed
objects, of a space whose character is already decisively marked,
in historical terms.[14]

What can certainly be stressed, by contrast, is the systematic
character of Du Sommerard's representation of the past. Compared
with the other figures mentioned here, he gives pride of place to

Plate 6 Guerschau and Godard, 'Bedroom of Marie de Médicis at the Luxembourg' reproduced from Du Sommerard, *Les Arts au Moyen Age*, (1838–1846)
Photo: British Museum

61

the process of integration; like so many Romantic myth-makers, he is ultimately vindicating a notion of resurrection from the dead – 'let these bones live!' On a more mundane level, his concern to recuperate every small item in order that the whole should be complete and convincing is represented, on a rhetorical level, in the plate of the 'Bedroom of Marie de Médicis at the Luxembourg' which also adorns *Les Arts au moyen âge*. A tiny object *might* have gone astray in this otherwise beautifully coherent milieu, and the lady in waiting bends down to recover it. The 'view of the past' is confirmed in its coherence by the admitted possibility that here, in an object that almost eludes our vision, a lack might have occurred.

Notes

1 See British Library Exhibition notes for 'Views of the Past: drawing as a record of place', 25 September 1987 to 31 January 1988, unpaginated. The watercolour is classed Additional MS 5677, f.49.
2 For a recent and brilliantly stimulating review of the issues, see Hubert Damisch, *L'Origine de la perspective* (Paris: Flammarion), 1987, especially pp. 21–63.
3 The first notion was developed by John Dixon Hunt, and the second by Michel Conan, at the recent conference, 'Hypothèses sur une troisième nature', held at the Palais du Luxembourg, Paris, 4–5 September 1987.
4 The work is classed under Additional MS 8797, f.88 (British Museum); the quotations from Martin and Walpole are included in the unpaginated exhibition notes.
5 For a further consideration of the Faussett Pavilion, see Bann, 1987.
6 See Bann, 1984: 93–111 for an approach to the question as it can be applied to Scott and Byron: the point of reference in psychoanalysis used here is the work of Melanie Klein.
7 A paper on Faussett's collection which dates from 1854 refers to 'the sudden notoriety it has acquired in being rejected by the Trustees of the British Museum', and mentions that one of the Trustees 'urged that they were not works of *high art*' (see p. 3, in anonymous pamphlet, 'The Faussett Collection of Anglo-Saxon Antiquities', London, 1854, included in *Collectanea Antiqua*, Vol. III, British Library).
8 The much grander gallery constructed by the Marquess of Lansdowne at Bowood in Wiltshire is remarkable for the seamless repairs effected on some of its finest pieces; another surviving example is the gallery at Petworth, in West Sussex.
9 For the absorbing story of the salvaging and reception of the Elgin Marbles, see Woodhouse, 1969.
10 Alexandre Lenoir was born in 1761 and originally trained as a painter, although he does not seem to have practised his art. When, in 1790, the Constituent Assembly took over the property of the French Church, it was decided to store a large number of works of religious art in the former Convent of the Petits-Augustins, on the Left Bank of the Seine in Paris. Lenoir was chosen to supervise this provisional depository, and immediately set himself to the task of conserving the objects stored there. In 1795, after a personal plea to the revolutionary Comité d'instruction, he took it upon himself to open the

collections to the public. It was decided to class the objects chronologically in the separate rooms of the convent, which was a system of classification never employed before. Lenoir's newly named 'Musée des Monumens français' persisted until the early years of the Bourbon Restoration. But in 1816 it was definitively closed, partly as a result of the violent campaign undertaken by the art critic Quatremère de Quincy. Part of his collection entered the Louvre in 1817, and at a later stage was amalgamated with the Musée de Cluny.

11 This visual effect is most pronounced in the watercolour studies by Gandy which so effectively document the museum (see the illustrations in Summerson, 1982).

12 Alexandre du Sommerard was born in 1779, a member of the provincial *noblesse de robe*. He volunteered for service in Bonaparte's Italian campaigns, and in 1807 received a post in the Cour des Comptes, where he had a successful career. Originally a collector of paintings and drawings (mainly of contemporary artists), he began to concentrate more and more exclusively on his highly original collection of precious and everyday objects from the Middle Ages and the Renaissance. However it was only with his installation in the medieval town-house of the Abbots of Cluny, close to the Sorbonne, that he had the chance to display this outstanding collection of objects. He chose to use the existing rooms of the Hôtel de Cluny (including the Chapel), and to give each of them a special unity, through the accumulation of particular types of object. After his death in 1842, the Museum was acquired by the French state.

13 See C.-M. Bouton, Monk in prayer in a ruined church (1824), Museum of Saint-Lô, reproduced in *Le Gothique retrouvé*, 1979: 124.

14 The curator of the Museum, Alain Erlande-Brandenburg, shows himself to be as far removed as possible from the ideas and practice of Du Sommerard in his choice of the Italian architects Gae Aulenti and Italo Rota for the recent installation of a group of statues from Notre-Dame in the former courtyard of the Hôtel de Cluny. It would be absurd to expect a contemporary museum to preserve the features of its original foundation. At the same time, it would be usefully informative as well as respectful if the present Musée de Cluny offered some documentation of the way in which the installation was conceived in Du Sommerard's time – to supplement the rather disparaging remarks in the official guide.

Bibliography

A New Description of Sir John Soane's Museum (1986), London, Trustees of The Museum.

Bann, S. (1984), *The Clothing of Clio*, Cambridge, Cambridge University Press.

Bann, S. (1987), 'Clio in part: On Antiquarianism and the historical fragment', in *Perspecta – The Yale Architectural Journal*, No. 23, New Haven.

Barrell, J. (1986), *The Political Theory of Painting from Reynolds to Hazlitt*, New Haven, Yale University Press.

Barrell, J. (1987), 'The public prospect and the private view', in J. C. Eade, (ed.), *Projecting the Landscape*, Canberra, Australian National University.

Harper, C. G. (1906), *The Ingoldsby Country*, London, Black.

James, H. (1960), *English Hours*, London, Heinemann.

Jullien, B. (1986), 'An investigation of the importance of the picturesque aesthetic theories in Soane's representation of history in Lincoln's Inn Fields', unpublished conference paper in *Der Geschichte ein Zuhause* Reader, Bochum, Museum Bochum.

Le Gothique retrouvé (1979), catalogue of exhibition at Hôtel de Sully, Paris, Caisse Nationale des Monuments Historiques.

Levine, P. (1986), *The Amateur and the Professional: Antiquarians, Historians and*

Archaeologists in Victorian England 1838–1886, Cambridge, Cambridge University Press.

Middleton, R. (1986), 'The Sculpture Gallery at Newby Hall', in *AA Files* No. 13, London, Architectural Association.

Nietzsche, F. (1969), *Vom Nützen und Nachteil der Historie für das Leben*, Stuttgart, Reclam.

Piggott, S. (1985), *William Stukeley: An Eighteenth Century Antiquary*, London, Thames and Hudson.

Riegl, A. (1982), 'The Modern Cult of Monuments: Its Character and Its Origin', trans. K. W. Forster and D. Ghirardo, in *Oppositions* No. 25, New York, Rizzoli.

Summerson, J. (1982), 'Union of the Arts: Sir John Soane's museum-house', in *Lotus International* No. 35, Milan, Electa.

White, H. (1978), *Tropics of Discourse*, Baltimore, Johns Hopkins Press.

Woodhouse, C. M. (1969), *The Philhellenes*, London, Hodder & Stoughton.

Art and its objects: William Ivins and the reproduction of art

Gordon Fyfe

Abstract

This paper is a critique of the contribution of William Ivins's *Prints and Visual Communication* (1953) to an understanding of the meaning of fine art reproductions. Ivins showed that photographic reproduction was constructed in relation to, and displaced, older ways of reproducing art which were carried out by handicraft engravers. His analysis alerts us to the fact that ambiguity characterized art reproduction before photographs. Art reproductions, then, were interpretations in line based on conventional modes of representation – what Ivins calls a visual syntax. In this respect he enhances our understanding of the social construction of the artist. For Ivins the social history of reproduction seems to end with the camera. This completed an individuation of creativity ushered in with the Renaissance, but which was always qualified by the interfering visual syntax of craftsmen-interpreters. It is argued that the value of Ivins's account resides in its reconstruction of the relationship between handicraft engraving, fine art reproduction and aesthetic objects that have long since slipped from our consciousness.

The Spartan Boy

The collection of the National Gallery of Ireland contains two *trompe l'oeil* paintings of prints, *Lowry* and *The Spartan Boy* (Plates 1 and 2), painted about 1800. These images deceive the eye in a game with reality. Surface textures are effaced in favour of a perfect depiction which persuades a spectator to address the paintings as engravings. There are tell-tale plate marks that distinguish intaglio images from other prints and from drawings or paintings. The paintings convey the rich tonality that is the hall-mark of the mezzotint.[1] Signs of wear and tear are symptomatic of casual display, perhaps in an artist's studio. The key and the tacks, along with the curling and furling of paper against wood grain, provide depth cues that these images are made from ink on paper

65

Plate 1 *Trompe l'oeil* painting of engraving of Lowry, painted circa 1800
Courtesy of National Gallery of Ireland, Dublin.

Plate 2 *The Spartan Boy*. Anonymous *trompe l'oeil* painting of an engraved reproduction, painted circa 1800. Courtesy of the National Gallery of Ireland, Dublin. The legend reads: 'Having stolen a Fox conceals it under his Garment, when being observ'd he suffers it to bite him Mortally'.

attached to wooden panels and not from oil on canvas. The engravings bear the signs of use and of their making.

Within *The Spartan Boy*'s plate mark there is the usual information concerning authorship of engraved reproductions, evidence that we are looking at a reproduction by W. Humphrey of a painting executed by Nathaniel Hone. The artist's skill brings the print so fully and frankly into our presence that the existence of another image, a second painting, is signified. Hone (1717–1784) exhibited a painting called *The Spartan Boy* (now in a private collection) at the London Royal Academy of Arts (RA) in 1775, and this is known to have been engraved by W. Humphrey.[2] The subject of our painting is not only a Spartan boy, not merely a mezzotint but a mezzotint reproduction of a painting. As a reproduction of a mezzotint the painting reverses the usual relationship, whereby engraving reproduced the effects of oil painting. Qualities that distinguish mezzotint as a medium for reproducing oil are now captured in oil.

Our painting depicts the qualities of a mezzotint, but in a world without photomechanical reproduction, the engraving-as-reproduction would usually have conveyed those of a painting. There are three levels of authorship – the anonymous *trompe l'oeil* painting, Humphrey's engraving and the original painting by Hone. The mezzotint reproduces a painting by Hone. The anonymous painter repossesses, as it were, the engraved image for painting. There is no signature and that is appropriate, for indication of authorship would threaten the perception that this is a reproduction of a painting. The anonymity of the painting's artist is a part of the illusion that we have the real thing – that this is a real reproduction! If the graven image is repossessed by painting then the authorship of our painting is concealed through the transparent effects wrought by the anonymous painter.

It is impossible to appreciate the image and not to register ambiguity. Signifiers and signifieds are always on the point of being reshuffled. Appreciation gives chase as the eye momentarily captures one image, acknowledges one authorship, whilst the others are concealed from sight. The sky behind the boy will be a mezzotint only while it cannot be one of two oil paintings. As the curling of the paper suggests, and as the partly obscured legend reveals, concealment is at the heart of the picture. Its subject is the Spartan boy's failure to hide a stolen fox which is suffered to bite the thief mortally when he realizes that he has been observed. Spartan subjects had currency at RA Exhibitions in this period and it seems that the story of the boy and the fox was especially widely known.[3]

The allusions of this picture to authorship and concealment would surely have been appreciated by contemporaries familiar with the print trade. Photography did not inaugurate the age of art reproduction which was a component of European visual culture as early as the sixteenth century. Throughout the eighteenth and nineteenth centuries reproductions ideally took the form of line engravings.[4] In a pre-photographic age, works of art might be known as reproductions engraved in line: 'pictures interpreted by engraving, had *become* engravings' (Malraux 1967: 11–12). The reputations and fortunes of successful artists, particularly those of painters were heavily dependent on a lucrative trade in engraved reproductions of their works. A print collection was an important and accepted working library for any artist and forays into the print shops were a natural part of the formation of a young artist's knowledge and sensibility.

By Hone's time the trade employed a variety of skilled and semi-skilled craftsmen/women whose cultural identity was ambiguous, not artists but not without a publicly acknowledged claim to creativity. Technical innovation perfected the means of reproducing paintings but was linked to a fragmentation and submerging of the engravers' occupation that was also an aspect of the making of the profession of the fine artist – a profession that was struggling both to regulate its relationship to patronage and to exploit the growth of a consumer society. There were two aspects to this. The first was a power struggle over the status of engraving and its place within the fine arts. In London the constitutional politics of exhibiting societies registered this well into the nineteenth century (Fox, 1976; Fyfe, 1985). Fine artists succeeded in containing the ambitions of engravers through an ideology that interiorized creativity as originality. What distinguished the Arts were their 'intellectual qualities of Invention & Composition, which Painting, Sculpture & Architecture so eminently possess, but of which Engraving is wholly devoid' (Hutchison, 1968: 90). Nonetheless, reproductive engravings were accepted as exhibits by the RA which also admitted engravers as junior members.

Second, at workshop level, the exploitation of the market for reproductions was associated with a separation of the labour of reproductive engraving from the intellectual means of production (Fyfe, 1985). Capital accumulation within cultural production endorsed and accentuated the difference between the artist and the craftsman that had been ushered in by the Renaissance. Consumption of art prints increasingly presupposed a division between mental and manual labour that was internal to pictorial production – a division between the activities of painting and engraving. Whilst it is true that there were artists such as Hone who straddled painting and engraving, the dominant ideology of creativity and the structure of the market made this an increasingly difficult position to sustain after Hogarth (1697–1764). As a successful artist a person was unlikely to have a public reputation for print making.

Reproductive engraving was the site of the aesthetic tension between the authorship of the painter and the translation of the reproductive engraver. Engraving was associated with an occupational ideology which asserted the creativity of reproduction as translation. There was an indeterminacy in the relationship between artist and engraver which sometimes erupted into disagreement and conflict and which could yield images whose authorial status was ambiguous. The effects of handicraft reproduction threatened to challenge and obscure the pictorial intentions of artists. Whilst print making extended artists' powers of communication it brought problems of aesthetic control and dependency that were perennial sources of conflict and gossip in the art world to which Hone and Humphry belonged. Who had executed the plate? Had assistants been employed? The answers to such questions sometimes suggest deception and fraud – see for example William Blake's 'Public Address' (Geoffrey Keynes, 1966: 594) and Farington's diary for 18 July 1816 and 10 January 1818 (Greig, 1922–8).

Engravers fought to retain a place within the cultural apparatus, but in the nineteenth century they did so on a terrain that was increasingly defined by a photographic way of seeing (Jussim, 1983; Fyfe, 1985). By the 1880s there were engravers who could deliver an impressionist brush stroke (Plate 3). For the critic Hamerton American wood engraving was superior for its 'tone and texture' (Hamerton, 1882: 324). At the end of the last century American engravers were still associated with a discourse of reproduction which had not completely submerged the authorship of reproductive craftsmen. Process reproduction could *not* interpret: '[h]ow much of the beauty of these admirable cuts [wood engravings of Italian old masters] depends upon the temperament, the originality, the artistic skill, the "personal equation" . . . of the man behind the graver' (*The Century*, 1890: 312).

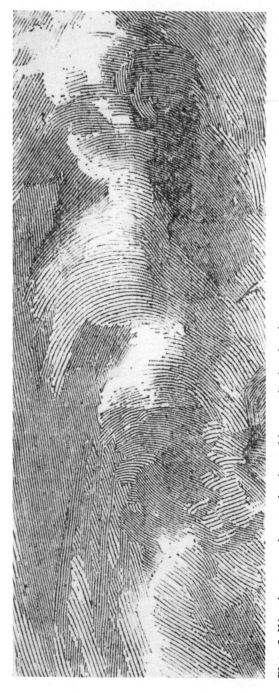

Plate 3 Wood engraved reproduction of impressionist clouds
The Magazine of Art, (1885)

Connoisseurship was sensitive to ambiguities that attended the meaning of reproductive prints: '[w]e want to forget that they are Engravings; and this sort of Engraver [Desnoyers] who glories in the freedom of his stroke, is, . . . continually trying to remind us of its power, freedom and elegance' (Cumberland 1827: 8). Anxieties about the effects of reproduction on art were not born with the photograph. What is surprising is that authorship of reproductive engravings might be granted an artistry of its own – one that might enhance, even improve on the original and which co-existed with that of painting. The legitimacy of this claim to creativity, promoted by engravers, was an issue in a profession that was tending to marginalize engravers as artists. The metaphor of poetic translation recurs as a contested claim to creativity (Strutt, 1785: 5; Landseer, 1807: 177–8; Blake, 1810; Pye, 1845: 208). Exploitation of the print trade went hand in hand with a connoisseurship that sought to determine the meaning of originality in relation to the authority of painting, but which could not wholly deprive reproduction of its own claim to originality (Richardson, 1774: 165).

It seems likely that *The Spartan Boy* was conceived as more than an exercise in *trompe l'oeil* virtuosity. It may have constituted a reflection on the ambiguities that attended art reproduction prior to the introduction of photo-mechanical methods. It must have articulated the experiences of painters and engravers where the fine arts were in the business of capturing engraving as reproduction. That the subject is a mezzotint, rather than a line engraving, is also connected with the meaning of the painting. Frequently used for the reproduction of portraits, mezzotint was more aesthetically subordinate to painting than other methods and particularly vulnerable to deskilling. (It was also commonly hybridized with line engraving and etching.) The mezzotinter's art was concealed that painting might be witnessed; there was not 'the line engraver's opportunity of asserting autographic mannerisms' (Godfrey, 1978: 28). The ambiguity remains. In what medium does the spectator witness the truth of the Spartan Boy's act: in the anonymous oil painting, in mezzotint reproduction or in Hone's original painting? If *trompe l'oeil* typically depicts minor cultural signs (Baudrillard, 1988) then just how minor is this image? The key is that the *trompe l'oeil* paradies the mezzotints pretence only to meet ridicule with the reality of art reproduction.

Anyone familiar with Hone's career would know that in the year in which he exhibited *The Spartan Boy*, 1775, he was the centre of a scandal concerning pictorial deception. This involved a libellous painting, submitted by Hone to the RA Summer Exhibition, which the Academy forced him to withdraw and which he subsequently exhibited independently. Called *The Pictorial Conjurer, displaying the Whole Art of Optical Deception*, it depicted Joshua Reynolds, pre-eminent in the profession and President of the RA, in the act of conjuring a painting from a cascade of reproductive engravings after the works of the Old Masters. The libel amounted to a charge of plagiarism against Reynolds. It was also comment on a problem that exercised Reynolds, Blake and other artists: how to distinguish originality from plagiarism in a profession which recognized the Masters as the point of creative departure. However, what I want to stress is the uncommon and explicit reference, in painting, to the role of reproductions in the gestation of art – the admission to the importance of their presence in the studio. With *The Conjurer*, the art of reproduction that fine artists were in the process of containing bursts through into the public domain, disclosing the creative life of the studio. The accusation of artistic theft could not be tolerated at the RA. What remained was *The Spartan Boy* reference to theft and concealment, a painting that was later to be a pretext for reflection on the meaning of reproduction. What may not have escaped the attention of Exhibition visitors in 1775 was a twist in the Spartan tale; that stealing might not be dishonourable if it was not discovered.

Ivins (1953) has it that with the invention of photographic reproduction ambiguity was resolved. To know art by means of modern reproductions is to be given access to pictorial effects denied to those who depended on handicraft reproductions. What is at stake here is the pictorial authority of artists. There has been an interest among sociologists in the question of the social construction of the artist, in the decentring of the artist and in the discursive role played by the artist-as-creator (Pollock, 1980; Bourdieu, 1980; Becker, 1982). Two issues arise in connection with these matters and Ivins's thesis. One is the dissemination of the idea of the artist as expressing the free-play of a coherent creative will, to which pictorial means are subordinate. The other relates to the institutional sites and art practices which have been loci for the production of the artist-as-creator. Here I am concerned with the cues through which a spectator recognizes the presence of an artist. Examples include art exhibitions and museum displays, the restoration and cleaning of pictures as well as the subject of this article – the reproduction of works of art. Ivins has much to say about visual communication that is pertinent to an understanding of these matters. This concerns the *centring* of the artist through the medium of art reproduction.

Prints and Visual Communication

William M. Ivins Jr (1881–1961) was a print curator. His ideas about visual communication had an impact beyond the Metropolitan Museum of Art in New York where he held a post from 1916 until his retirement thirty years later. In *Prints and Visual Communication* (1953) (hereafter *PVC*) he advanced a seminal thesis concerning the difference that photographic reproductions had made to art. *PVC* melds a socio-technical and aesthetic history of art reproduction with Ivins's experiences as a connoisseur and curator. *PVC* contributes to an understanding of the meaning of photographic reproduction partly because of its insights into the marginalization of a connoisseurship associated with handicraft reproductive prints. The camera had to meet the challenge of dissidents and the visual *anomie* of those who experienced photographic distortion rather than truth to originals. Ivins registers this, indexing a taken-for-granted aesthetic that differs from our own. Footnotes from long forgotten treatises, anecdotes from his youth and early career at the Metropolitan, when the residues of older attitudes to reproductions still survived, allow us to glance at the making of a photographic way of seeing art (Ivins, 1953: 90, 174)

Much of *PVC* is dedicated to a phenomenology of reproductive engraving. Ivins reconstructs the connoisseurship that accompanied pre-photographic reproductions and argues that the meaning of photographic reproductions was determined in relation to their merits vis-à-vis reproductions delivered by engraving. In a nutshell, the photograph magnified a difference that could only be furtively glanced under the regime of the reproductive print. This was the difference between mere pictures of things and works of art.

Two concepts are central to the thesis: *viz.* the exactly repeatable pictorial statement and visual syntax. The first signals the importance of the printed image for science, technology and mass culture as well as for art: 'far from being merely minor works of art, prints are among the most important tools of modern life and thought' (Ivins, 1953: 3). Ivins argues that a culture without exactly repeatable pictorial statements is different from our own. It is bereft of a visual communication that has made possible our sciences, technologies, archaeologies and ethnologies. It is a key to the development of a visual culture that has been a component in the modernization of the world, a world that has, since the Renaissance, been rendered more visual.

Visual syntax conveys the sense that visual depictions are of a different order from verbal accounts. Since the Renaissance both science and art have emerged as discourses which are intimately associated with the production and dissemination of illustrated arguments: diagrams, sketches, engravings, handicraft reproductions, photographs, half-tones – yet these images are always more than mere 'illustrations'. They are not derivative of a privileged and ongoing discourse; as *printed* images they are marked by syntactical forms, depictive conventions, which realize the scientific or the aesthetic character we assign to scientific reports and art criticism.

Ivins shows that interpretations of reproductive engravers did not emerge *de novo* from craftsmen's encounters with art works. Early sixteenth-century engravers evolved visual conventions that represented the world evoked by the conventions of painting. The making of a printed image involved one of several possible visual conventions or languages whose qualities were bound up with available or chosen technique. A print-making hegemonized by painting, was charged with solving the problems of representing the distribution of objects in a rational space – chiaroscuro and volume.

Credit for devising a print that could, in a world without photo-mechanical methods, substantially express such qualities goes to Marc Antonio (c.1480–1530). He developed a linear system, 'a kind of shading that represented not the play of light across a surface, and not the series of local textures, but the bosses and hollows made in a surface by what is underneath it' (Ivins, 1953: 66). It was as though a net had been cast over the objects represented. Imagine, suggested Evelyn, in *Sculptura* (1662) a shadow cast by the sun, through a mesh of threads onto an object such as a bowl or a person's head: 'it is evident, that these Threads, in whatever manner you interpose the said Frame 'twixt the Bowle and the Sun, that they will perpetually cast their shadows' (Evelyn, 1905: 122) (Plate 4). Marc Antonio and those who followed him used a language, or engraved syntax, into which

Plate 4 Illustration of the principle of line engraving from Evelyn's *Sculptura*, (1662). The pictures show the principle by comparing the lines of the engraver with the shadows cast onto solid objects by threads stretched on a frame: 'it is evident, that these Threads, in whatever manner you interpose the said Frame 'twixt the *Bowle* and the *Sun*, that they will perpetually cast their shadows parallel *inter se*, cutting it as it were, into several planes, uniforme and parallel also' (Evelyn 1662: 121).

works of art and other images could be translated. What the viewer saw was not just a picture, but one composed from a system of lines and dots which translated a painting (Plates 5 and 6).

The development of a European trade in printed pictures was linked to a withdrawal by artists as designers from the labour of engraving. By the end of the eighteenth century it was rare for artists to have reputations for carrying out their own engraving and printmaking (Ivins, 1953: 96–7) (Plate 7). Innovations associated with line engraving and its hybridization with other techniques went hand-in-hand with structural changes in the trade. Seventeenth-century print making passed into a manufacturing phase with houses such as those of Rubens where the labour of engravers was regulated according to a house style: '[a]ny sketch, no matter how fleeting its indications and any most elaborately detailed oil paintings of the Rubens type, could be tossed into the hopper of the engraving shop, and out of the other end would come a print that had all the familiar trade-marked Rubens look' (Ivins, 1953: 73).

In the eighteenth century intensification of the division of labour combined with technical innovations to drive a wedge between design and the labour of reproduction. Execution of plates devolved onto teams of craftsmen with individuals increasingly confined to semi-skilled labour, some specializing in a particular stage of production. For Ivins there is aesthetic scandal here. The world was engulfed in pictures which lacked authenticity: 'second- or third- or fourth-hand accounts, or even badly jumbled accounts by different people, of what things were supposed to look like' (Ivins, 1953: 99). The visual syntax of engraving shops intersected with the economics of the print trade to produce images executed by craftsmen who might never have seen the originals.

Ivins shows how the use of a linear scheme had consequences for what could be communicated about art. What was admitted was more a knowledge of iconography and composition than an understanding of the 'personal characteristics of the original works of art, their brush strokes and chisel marks' (Ivins 1953: 166). The meaning of a work of art was refracted through the engraver's language: '[p]ainstakingly as Durer might copy a real rabbit . . . in his own syntax, when it came to copying a print by Mantegna he refused to follow Mantegna's syntax, and retold the story, as he thought, in his own syntax' (Ivins, 1953: 61). What could not be communicated was the authority of the original artist as it related to the quality of the medium. What could be communicated were

Plate 5 Mid nineteenth century steel line engraving by H. Bourne after *The Last of England* by Ford Madox Brown. In the eighteenth century reproductive plates were made on copper engraved with a burin. In the nineteenth century the introduction of steel plates led, as here, to the combined use of etching and line engraving

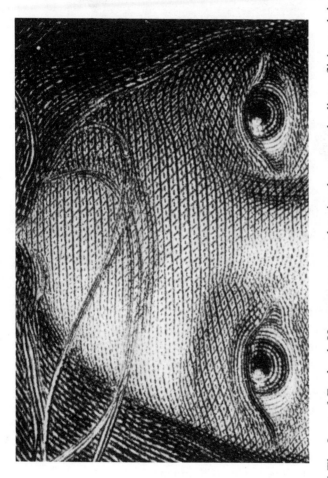

Plate 6 Detail of *The Last of England*. Here we can see the visual syntax, the lines, flicks and dots that formed a convention for reproduction before half tone photographs. This is lost by reproduction in Plate 5 but is visible at reading distance in the original. Ivins shows how a systematic laying down of lines, that he calls a 'net of rationality', could only catch certain kinds of aesthetic objects.

Plate 7 An Engraver's Workshop, *The Universal Magazine*, 1748. This illustration accompanies an article on engraving in which the author explains: 'I have represented a genius *a*, inspiring the draughtsman *b* with the design, which he afterwards cuts with his graver' (*The Universal Magazine* 1748: 179). (An earlier, more decorative but similar, depiction of an engraving shop takes the form of a trade card for John Burton, Engraver of Holborn (1720). Again there are the sculptural references to the antique and other allusions to the world of learning. See the trade card collection of the Guild Hall Library, City of London.)

the differences between the achievements of reproductive engravers some of whom established reputations as virtuosos. The engraver-as-interpreter occupied and extended a space that was to be closed off by photographic reports, a space between original work of art and reproduction.

In this space flourished an aesthetic. It had two aspects which together yielded an indeterminacy in experiences of works of art. There was a connoisseurship which flowed from the virtuosity of the reproductive engraver in handling the swelling lines, the dots and flicks from which a printed picture was composed: 'the things that counted in public estimation were the brilliant moire of the damask of the engraved lines' (Ivins, 1953: 172). Engravers 'chose the pictures they were to make or reproduce not for their merits but as vehicles for the exhibition of their particular skills' (Ivins, 1953: 69).

> The laying of lines, swelling and diminishing, the creation of webs of crossed lines, of lozenges with little flicks and dots in their middles the making of prints in lines that all ran parallel or around and around – one engraver made a great reputation by the way he rendered the fur of a pussy cat, and another made a famous head of Christ that contained but one line, which beginning at the point of the nose, ran around and around itself until it finally got lost in the outer margin. (Ivins, ibid.)

Secondly, the circulation of engraved reproductions accommodated a connoisseurship sensible of authority that resided not in the picture but elsewhere – a hypostasization of something that lay behind the engraved lines, the 'unreachable, the unknowable, *vrai verite*' (Ivins, 1953: 139). Ivins recites the vocabulary of eighteenth-century neoclassical doctrines: 'harmony, proportion, dignity, nobility, grandeur, sublimity' to indicate the discursive preoccupations of a connoisseurship that depended on reproductive engravings. Here there was no knowledge obtained of '[t]he wilful theatrical stroke of Ruben's brush' or 'the dominant expressive gouge of Michael Angelo's chisel' (Ivins, 1953: 173).

It was through photographic reproductions that the connection between such objects and the creative intention of the artist could first be widely experienced and demonstrated: the 'traces of the creative dance of the artist's hand' and the effects of a deliberate creative will' (Ivins, 1953: 144). They promoted a connoisseurship based on the distinction between pictorial expression and pictures which were statements of fact. Photographs enabled the transmission of images as works of art and the recognition of the difference between information and art. It enabled us to see 'the choice and manipulation of the paint', the difference between the founders of modernism and the Salon subject painters of the nineteenth century (Ivins, 1953: 144). Meissonier could now be recognized for what he was – a reporter!

Where should the line be drawn between art and dross? What is worthy of a place in a museum collection? Ivins's answer presupposes both an ontology of art and a discrimination on the part of the art lover whose sensibilities have been subordinated to the purely visual. True creativity is defined in opposition to culture and convention: 'culture and intelligence are quite different things' (Ivins, 1953: 4). Creativity and convention have become antonyms for 'the greater a work of art is, the more it is a bundle, not of similarities to other things, but of differences from them' (Ivins, 1953: 139). The conventional modes of pre-photographic art reproduction render it unable to grasp images as Art.

> objects can be seen as works of art in so far as they have visible surfaces. The surfaces contain the brush marks, the chisel strokes, and the worked textures, the sum totals of which are actually the works of art. (Ivins, 1953: 143)

The argument of *PVC* was carried forward by means of the text *and* through the counterpoint of illustrations. Two images – the *Laocoon* and Rembrandt's *Old Woman Cutting her Nails* – are crucial. Ivins invites us to compare ten reproductive engravings after the *Laocoon* (made between the 1520s and the 1890s) with one half tone reproduction after the Rembrandt. The first are evidence for the subjectivity of the old ways of reproducing pictures. The meaning of the *Laocoon* is distorted, fragmented and dispersed as it is refracted through the syntaxes of different engravers. The second, a detail, provides evidence of the disposition and surface of the paintwork, evidence of the things that make this a work of art and which would have been concealed by an engraver.

The photograph gives us the image's presence as a work of art. With photographs, or more precisely the half tone reproduction,[5] the syntax of reproduction drops below the visual threshold of the viewer who now encounters the work of art in all its immediacy:

the lines of the process as distinct from the lines of the visual report could be below the threshold of human vision. In the old hand-made processes the lines of the processes and the lines of the report were the same lines, *and the process counted for more than the report in the character of the lines and the statements they made*. (Ivins, 1953: 177, my emphasis)

The dots produced by the half-tone screen are interpreted as continuous tone. It is the quality of the lens not the interpreter that matters when it comes to photographic reproduction (Ivins, 1953: 138). The camera objectively draws art lovers into a communion with image-as-a-work-of-art. Those who have communed with art do not expect art to be conflated with anecdote or journalism. They know the difference between reporting and creation.

Critique

Zigrosser, noting Ivins's 'mutation . . . as a minor prophet in the pantheon of Marshall McLuhan', doubts if he would have relished this (Zigrosser 1975: 208).[6] The doubt is well founded. Ivins's thesis is not that photography determines the message of art, but that in photography art has found a medium that is adequate to the reproduction of its meaning. Photographs and half tones have assisted our escape from the confusions of handicraft engraving to the truth that is the work of art. He reverses the periodization associated with McLuhan and more recently Baudrillard. Far from photographic reproduction proliferating images at the price of authentic meaning it rescues us from confusion. This is his point concerning engravings after the *Laocoon*, and the instability of pictorial meaning under the regime of handicraft reproduction: '[h]ad they represented butterflies instead of a known single statue, one would have said that they represented different families of the genus Laocoonidae' (Ivins, 1953: 89).

However, neither position, either McLuhan's materialism or Ivins's idealism, is adequate to signification as it relates to the reproduction of works of art. Both dissolve the social production of meaning, ignoring the dialectical relationship between 'reproduction' and 'originals' that is the contingent and situated meaning of a work of art. In assessing *PVC* it is necessary to make the following points:

(1) Art reproduction is exegesis about an original which changes the relationship between the artist and the public meaning

of the work of art. It cannot be judged as posterior to the authorship of the original. Reproduction does not translate or encode a pre-established authorship, it is a medium through which authorship is produced. There are no works of art which are original in the sense that the social is an addition to their meaning (Bryson, 1983). Reproduction is *argument* about images whose meanings have already been socially transacted. The camera constructs a viewpoint and a spectator as do the chapel, the palace, the exhibition, the museum or the artist's studio. There are differences, but what is at issue is the regulation of relationships between these different viewpoints. Regulation of the meaning of printed images as fine art – as originals and reproductions – has been an aspect of the extension of art markets since the eighteenth century. The production of artistic value has emerged from a dialectic of differentiation and regulation in which a measure of originality is the socially constructed impersonality of reproductive craftsmen.

(2) Reproductive engravers' claims to creativity may seem to be of antiquarian interest but their suppression was part of the making of the modern artist. They *were* antiquated in favour of the personal gesture of the artist. From the eighteenth century an *impersonalization* of reproduction went hand-in-hand with a *personalization* of the artist. If we are to talk about the social construction of the artist then we must also talk about the social construction of impersonal process work. The individuality of the artist has been produced through a struggle to determine the meaning of reproductions. Determining this meaning has been a feature of art politics (e.g. Francis Seymour Haden's campaign for autographic etching, the James Whistler/Joseph Pennell court action of the 1980s to secure their definition of original lithography and the post-war definitions of the original print offered by agencies such as the Print Council of America, the International Association of Plastic Arts or the French National Committee on Engraving). It is this meaning which is most commonly promoted by dealers and print publishers today and it is the ontology which is at the heart of *PVC*.

(3) At stake is the consolidation of a regime of signification where originals and reproductions are insulated from each other. Since the late nineteenth century the cultivation of art by the bourgeoisie has involved a prioritization of this dichotomy. What does it mean to say that a work of art is 'original'? The keys to this are cultural practices, such as art exhibitions or reproductions,

which centre the artist-as-creator, securing the creator as 'the first and last source of the meaning of his work' (Bourdieu, 1980). Yet these practices constitute the artist as an interdependent agent whose sense of what his or her art means may be produced through the medium of, say, exhibitions (Fyfe, 1986). In a different context Elias has insisted that 'meaning' is a social category: 'the subject corresponding to it is a plurality of interconnected people' (1985: 54). What a famous painting, and the life of its artist, mean today depend on the activities of a chain of agents (critics, dealers, art historians, curators, reproductive craftsmen etc.) involved in interpretation, including the work of reproduction – and even on an artist's guess as to what such interpretation will be. Interpretation may take the form of written criticism, but it can also be the *argument* of exhibition or reproduction.

(4) Ivins contributed more than most people to an appreciation of what photographic reproductions meant. Yet *PVC* elides the agency that is art reproduction. It stabilizes signification in favour of a unitary creativity that is the touchstone of modernism – the artist-as-creator. Inquiry is closed off at precisely the point where signification escapes the artist and where the social production of pictorial meaning would be revealed. There are frank admissions about curators' use of reproductions – the image of the artist-as-creator flickers for a moment. However, photographic reproductions are not to be taken as substitutes for originals (Ivins, 1953: 94, 138; Ivins cited in Fawcett, 1982). The camera is judged to be capable of objective and authoritative statements of which the older handicraft modes of reproduction were incapable. Yet it is clear that the truth of the *illustrated* argument proposed in *PVC* could not be guaranteed by *any* photographer. It required Ivins's eye to be at the view finder.

Freitag (1979) and others draw attention to aesthetic choices that may attend production and consumption of photographic reproductions. Their significance was debated in arguments that divided a fledgling art history profession during the last century. The outcome of these debates was not a consequence of the camera's technical superiority but of its mobilization in arguments about the nature of creativity. For some, photographic reproduction endorsed a way of seeing that was a corruption of the eye, neglecting 'the shape of ideas' and the truth of art as it might be conveyed by the creative intervention of the reproductive craftsman (Fawcett, 1982; Freitag, 1979). Photographs yielded copies that were not interpretations: 'what interests us is no longer the likeness of the original that has been faithfully poeticized by a gifted intermediary. No! nothing else satisfies us but the absolute physical identity of the reproduction with the original' (Delaborde quoted in Freitag, 1979: 118). For Delaborde[7] what mattered was loss of meaning as photography separated experience from authentic art and from aesthetic objects that were presupposed by what the artist *and* the engraver might have to say.

Today there are doubts about the use of reproductions in teaching and research. The contrast between a way of seeing cultivated through the luminosity of the lecture slide or television screen and the apparent unexciting flatness of the original has been noted (see for example Freitag, 1979: 123). What is ignored by Ivins is the creativity of art historians who may judge the manner in which an image should be photographed or process workers whose technical knowledge is brought to bear on the requirements of art. Wind argues that the spectator's eye has been alerted to aspects of art that are endorsed by the camera and that effects pursued by artists may be mediated by a vision shaped by photographs: '[t]hat Picasso has consciously adjusted his palette to the crude requirements of the colour process I would not say, but his paintings suffer remarkably little in this singularly coarse form of reproduction. They suit it almost as well as Van Gogh' (Wind, 1963: 76–7).

Ivins says nothing about engravers' reactions to the camera or their resistance to economic and artistic displacement. Photographic reproductions are treated largely in isolation from their production and as products of optical and chemical agents unaffected by human subjectivity and experience. Ivins tends to treat photo-reproduction as a unity whose history has been completed with the advent of the modern half tone. He omits assessment of the aesthetic/economic possibilities, choices and judgements that attend innovation in art reproduction. Decisions about lenses, location, lighting, exposure and about processing an image are matters that presuppose argument about the meaning of originals. They are also decisions about *who* should be making the decisions – professional photographers, artists, art historians, curators?

The omission is surprising given that it was not caused by ignorance and considering Ivins's participation in the manufacture of the illustrations for *PVC*. Correspondence with his publishers, and others, shows that Ivins regarded the illustrations to *PVC* as crucial to his argument, that he exercised a high degree of control

and surveillance over their production (*Ivins Manuscripts*, Routledge and Kegan Paul Archive, University College, London).
Many of the photographs were made by the author on the grounds
that a standard photographer would not provide illustrations
showing what was intended (*Ivins Mss*: Ivins to Herbert Read 7
May 1950). Nonetheless, correspondence between Routledge and
the plate makers reveals the role of both these parties in
determining the quality of the images at proofing: 'Many of the
illustrations show some faults, thickening of the shadows but
particularly vanishing or fading detail in the highlights' (Routledge
and Kegal Paul to Waterlow and Sons, 19 September 1952). Detail
had been lost. Had the plates, Routledge wondered, been printed
in black enough ink? They needed assurance from the platemaker
that the detail would be recovered: 'the point about printing in
collotype is that it should bear examination under the glass' (*Ivins
Mss*, Routledge to Waterlow and Sons, 19 September 1952). This
helps to explain Ivins's remarks in the preface concerning the
publisher's generosity and his choice of three kinds of reproduction
– line cuts, half tones and collotypes. Out of a total of eighty-four
illustrations fifty are collotypes. Collotype, an expensive, tricky
method of photographic reproduction, gives a limited run (about
1,500 impressions) and is capable of producing continuous tone
(no intervening screen). Particularly suitable for the reproduction
of delicate line work and washes, it was considered by Ivins to
have virtues that were necessary for his book. At mid-century he
knew that most readers would be unfamiliar with the linear
qualities and textures of handicraft reproductions and determined
that collotype rather than half tone was appropriate for conveying
them.

PVC is about the effects of photographs, more particularly half
tones, yet the majority of its illustrations are collotypes. The
inescapable conclusion is that collotypes tell readers something
about prints that half-tones could not. Moreover, a collotype was
used to reproduce a half tone! Ivins's book is a composition with a
counterpoint of half tones and collotypes. This turns out to be an
unwitting admission of the limitations of half tone reproductions.
It seems that the reader was to *look* at the illustrations in a way
that half tones do not invite – to take the glass and recover
something of the old connoisseur's sense of line, something
that would have exposed the dots of a half tone screen (*Ivins
Mss*, Ivins to Jennett, 23 February 1951). Collotypes were to serve
as a 'meta-language' for the visual syntax of the prints (*Ivins Mss.*

Ivins to Read, 7 April 1950; Ivins to Read, 10 May 1950).

The depictions in *PVC* are an unintended challenge to the notion that photography is a thing, a unity, that completes itself. The illustrations convey the heterogeneity of photographic art reproduction, unconsciously subverting the text's argument concerning photography's revelation of the unity that is art. Ivins used collotypes, but the economic and technical problems of their production had made it an unusual venture by the mid-twentieth century. He had reason to thank his publishers. *PVC* did not arrest the development of art reproduction. By the 1970s offset lithography (used for the 1969 reprint of *PVC*) had displaced letter press (used in the first edition of *PVC*) as the most common means of reproduction.

The histories of reproduction and print-making are neither aesthetically nor technically complete. The verities of the original print are sometimes challenged in a world that is more complex and potentially open in its meanings than that definition. In the 1960s some artists were crossing the boundaries of fine art and commerce, reflecting on their relationship, blurring the distinction between art and process work, qualifying and challenging the ideology of the artist-as-creator with admissions that creativity might not be unitary.[8] Ivins could see only exhibitionism in the art of the old line engravers where others have discerned a distinct aesthetic, one with different possibilities from a painterly aesthetic based on revelation of self (Gilmour, 1978: 48–50). What was not entertained in *PVC* was the possibility that art might reflect on the meaning of reproduction.

Reproductive engravers were eliminated from the canon but so were Salon painters who had traded in mimesis and whose art engravers had served – those nineteenth-century subject and narrative painters whose copyrighted popular works were academy draws. Ivins argues that it was photographs that enabled us to see differences pertinent to art. *PVC* is part of the story of the institutionalization of a modernist aesthetic in the early twentieth century – one that eschewed *kitsch*, the merely popular, the gaudy and the sentimental. Outside the museum photographs rendered the difference between art and convention visible – the eye of the art lover was captured and brought under the thrall of the singular artist's charismatic authority. I now turn to the question of what that difference meant.

Art and its objects

The circulation of photo-mechanical reproductions has prompted questions concerning the sovereignty of originals. How are the meanings of art affected by reproductions? What is the difference between originals and reproductions? Can works of art be reproduced? Are reproductions duplicates or merely imitations of originals? Reproductions have been experienced as ambiguous. They have seemed to threaten the authority of originals, substituting medium for message, displacing authentic encounters with works of art with experiences of inauthentic copies.

The most perceptive accounts of art's relationship with photography have been those identifying a normalizing of aesthetic judgements that attend the camera (Wind, 1962; Berger, 1972; Freitag, 1979). But normalizing in relation to what? An innocent, unmediated and authentic encounter with original works of art? No. The difference made by the earliest photographic reproductions was to eyes schooled in art through engravings. Moreover, the merits of photographic reproductions were not evident to all who encountered them.

Ivins argues that modern reproduction is part of the making of new ways of writing and knowing about art in the wake of the disintegration of a nineteenth-century cultural apparatus hegemonized by the academy. This was related to the formation of the art historians' profession (Freitag, 1979). It was also related to a separation of art academies from the means of determining art history. Elsewhere I have argued that these were discursive changes in which the relationship between art and power disappeared from sight to be re-presented as an apparently fortuitous association between discrimination, discovery and the artist-as-creator (Fyfe, 1988). They were also changes in state forms which put the links between professional art academies, the state and national art institutions at issue.

Since the seventeenth century, the bourgeoisie has followed a distinct cultural strategy (Bourdieu, 1980, 1984; Clark, 1985). Its class situation compelled cultivation of an autonomous Art experienced as 'essentially detached from the pressures and deformities of history' (Clark, 1985: 86). The social function of art concerns its removal from the contexts of practical life: a cultivation of a sensuousness by 'members of those classes which, at least at times, are free from the pressures of the need for survival' (Burger, 1984: 46). Art no longer expresses the arbitrary power of patrons but celebrates a contemplative mode that is the separation of creativity from power, convention and society. This illusion has been linked to the promotion of a charismatic aesthetic through technologies of cultural power associated with art reproduction, exhibitions, catalogues, museum display as well as other institutions and practices. These have metamorphized the spectator's participation and marginalized certain kinds of knowledge – those that are not of purely pictorial effects wrought by the artist. This involved a realignment in the relations between power and art, an erosion of the transcendental power of the patron/aristocrat.

Academies, royal and aristocratic collections were sites of struggles for cultural power and legitimacy by the bourgeois state. Aspects of this concern academies' exploitation of cultural markets through strategies which defined and defended the meaning of art. Transformation of the means of reproduction was always in the process of fragmenting pictorial meaning, sometimes yielding print making techniques that had no obvious artistic purpose (lithographs, chromolithographs, wood cuts). By 1859 there were said to be 156 different reproductive techniques. The market was a site of struggles for cultural capital which shaped a public sense of which differences between images were pertinent to art. Fragmentation was contained through hierarchy and through a system of art reproduction (whose ideal form was the line engraving) that was hegemonized by academies of painting and sculpture.

Shifts in the locus of cultural power were mediated by changes in the rules governing aesthetic judgements, including judgements about the reproducibility of art. Print making is a means of pictorial distanciation in which a transcendant power or ideology may be made palpable – for example, glorifying monarchy as patronage through reproductions of the King's image and works. Prints may be visible signs of the patron's power, establishing the connection between art and his/her authority – prints of pictures which reside in the patron's collection, prints of pictures which society has endorsed at salon or exhibition and which are sanctioned by the presence of patrons.

The linear syntax of engraving could be cultivated for itself, yet it placed spectators at a distance from the truth of art, except in so far as the reproduction was treated as a work of art in its own right. This distance nurtured a vocabulary of the unreachable and unknowable (Ivins) and registered the aura of the art work

(Benjamin, 1970). Here was a language which spoke of the existence of originals which were located elsewhere (for example in the palace) and referred the art lover to the existence a painted canon, ownership of which is beyond the means of those who did not wield economic and social power. Art reproduction explicitly indexed aesthetic difference as social difference, as hierarchy.

A *patent* relationship between power and art is evident. In England, the Victorians reconciled art with its mass production through a terracing of taste associated with artists' proofs, proofs before letters and stamped editions published under the authority of the Print Sellers' Association. Print entrepreneurship involved a subtle interplay between matters of authorship, accessibility, technical innovation and substitution, quality and morality – matters which were questions of class participation regulated by differentiating rituals. Taste in reproductions formed a hierarchy which knew certain materials as intrinsically artistic before an artist said anything. In so far as the RA presided over the qualified status of engraving this cultural system was sanctioned as one of aesthetic hierarchy. In America:

> there was a strongly and generally held opinion that etching was more artistic than line engraving, that both were more artistic than wood engraving and that all were more artistic than lithography. Lowest of all and utterly contemptible, were photography and any medium that bore the name of some process. (Ivins, 1953: 114)

Ivins the curator was seeing off the old school, disposing of the hierarchies and orthodoxies of the academy and the notion of 'beauty with a capital B' through curatorial innovations in the new Department of Prints at the Metropolitan. We learn of his encounters with an older connoisseurship. Its authority is transmuted into the eccentric preferences of gentlemen who scolded Ivins for purchasing 'horrid rough old wood cuts by such artists as Durer and Cranach when I could have bought the . . . white line reproductive engravings of such modern masters as Timothy Cole and Elbridge Kingsley' (Ivins, 1953: 114). In 1916–17 there was 'much talk and argument about what the character of [the] collection should be' (Ivins, 1953: 1). New rules of cultural classification were being instituted. For Ivins it was necessary to exclude the vast majority of the '"ana", topography, sporting and theatrical prints, costume, portraits, and reproductive work as such' (Ivins, 1927: 5). In the main 'prints gathered for a museum collection shall be of importance for the manner in which they represent things, and not for the things they represent' (Ivins, ibid.; cf. Bourdieu, 1984).

Ivins's account of the photographic reproduction portrays a relationship in which the meaning of the image for the spectator has become purely visual. It is no longer trammelled by the codes of engravers. His assessment of this meaning may be interpreted in relation to the changes in cultural power discussed above. His activities at the Met are part of the story of how in the early twentieth century some art museums began to authorize a modernist aesthetic which eschewed mimesis – one that secured the difference between art and mere pictures as the *sine qua non* of an authentic aesthetic. From the mid-nineteenth century museum directors increasingly engaged problems of space and display through policies that acknowledged the existence of a fissured audience (Dimaggio, 1982; Fyfe, 1986). The production and transmission of this difference was naturalized through acts of cultural classification which informed acquisition and display – acts which were in turn related to a transformation of the internal organization of museums and progressively differentiated the curator as a professional from older patrimonial/aristocratic principles of cultural domination (Zolberg, 1981).

Photographic reproduction did not endorse and extend a knowledge of art that was already *there*. It ushered in aesthetic objects that were encountered as strange by eyes that had experienced art as reproductive engraving and which knew mimesis as the norm of artistic appearance. Ivins's account contributes to our understanding of the camera's role in endorsing a taken-for-granted assumption of modernism – that art is the artist's search for originality. The camera provided a knowledge of art that could be conveyed neither by verbal communication nor by the visual syntax of handicraft reproductive print-making. Before, it was impossible to mass produce the difference, say, between the achievements of an academic artist such as Bouguer-eau and Manet: '[i]f Manet and Bouguereau had painted the same model, in the same light, with the same accessories, and the same iconographical composition, any engravings made from them by the same engraver would have been remarkably alike' (Ivins, 1953: 150 and 144).

The meaning of photographic art reproduction for Ivins is that it is communication without syntax: 'the actual surfaces of the objects reproduced are made visible' (Ivins, 1953: xxv). It is not that. What the photographic reproduction did was to mediate a change in the relationship between spectator and print. Prior to photographs, reproductions reproduced an aesthetic *distance* between the art work and the art lover/connoisseur – an unapproachability which was the aura of the art work. For Ivins, the photograph conveys a sense of the visibility of the work of art – enhancing the image's sensuous presence and securing a necessary primacy for the artist as the creative subject. In the modern half-tone there is pictorial communication apparently without exegesis – the babble of voices is silenced in favour of mute, ascetic contemplation. Our art lover has become something of a Prigsby:[9] '[i]t is interesting to note how dry and tongue tied so many of the people are who have had a long and intimate first hand acquaintance with works of art as compared with the volubility in abstractions of the persons who know about art through words and verbalist doctrines' (Ivins, 1953: 139). To put it another way: 'the only context which we are expected and encouraged to bring to a given content is contentment, the sighing "Aaaah" of plenitude and self (mis)recognition as *being there*' (Corrigan 1985).

Works of art are not things-in-themselves. Images gain admission to the realm of art through the medium of discursive rules that are knowledgeably applied by experts and art lovers. Such discourse does not float free of power, interests and the social contexts in which art lovers come to know art objects although their meanings may be constructed around a denial of such contexts (Bourdieu, 1980). The experience of photographs has been linked to a revision of the idea of a masterpiece. Until the nineteenth century the truly great work of art was one that was 'most perfectly in accord with a tradition', it was the most complete, the most "finished" work'. The masterpiece has become 'the one in which the artist, in relation only to himself, has touched the pinnacle of his style and stripped away everything that is not uniquely his own' (Malraux, 1967: 80).[10] It is in part the photographic reproduction that allows us to know this as the difference that an artist has made to art. It enabled us to know style as deviation from what has gone before. If the dots and flicks of the engraver's burin have disappeared then it may be that *our* visual syntax is composed from the paintings themselves.

The question of what reproductions meant was contested in the eighteenth and nineteenth centuries as it is today. Ivins wanted to

Gordon Fyfe

make the eye the locus of an aesthetic discipline where art was separated from mere pictures of things, from description, from illustration, from journalism, in favour of a universal and autonomous narrative. This was the story of art as it was accomplished by the heroes of modernism and as it was institutionalized by the modern state in the twentieth century.

Conclusion

If *The Spartan Boy* reflects on the ambiguity of reproductions it was not the camera which clarified or confused things. Modernization is partly a visual process involving a rationalization of the means of representation that has unleashed new powers of depiction. But what do they mean? The Conjurer posed the question: what does it mean to be an *original* artist in the age of reproduction? To be an artist in the modern world has been to be offered the *possibility* of answering this question. Here, as in other cultural contexts, simplification has been attended by complication and emancipation by constraint. Ambiguity has been experienced by generations of artists, connoisseurs and cultural agents who have been winning and losing the struggle to determine the meaning of reproductions and to keep up with the game of art. The matter of who won and who lost aesthetically has not been innocent in relation to the production of power and privilege in the modern world.

The circulation of reproductions has been associated with the dissolution of traditional aesthetic hierarchies, fragmentation of pictorial meaning *and* cultural strategies of containment. The visibility of images once confined to the collection and refracted through the steel grey of engraving has increased as the means of pictorial reproduction have been transformed. At the same time new meanings, differences and anxieties have been promoted. In the present century an ontology of difference, where originals and reproductions are antonyms, submerged the tradition of reproductive engraving in favour of original prints and photographic reproductions.

Ivins's history of art reproduction is less objective than it seems. The camera appears to give us visual communication without convention, without syntax, without exegesis. The art lover knows the difference that an artist has made to Art and can now celebrate Art *as* difference. There is a price to pay and it is paid by someone. No room for a Norman Rockwell here, but there is for a Van

94

Gogh. Creativity can now be experienced for what it is, deviation from convention. We have visual deadlock: where art is, the social is not. *PVC* is an argument about reproduction which resolves the ambiguity, indeterminacy and noise that attends the difference between reproductions/originals in favour of the artist-as-creator.

No thesis by a print curator can have gained such a wide currency in the field of cultural analysis as *PVC*. Thirty-five years on the book is to be judged a classic. It still informs critical debate about technical change in the making of pictures and reproductions (Jussim, 1983; Walker, 1983; Freitag, 1979). Sociologists have harnessed his ideas on representation, arguing that the notion of visual syntax sharpens understanding of the social determination of knowledge and art (Barnes, 1977; Becker, 1982). This is curious because the denouement of the story of art reproduction as retailed in *PVC* is a separation of art from life and the hypostatization of the creator. We should learn from Ivins but beware that an uncritical reading does not seduce us into underwriting cultural power that we need to understand.

Acknowledgements

I am grateful to University College, London for access to the Ivins manuscripts held in the Routledge and Kegan Paul archives. I am also grateful to Colin Ellis, Norman Franklin, Christine Fyfe, Belinda Loftus and Jim McLaverty for their advice on aspects of the argument.

Notes

1 The first prints appeared in Europe in the fifteenth century. As Ivins shows, between the eighteenth and the twentieth centuries the dominant tradition of fine art prints, was as reproductive print making after painting and sculpture. The mezzotint was first publicized by Evelyn in *Sculptura* (1662). The mezzotint plate is made by a graduated smoothing out of its roughened surface (which unworked would print black) to produce tonal values that are appropriate to oil painting. Intaglio, where the ink is held within the grooves and recesses of the plate is usually contrasted with relief printing (remember those school lino-cuts?) and planographic print-making (e.g. lithography). Ivins's half tones, in the 1953 edition, were printed letter press, that is relief. See Gascoigne (1986) for an extraordinarily lucid account of the differences between prints, but also see Harris (1968, 1969 & 1970) for a cautionary note on the reification of such differences.

2 See *Dictionary of National Biography* entries under Hone, Humphrey and Lowry as well as Lister (1984: 261). It is possible (Crookshank and The Knight of Glin 1978: 157–8) that Lowry is a self portrait of Stickland Lowry (1737c.–1785). His son, Wilson Lowry (1762–1824), was one of many eighteenth and nineteenth-century engravers who pioneered technical innovations in

Gordon Fyfe

reproduction. *The Spartan Boy* is a portrait of Hone's son John Camillus.

3 Rawson (1969: 355) explains: 'Many people in these years got their knowledge of Greece from the histories of Rollin, in original or in translation, and his not much more than epitomator Oliver Goldsmith. To this, not to any English obsession with foxes, is perhaps largely due the primacy that the Spartan boy and the fox begins to gain over the hundreds of ancient anecdotes of similar type. The prologue to Mrs Cowley's tragedy *The Fate of Sparta or the Rival Kings* (1787) shows that what the public is now expected to know about Sparta is the fox story.' Goldsmith, citing the authority of Plutarch, reports of Spartan boys' endurance training that: '[i]n order to prepare them for strategems and sudden incursions, the boys were permitted to steal from each other; but if they were caught in the fact, they were punished for their want of dexterity' (Goldsmith, 1809: 27–8).

4 In assessing the meaning of pre-photographic reproductions it should be realized that the original print has only achieved an importance in the fine art market in recent times. The original print, as it is sanctioned by the market, is intimately and ideologically associated with both the social construction of authorship and the capturing of a petit bourgeois audience for modernism. The hyperbole of the contemporary art market tends to freeze our thinking about image-making, naturalizing the distinction between reproductions and originals. The 'originality' of an original print is predicated on (1) the print's categorical difference from a reproduction, (2) its independent status as a work of art and (3) the assigning of complete pictorial authority to the 'artist'. There are ideological aspects to the original/reproduction dichotomy for it does not accommodate the range of images which have circulated as art in the past and which circulate today. Part of the difficulty is to do with the way in which the concept of originality elides the collaborative activity of artists and technicians/craftsmen and women. See Curtis (1972), Gilmour (1978), Simmons (1980).

5 Photographs of themselves did not yield mass reproduction capable of delivering the tonal values of say, a painting. As Ivins shows, from the 1850s, the first steps to the modern half-tone were taken, and perfected in the 1880s. The principle of the half-tone (half, because half the image is lost) is a breaking down of continuous tone into a mass of dots – accomplished by means of a cross line screen interposed between the image and a light sensitive printing surface. The effect is to translate tone into a pattern of dots which (with the exception of cruder newspaper pictures) normally *appear* as continuous tone.

6 A section from *PVC* was reprinted in McLuhan (1962).

7 Delaborde was Print Curator at the Bibliotheque National in Paris.

8 One artist, Joe Tilson, comments on his experiences of print-making at the Kelpra studio run by Chris Prater: 'Chris often uses the analogy of Composer-Conductor-Orchestra for the Artist-Chris-and the Team, but although the analogy is quite a good one I think it underestimates Chris's role. Because, without a conductor music can exist at least in manuscript, but without Chris Prater none of the work in this exhibition [Arts Council exhibition of Kelpra prints] would exist . . .' (Tilson, 1970). Also see *Studio International*, December 1967, vol. 174, (895): 293. For Roy Lichtenstein in the 1960s the mass produced newspaper cartoon strip was a point of departure for investigating the gestural quality of Abstract Expressionism: 'I was very interested in characterizing or caricaturing a brush stroke. The very nature of a brush stroke is anathema to outlining and filling in as used in cartoons. So, I developed a form for it . . . – that is, to get a standardized thing – a stamp or image' (Lichtenstein, 1968: 12).

9 Prigsby, a cartoon creation of George Du Maurier appeared in *Punch* (1881). Prigsby, stands contemplating a painting, he knows cannot be a Botticelli: 'Before a Botticelli I am mute'.

10 Ivins explains that he came across Malraux's book when *PVC* was almost completed.

References

Barnes, Barry (1977), *Interests and the Growth of Knowledge*, London, Routledge and Kegan Paul.

Baudrillard, J. (1988), 'The Trompe L'oeil' in N. Bryson (ed.), *Calligram*, Cambridge, Cambridge University Press.

Becker, H. (1982), *Art Worlds*, Berkeley, University of California Press.

Benjamin, Walter (1970), 'The Work of Art in the Age of Mechanical Reproduction', *Illuminations*, London, Jonathan Cape.

Berger, J. (1972), *Ways of Seeing*, London, BBC/Penguin Books.

Blake, William (1810), 'Public Address', in Geoffrey Keynes (ed.) (1966) *The Complete Writings of William Blake*, London, Oxford University Press.

Bourdieu, P. (1980), 'The Production of Belief: contribution to an economy of symbolic goods', *Media, Culture and Society*, 2, 3.

Bourdieu, P. (1984), *Distinction: A Social Critique of the Judgement of Taste*, London, Routledge & Kegan Paul.

Bryson, N. (1983), *Vision and Painting: The Logic of the Gaze*, New Haven, Yale University Press.

Burger, Peter (1984), *Theory of the Avant-Garde*, Manchester, Manchester University Press and Minneapolis, University of Minnesota Press.

Clark, T. J. (1985), 'Arguments about Modernism' in F. Frascina (ed.), *Pollock and After*, London, Harper & Row.

Corrigan, Philip (1985), 'In/Formation: A Short Organum for Photograph Working' in *Photocommunique*, Fall.

Crookshank, A. and The Knight of Glin (1978), *The Painters of Ireland c. 1660–1920*, London, Barrie & Jenkins.

Cumberland, George (1827), *An Essay on the Utility of Collecting the Best Works of the Ancient Engravers of the Italian School*, London.

Curtis, J. (1972), 'The Original Print: An Epitaph', *The Penrose Annual*.

Dimaggio, P. (1982), 'Cultural Entrepreneurship in Nineteenth-Century Boston', *Media, Culture and Society*, 2 pts, vol. 4, nos 1 & 4.

Elias, N. (1985), *The Loneliness of the Dying*, Oxford, Basil Blackwell.

Evelyn, John (1905), *Sculptura: or the History and Art of Chalcography*, Oxford, Clarendon Press (first published 1662).

Fawcett, T. (1982), 'On Reproductions', *Art Libraries Journal* 7, 1.

Fox, Celina (1976), 'The Engravers' Battle for Professional Recognition in Early Nineteenth Century London', *The London Journal*, 2, 1.

Freitag, Wolfgang M. (1979), 'Early Uses of Photography in the History of Art', *Art Journal*, 39, pt. 2.

Fyfe, Gordon J. (1985), 'Art and Reproduction: some aspects of the relations between painters and engravers in London 1760–1850', *Media, Culture and Society*, 7.

Fyfe, Gordon J. (1986), 'Art Exhibitions and Power during the Nineteenth Century' in J. Law (ed.), *Power, Action and Belief*.

Fyfe, Gordon J. (1988), 'A Trojan Horse at the Tate: the Chantrey Bequest, Art and the State', (forthcoming).

Gascoigne, B. (1986), *How to Identify Prints*, London, Thames and Hudson.

Gilmour, Pat (1978), *The Mechanised Image: An Historical Perspective on 20th Century Prints*, London, Arts Council of Great Britain.

Godfrey, R. T. (1978), *Print Making in Britain*, London: Phaidon Press.

Goldsmith, Oliver (1809), *The History of Greece from the Earliest State to the Death of Alexander the Great*, (two vols, tenth edition) London, R. Baldwin et al.

Graves, A. (1905), *The Royal Academy of Arts: A complete dictionary of contributors and their work from its foundation in 1769 to 1904* (5 vols) London, Henry Graves & George Bell (Kingsmead Reprint 1970).

97

Greig, James (ed.) (1922–8), *The Farington Diary*, (8 vols), London, Hutchinson.

Hamerton, G. (1882), *The Graphic Arts*, London, Seeley & Co.

Harris, E. M. (1968, 1969, 1970), 'Experimental Graphic Processes in England 1800–1859', *Journal of the Printing Historical Society*, 4, 5 and 6.

Hutchison, S. (1968), *The History of the Royal Academy*, London, Chapman & Hall.

Ivins, William M. Jr. (1927), *Prints and Books: informal papers*, Harvard University Press, Cambridge, (reprinted 1969, New York, De Capo Press).

Ivins, William M. Jr. (1953), *Prints and Visual Communication*, London, Routledge & Kegan Paul.

Ivins, William M. Jr. (1969), *Prints and Visual Communication*, Cambridge Mass. and London, MIT Press (reprint).

Jussim, E. (1983), *Visual Communication and the Graphic Arts*, New York and London, R. R. Bowker Company.

Landseer, J. (1807), *Lectures on the Art of Engraving*, London, Longman, Hurst, Rees & Orme.

Lichtenstein, R. (1968), 'An Interview' in *Roy Lichtenstein*, London, Tate Gallery.

Lister, Raymond (1984), *Prints and Printmaking: A Dictionary and Handbook of the Art in Nineteenth Century Britain*, London, Methuen.

Malraux, A. (1967), *Museum without Walls*, London, Secker & Warburg.

McLuhan, M. (1962), *The Gutenberg Galaxy*, London, Routledge & Kegan Paul.

Newman, J. (1986), 'Reynolds and Hone: "The Conjurer" Unmasked' in Nicholas Penny (ed.), *Reynolds*, London, Royal Academy of Arts/Weidenfeld & Nicolson.

Park, Cynthia (1980), 'Five American Collectors', *Print Collector's Newsletter*, 11, pt 3.

Pollock, C. (1980), 'Artists, Mythologies and Media – Genius, Madness and Art History', *Screen*, 21, 3.

Pye, John (1845), *Patronage of British Art*, London, Longman, Brown, Green & Longmans (Cornmarket Press 1970).

Rawson, Elizabeth (1969), *The Spartan Tradition in European Thought*, Oxford, Clarendon Press.

Richardson, J. (1773), *The Theory of Painting*, London.

Simmons, R. (1980), *Collecting Original Prints*, London, Studio Vista.

Strutt, Joseph (1785), *A Biographical Dictionary Containing an Historical Account of All the Engravers*.

Tilson, J. (1970), 'Kelpra Prints' in Kelpra Prints, London, Arts Council of Great Britain.

Walker, J. A. (1983), *Art in the Age of Mass Media*, London, Pluto Press.

Waterhouse, Ellis (1981), *The Dictionary of British Eighteenth Century Painters in Oils and Crayons*, London, Antique Collectors' Club.

Wind, Edgar (1963), *Art and Anarchy*, London, Faber & Faber.

Zigrosser, C. (1975), *A World of Art and Museums*, Philadelphia, The Art Alliance Press.

Zolberg, Vera L. (1981), 'Conflicting Visions in American Art Museums' in *Theory and Society*, 10.

Northern Ireland 1968–1988: enter an art historian in search of a useful theory

Belinda Loftus

Abstract

Publications and museum or art-gallery displays have tended to separate the visual images related to the Northern Ireland troubles into illustrations of history, works of art and media imagery. These distinct categories to some degree reflect the growing specialisation of art workers in Europe from the late eighteenth century onwards. But in the context of the Northern Ireland conflict visual images patently cut across such distinctions. Fine art works have direct political and therefore historical impact; media images use and are used by the producers of popular emblems; visual styles are held in common by all categories of imagery. The perpetuation of the separate history illustration/artwork/media picture categories when dealing with Northern Ireland imagery is therefore attributed to the formal and informal training of British and Irish historians and art historians. An alternative theoretical basis for examining the images related to the Northern Ireland conflict is suggested, in which those images are seen as parts of visual language codes, whose constant use and re-use simultaneously adds further layers of meaning to them, ensures their real impact on social, political, economic and religious developments, and modifies the overall visual language of their producers/users. This approach is related to the work of German and Austrian art-historians and their successors, American media studies focusing on the links between institutional organisation and visual style, anthropological analyses of ritual symbols and recent sociological use of linguistic theory.

A vast amount of visual images, falling into a wide range of categories, have been produced in relation to the Northern Ireland troubles, during the past twenty years. Press photographs, cartoons, advertisements, posters, Christmas cards, banners, badges, wallpaintings, craftwork, processional regalia, paintings,

99

drawings and sculptures have all taken up themes related to this conflict. Yet the analyses of these images are few in number and highly selective in their approach.

These analyses have been offered in two main forms, publications and permanent or temporary displays in museums and art galleries. In both there has been a marked tendency to separate the images related to the Northern Ireland troubles into illustrations of history, works of art and media imagery, each category being treated in a different fashion. This division in treatment can best be illustrated by considering first three publications in which troubles imagery is reproduced, and then a number of the relevant museum and art gallery displays.

Since the beginning of the present troubles in Northern Ireland in 1968, English and Irish publishers have produced a number of illustrated books attempting to set the conflict in a historical perspective. Some of these have been designed to be used as school text-books; others have been aimed at the general public. In the latter category a recent example is Robert Kee's *Ireland, A History*, published by Weidenfeld and Nicolson in 1980, to accompany his television series of the same title, first broadcast on BBC 2 and RTE between December 1980 and February 1981. In this book visual images related to the troubles are used as illustrations of history: This emphasis is conveyed by the way they are selected, the style in which they are reproduced, and the kind of written information which accompanies them.

Take for example the two colour pictures of Orange processions reproduced opposite page 64 of Kee's book (Plate 1). The juxtaposition of painting and photograph on this page places them on a level as sources of information, although the painting is accorded a small measure of superiority by virtue of its position at the top of the page, its size and the fact that it is not cropped, which the photograph obviously is. This interpretation of the two images is reinforced by the captions accompanying them. The reader is directed by these to see the pictures as interesting evidence of the Ulster Orangemen's continuing celebrations of William III's victory at the Battle of the Boyne in 1690, (illustrated on the following page), and to a question about an item of regalia used in those celebrations. The painting is given slight precedence by the naming of the artist responsible for it; anyone interested in the name of the photographer who took the picture of contemporary Orangemen will have to search in the acknowledgements at the back of the book. The reader is not however encouraged to

above: Celebrating an ancient victory. Orange parade, 12 July 1926 (painting by Sir John Lavery, who also designed the Irish Free State bank notes).

right: Contemporary Orange Day celebrations. But why in bowler hats?

Plate 1 Colour illustrations opposite page 64 of Robert Kee, *Ireland, A History*, Weidenfeld and Nicolson, (1981)

reconstruct Lavery's work as a painting. Neither its size, nor its medium are given, and its location can again only be traced through the acknowledgements. The presentation of these pictures as illustrations of historical information is further emphasised by their relationship to chapter three of Kee's book, in which he explains the Orangemen's celebrations as an assertion of their resistance to and victory over the encircling Irish Catholics at the period of plantation, during the bitter political and religious conflicts in the 1640s, during the Williamite campaign of 1689–90, and at the time of the fight against Home Rule in the early years of this century.

In the notably few art publications discussing visual images related to the present conflict in Northern Ireland, a radically different approach is taken. The most coherent of these publications is Mike Catto's chapter titled 'Notes from a Small War/Art and the Troubles', in his *Art in Ulster 2* (1977, Belfast, Blackstaff Press). What Catto offers is a selection of images in which artists and a handful of cartoonists, photographers and graphic designers have reacted to or handled the troubles. These images are all accorded individual importance by their separate reproduction, but a hierarchy in their status is implied by the caption information supplied with them. In the case of fine art works, like Denis McBride's *Northern Incident (Peaceful)* (Plate 2), the reader is given the artist's name and the title of the work, together with its date, medium, size and location. This information urges the insertion of the work into the artist's total output, and the reconstruction of its original appearance. The same kind of artwork information is provided for the *Don't Fraternise* poster (Plate 3). Indeed by categorising it as the work of 'Anonymous' rather than of a member of the political group which produced it, it is removed from a political into an artistic context. For Rowel Friers' *Miss Free Derry* cartoon (Plate 4) however, no medium or dimensions are given, the implication being that not being a work of art such information is not appropriate. Yet the lack of dimensions deprives the reader of a particularly important piece of evidence about the cartoon, for much of its impact at the time it was issued in the *Belfast Telegraph* derived from the very large scale of its reproduction. The implied scale of values in these captions is further endorsed in Catto's text in which a constant opposition is proposed between the independent view of the troubles presented by the fine artist who is seen as being above political divisions and 'the futility of violence' and the mindless

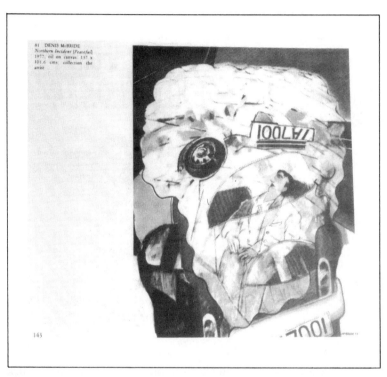

Plate 2 Black and white illustration on page 143 of Mike Catto,
Art in Ulster: 2, Belfast, Blackstaff Press, 1977

Plate 3 Black and white illustration on page 127 of Mike Catto, *Art in Ulster: 2*, Belfast, Blackstaff Press, 1977

73 ROWEL FRIERS
Miss Free Derry
13 November 1971; *Belfast
Telegraph* cartoon

129

The example here (no 73), is typical of his style of draughtsmanship. His gallery of working urban or rural 'types' is generally a pithy form of human observation. Friers' political cartooning has a sense of fair play: it provokes a tut or a chuckle (in itself no bad thing) rather than giving the cruel flash of insight that one gets from commentators as diverse as Daumier, Scarfe or Heartfield. There have been some exceptions, notably the example illustrated, which is deservedly one of the most famous of the 'troubles' cartoons. Rowel Friers' art, however, is not specific to the troubles; for him this past decade probably represents yet another daft episode in the history of a fascinating but daft community.

Another Ulster artist who has specialised in cartooning with a political slant is Kenneth Mahood whose work appears regularly in *The Times* and *Punch*. Mahood was one of the young painters of promise in the mid 1950s but his subsequent move to London saw the spiky line of hi. paintings develop into an almost baroque graphic style which delights in curls and swirls. Although he has produced a fair number of scathing visual comments on the Irish situation, he has no great

Plate 4 Black and white illustration on page 129 of Mike Catto, *Art in Ulster: 2*, Belfast, Blackstaff Press, 1977

sectarian propaganda of makers of political imagery, from which category the maker of the *Don't Fraternise* poster escapes by virtue of his or her involvement in a form of poster-work popular amongst art students and sanctioned by art fashion in the late 1960s.

Mass-media photographs of the Northern Ireland troubles have been analysed in a number of publications, notably in various issues of *Camerawork*, a photography magazine produced by a leftwing collective in London. Issue no. 14 of the magazine, which appeared in August 1979, was entirely devoted to the subject of *Reporting on Northern Ireland*. The overall message about press photographs of the Northern Ireland conflict conveyed by this publication is that the production of such photographs for the mass media is subject to strong political and technical pressures, to which certain committed leftwing photographers respond by seeking more independent ways of issuing their pictures so that their aesthetic and political content can be given unhindered expression. Except in the first three pages of the magazine, which carry an illustrated 'Short History of Ireland' based on a slide show compiled by the Troops Out Movement, the photographs in the magazine are beautifully reproduced, generally on a very large scale; they are grouped in photo-essays and articles on particular political aspects of the Ulster conflict, such as 'Catholic West Belfast', or 'Camera on Patrol' (an article on the use of cameras by the British Army in Northern Ireland); they are captioned in such a way as to emphasise their political content; and they are credited with the name of the photographer responsible. The same implied antithesis between the independent photographer observing developments in Ulster with political and aesthetic correctness, and the manipulation of photographic images by the mass media and the British Army, can be found in the articles in this issue, in which analyses of press distortion and army surveillance are counterbalanced by a series of interviews with a number of photographers who have worked in the province since 1968.

To sum up then: two different relationships between visual images and political conflict are generally proposed by the few published analyses of the visual material linked to the Northern Ireland troubles. On the one hand the history books, by concentrating on the content of visual images, imply that they are reflections or illustrations of political developments, and as such have an equivalent value, whether they be paintings, photographs, prints or wallpaintings. And on the other hand the art books, and to a large extent the publications dealing with media photographs, by concentrating on the authorship of images, emphasise their role as creations of finely-tuned aesthetic individuals, who are essentially independent of political constraints, and whose output is graded according to a hierarchy of artistic categories, and an estimation of value based largely on the degree of independent integrity involved.[1] Neither approach exhibits much interest in the function of these images or situates them in their original context. Neither approach develops an analysis of the political messages coded in their style as opposed to their content. In fact neither approach is concerned with them as evidence in themselves. The relationship between image and conflict is collapsed by focusing too exclusively on image or conflict.[2]

Similar limited and divided approaches can be found in the museum and art gallery displays of visual imagery related to the Northern Ireland troubles. In the Ulster Museum in Belfast various kinds of visual images ranging from a painting of William III to a penal cross and transfer-printed volunteer jugs illustrate the province's political traditions in the Local History galleries, opened in 1978, and at the end of these galleries a wall-panel of photographs surveying various aspects of Ulster's past and present concludes with a small selection of carefully balanced, tasteful press pictures of the present conflict. Several floors above, the few works of art referring to the troubles which the museum owns are displayed in the art galleries reserved to the Irish school or to international modern art.

Temporary exhibitions, normally regarded as a more flexible and experimental way of handling visual imagery than permanent museum and art gallery displays, have in fact generally offered the viewer the same kind of limited and divided presentation of troubles imagery. There have been various shows of personal, aesthetic visions of the troubles by fine artists from Ulster, the Republic of Ireland and Britain. Some of the political images produced by loyalist and republican groups were displayed in photographic form in an exhibition surveying political attitudes in the province, compiled by Conrad Atkinson in 1975. Actual photographs of the troubles have been shown in exhibitions mounted by organisations like Camerawork, Camerawork Derry and Belfast Exposed. Only very rarely, as in the People's Festivals in Armagh and Dublin early in the conflict, or the Troubled Image contributions to Queen's University Belfast's Fringe Festival in 1972, or the Almost Free Art Show in Belfast in 1978, have fine art, popular and media images relating to the troubles been presented together, avoiding division into subject and object, illustration and art.

Clearly the bulk of the permanent and temporary displays of visual imagery relating to the Northern Ireland conflict propose, like the publications, that such images are either reflections of political developments or creations of artistic individuals independent of political constraints, whose output is graded and separated according to a hierarchy of existing categories, and a valuation system based largely on the degree of independent integrity involved.

It is possible to argue that at least the second assessment of the relationship between visual imagery and politics has some foundation in existential reality. From the end of the eighteenth century onwards the makers of visual imagery were increasingly divided into separate and graded categories, headed by the fine artist who was expected to stand somewhat aloof from society so as to be able to present it with the independent creations of his individual genius. The artist/craftsman working to a patron's commission in a range of images from murals and easel paintings to designs for jewellery, stage scenery or propaganda prints, was gradually replaced by the fine artist, committing his individual visions to a more limited range of paintings, drawings and sculpture, while other forms of imagery were produced by a growing army of specialist craftsmen, such as medallists, print-makers and stage-designers. This was part of a more general split between high and low culture during this period, which was deepened by the far greater rate of change in high culture, its increasing reservation to institutions such as universities and art-dealers, to which the general populace had very little access, and its absorption of the romantic conception of the artist as a heroic rebel against social conventions (Burke, 1978 and Neuburg, 1977).

It is also true that the development of the mass media during this period, and most particularly after 1900, did effect a further major division in categories of visual imagery. It is as well to remember that mass-production on a limited scale was already being used for objects such as coins, medals and wood-engravings (Ivins, 1969). But the changes in scale and speed of output which now took place were enormous. Contrast for example the implications of a newspaper photograph to those of an Orange or Hibernian banner. The former is produced in enormous numbers, available to all, largely uncontrollable by the individual, designed to be thrown away, demands a speedy response and may well refer to far distant events. The latter is a single image available to a select group, geared to their taste and chosen by at least one of their number, designed to be kept, demands repeated reflections and refers to local allegiances. It is clear that with the development of the mass media a totally new kind of image did come into existence.

However the situation in Northern Ireland makes it plain that the existential separation of visual imagery from politics and society, and its organisation into a hierarchy of categories, has been less clear-cut than is often assumed.

Images in Northern Ireland have direct political roles. Wearing the wrong tattoo or ignoring the territorial claim of the wallpainting (Plate 5) can lead to injury or death. Not only popular images function in this way. Oliver Sheppard's dying *Cuchulain*, made in 1911, and later erected in the Dublin GPO as a memorial to the 1916 rebels, has subsequently been featured in army medals issued by the Republic of Ireland, a republican wallpainting in the Bogside area of Derry, a photo in the headquarters of the Ulster Defence Association, a butter-sculpture in a Dublin competition and trophies from innumerable events, ranging from the sporting to the scientific (Plate 6). And in 1950 Belfast councillors vetoed the purchase for the city's museum of a Wyck painting of King William III (*Irish News*, 1950), because the monarch was shown astride a brown horse, not the white steed hallowed by traditional association with the House of Hanover and the Saviour in the Apocalypse (Plate 5).

Both of these latter images have their political message reinforced by religious overtones (the Cuchulain figure was clearly influenced by traditional representations of the Deposition and Entombment of Christ, particularly those by Michelangelo). Such blending of religion and politics is generally shared by both nationalist and loyalist political images in Northern Ireland. But the *style* of the images employed by the two political groupings is very different, as is made clear by the symbols they have employed to appeal for support for their political prisoners and internees (Plates 7 and 8). Whereas imagery associated with the nationalist community tends to be highly figurative, handled in a free, expressive, emotive fashion, with a strong emphasis on rebellion, imagery associated with the loyalist community tends to be predominantly decorative or heraldic, handled with a semi-industrial precision, and a constant emphasis on secret symbols

Plate 5 Mural of King William III, first painted in 1939
Photo: B. Loftus (1979). Blackstaff Press, 1977

Plate 6 Photo of the 'Young Computer Person of the Year', Mr Gerald Newman in *The Irish Times*, Wednesday, 3 December, 1986, page 7

ULSTER LOYALIST

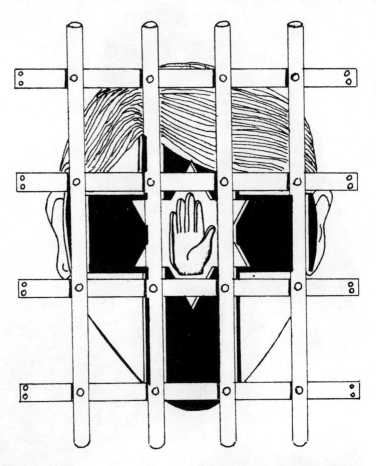

POLITICAL PRISONERS

Plate 7 Loyalist prisoners' emblem in *Orange Cross*, (Ulster Volunteer Force newsheet), May 1972, Linen Hall Library, Belfast

Plate 8 Northern Ireland Civil Rights Association Christmas Card, 1972
Collection: B. Loftus

and legitimacy. This division in style extends to fine art and even mass media imagery in Northern Ireland (Loftus, 1983 and 1986).

In both communities the public and private roles of visual images constantly intersect. Prison crafts made as presents for friends or relatives become public assertions of defiance when displayed in windows facing onto the street, or pointers to a familial and national heritage, in which Irish mother and Celtic motherland become one, enshrined over the family hearth (Plate 9). The sash or collarette which forms part of the marching regalia of Northern Ireland's Orange organisations (Plate 10), may literally be the one 'my father wore', for family traditions play a large part in the survival of these societies.

Partly as the result of this mingling of private and public, visual images in Northern Ireland can fuse apparently conflicting meanings. A republican funeral is a time both of private grief and public celebration of a cause. An Orange procession has both a tight hierarchical structure and a strong element of licence, with drinking, courtship and uninhibited music and dancing traditionally associated with it.

Indeed, if one looks at the total function of visual images in everyday life in Northern Ireland, rather than at the particular question of their initial production, the existential basis for a view of them as separate from society and politics and isolated into different categories crumbles very rapidly. Consider for example the various interrelated roles of visual imagery in the life of a man who lives in Derry, paints Orange banners and Catholic statues, displays his own paintings of Irish landscapes on the sitting-room wall, has access to books reproducing Dutch oil paintings and medals of William III, makes a ritual effigy every year, attends a Church of Ireland cathedral, walks in Apprentice Boys processions, and therefore may be photographed by the British Army and various Irish newspapers, has a house-painter's training, and reads the *News Letter*, the *Londonderry Sentinel* and the *Orange Standard*. For such a man visual images are very much part of his involvement in society and politics, and divisions between fine art and popular imagery are virtually meaningless.

If the existential basis for the commonly held views of the relationship between visual imagery and political developments is debatable rather than fixed, why are those views so persistent? To a certain extent one must recognise that they are rooted in both overall and specific practical considerations. Analysis of a wide range of imagery, produced by image-makers who assume

Plate 9 Decorated wooden plaque made by an internee in Long Kesh in 1977, Falls Road, Belfast, 1982
Photo: B. Loftus

Plate 10 Orangemen at a demonstration outside Belfast City Hall, 15 March 1980

116

themselves to be in very separate categories, displayed and stored in museums and archives which reflect those separations at the point of production, and similarly discussed and analysed by different groups of commentators, requires considerable time, energy and money.

Moreover one can argue that the modes of presentation and analysis of visual images relating to the Northern Ireland conflict have also been considerably affected by the more immediate practical circumstances surrounding their production, notably the intention with which they were made, and the way in which they were constructed. This may become clearer if we look at some of the specific examples already cited.

The intention of Robert Kee's book, as of his television series, was to present to a wide public in England and Ireland,[3] an account of Irish history which would facilitate a solution to the present conflict in Northern Ireland.[4] Like the majority of such popular illustrated history books it used visual images as a means of attracting readers, and thereby increasing sales, and as teaching aids, stimulating an interest in the written text. These images were selected not by the author but by a picture researcher. Most picture researchers are underpaid, work to tight deadlines, under pressure to find cheap, easily obtainable images, and move speedily from one project to another – today the First World War, tomorrow Northern Ireland. Often these conditions of work result in their producing images which are only loosely appropriate to the text, and lack even the most basic information about their relationship with the historical point they supposedly illustrate.[5] Even educational publications use picture researchers for their illustrations (e.g. Schools Council, 1977), and it is only very occasionally, when a historian selects and analyses his own illustrations (e.g. Public Record Office of Northern Ireland, 1976), or a particularly talented picture researcher is involved in the writing and making of a history book (e.g. Downing, 1970), that its illustrations are used and analysed as historical documents presenting their own particular kind of evidence. Clearly the tendency of historians to present visual images as illustrations or reflections of political developments is closely linked to current practices involved in making and selling history books.

Mike Catto's *Art in Ulster: 2* is an example of a very different kind of publication, aimed at a specific, limited audience. It was written principally for the Northern Ireland market, and chiefly for use in teaching the province's new alternative syllabus Art GCE exams, introduced in 1975, for which study of Northern Ireland art history is required. In dealing with the visual imagery related to the Northern Ireland troubles, Catto was therefore limited to a brief, straightforward, factual account of who did what within the limits established by the concept of 'art history' as a school subject, and his awareness of the need to be careful in handling political issues given the need to consider both his audience and his subjects (who might conceivably suffer attack for too close identification with a particular political standpoint). These practical consider-ations appear to be strongly linked to Catto's emphasis on the role of the independent artist in his analysis of visual imagery relating to the troubles.

Somewhat similar considerations have affected the limited and divided displays of such material in the Ulster Museum. Museums are habitually cautious about putting on show imagery which relates in any way to contemporary political issues. Their administrators are very conscious of their practical responsibilities towards the safety of both the public entering their premises, and the objects on display in their showcases. Anything which might provoke the half-brick or the firebomb is therefore to be strenuously avoided. Such administrators are also sadly aware of the way in which any display which could be regarded as political will be regarded as such, and will normally be interpreted as favouring one 'side' or another. This is a situation normally regarded as highly embarrassing by an institution in receipt of public funds, particularly if, as in the case of the Ulster Museum, it is responsible to a governing body largely composed of local and central government representatives, and the political issues in question are close to home. These factors largely affect the limited, tentative nature of the museum's displays of visual imagery relating to the troubles.

However the categorisation and separation of those displays is linked to a somewhat different practical limitation, that imposed by the usual internal organisation of a museum into departments which acquire, document and display their own separate collec-tions. Thus in the Ulster Museum visual images relating to the present troubles and to the traditions connected with them, are handled by either the Art Department or the Local History Department. Paintings, sculptures, drawings, quality prints, glass and china are the province of various specialists in the Art Department, while Local History handle popular prints, flags, banners, badges, coins, medals and photographs. There is collaboration in mounting displays – the Cobbe cup which forms part of the Art Department's collections was at the time of writing in a case of Williamite objects in the Local History galleries – but the separation of categories and treatment of troubles imagery previously described is closely related to the departmental organisation of the museum. And that organisation in turn is linked to the way museum staff are trained, normally taking a degree in a relevant discipline and an additional Museums Diploma, primarily intended to certify a level of competence in current administrative practices in such fields as preparation of estimates, security and conservation.

For the practical factors affecting the ways in which the relationship between visual imagery and the troubles is handled in Robert Kee's book, Mike Catto's book and the Ulster Museum displays are all linked to the formal and informal training in handling such material received by those involved. In the majority of cases they have a university degree and subsequent employment in either history (Kee,[6] and the staff of the Local History Department in the Ulster Museum), or art history (Catto,[7] and the staff of the Art Department in the Ulster Museum). The teaching and practice of these two academic disciplines in Britain and Ireland predispose those trained in them to the two very different attitudes towards the relationship between visual imagery and political developments which I have just outlined.

On the one hand British and Irish historians are not trained to analyse visual imagery as historical evidence, and rarely see their elders or their peers doing so. And on the other hand the majority of art-historians in Britain and Ireland have until very recently been trained to document, evaluate and categorise artworks in a manner associated with their status as collectable objects, and have often found employment in art world jobs involved with collecting (museums and art-dealers), and its promotion (art-criticism and art-administration). This slant to their training and professional careers naturally orients them towards emphasis on visual images which are unique, set apart from political and social developments and preferably the creations of individual geniuses. For collecting by its very nature removes visual images from their social and political contexts into an association normally deter-mined by the purely artistic concepts of the medium (oil paintings, drawings, prints, medallions, ceramics, etc.) or the artist, or the style (Gothic, Mannerist, Baroque, etc.), or the school (which may have a political element, as with the British or Irish schools, but equally may be related to a particular centre attracting artists from a number of countries, as with the Paris or New York schools).

Attempts to break away from this mainstream of art history by studying art and politics, popular imagery or the mass media have generally failed to break with overall tendencies within the discipline. Thus most existing discussions by British and Irish art-historians of the relationship between art and political develop-ments in past conflicts appear to be strongly confined to traditional interest in the commissioning and production of art (e.g. Miller, 1966; Leith, 1965; Willett, 1970; Joll, 1960 and Rye, 1972), heavily slanted by political loyalties,[8] and committed either to unsupported associations between political developments and the nature of an artist's work,[9] or to so cautious an awareness of the complexities of the relationships between imagery and politics that attempts to assess it are virtually abandoned (Honour, 1968; Barrett, 1975; Sheehy, 1980).

Discussions of popular imagery are similarly predominantly constrained by value-assumptions and modes of analysis inherited from existing disciplines. To this day analysts of popular culture tend to focus on 'good' rural folk traditions, for much the same reason as those who first worked in this field, namely because of a desire to preserve the rapidly disappearing past, a reaction against the effects of industrialisation and modernisation, and a belief that in such traditions lie the ethos of the nation (Burke, 1978: 7–16; Bigsby, 1976). In Ireland this has resulted in a large body of writing extolling the national virtues of the traditionalism of the Irish peasant, and implicitly separating them from urban and English culture, and a smaller number of works (e.g. Evans, 1957), seeking in rural folk culture something older, wiser and separate from the country's political conflicts, whether past or present.

Clearly this concept of popular culture has been inimical to the incorporation with it of the mass media. Those who have pioneered the study of media imagery have done so from a position of horrified fascination. Their attitude seems to derive from that peculiarly English half-literary, half-artistic tradition of revulsion from the effects of industrialisation and mass-production which runs from Matthew Arnold and William Morris to F. R. Leavis (Swingewood, 1977). Thus Marshall McLuhan characteris-tically describes production and sales executives as 'thinking in military terms, smashing public resistance with carefully planned barrages followed by shock troops of salesmen to mop up the pockets' (McLuhan, 1967: 34).

It is significant that McLuhan was a Professor of *English*.

The same line has been adopted in the recent publications on the mass media and Northern Ireland such as *Camerawork no. 14*. The message is sharpened by the particular political anxieties involved, i.e. Irish distrust of the English and leftwing English distrust of capitalist control of the organs of opinion, but it is basically the same message: 'Big Brother is watching and controlling you with his evil technology which is capable of perverting you without you realising it.'

This is the view of outside critics of the mass media. A second strand in the development of media-studies in recent years has been the provision of inside knowledge about the tricks of the trade. Harold Evans for example, appears to offer the viewer a fairly comprehensive guide to the way photographic images of events can be altered by photographers and picture editors, by virtue of such techniques as use of different lenses, selection, juxtaposition, cropping and downright faking (Evans, 1978). This is the kind of approach employed by Frank Webster in his analysis of the photo coverage of Maire Drumm's funeral, although he considers a wider range of factors than Evans does (Webster, 1977). Yet by their focus on these kinds of alterations Evans and Webster implicitly distract the viewer from the effects on photographic images of the wider context in which they appear. They make no mention for example of the juxtaposition of news photographs with advertising material and of their consequent reduction to objects for consumption. Just as McLuhan and similar critics of the mass media are limited by their position as outsiders to it, so Evans and Webster are limited by their role as insiders.

The other kind of inside information which the viewer needs to consider alongside that made available by Evans and Webster is the specialised analyses of advertising researchers, published in journals such as *Admap*. Here there is constant discussion of such considerations as the location of images, the relative impact of descriptive or illustrative layout and the *varying* use made of publications by their readers. Yet this kind of research on visual imagery is rarely considered by academics or the general public.

Even within media studies therefore, there are divisions of approach which hamper the viewer's ability to decipher the images with which he or she is confronted. Indeed the existing studies which move outside the mainstream of art history to consider art

121

and politics, popular imagery and the mass media have little to offer anyone interested in the relationship between visual imagery and political developments, for they take with them many of the assumptions traditional to the kind of art history generally practised in Britain and Ireland.

Far more useful to anyone attempting to discover the nature of this relationship are the works of the German and Austrian historians working in the first half of this century, notably Erwin Panofsky and Fritz Saxl. In Panofsky's studies it is possible to find the kind of sensitive and complex analysis of the interplay between various cultural and social factors within a given area of time and space that has been so lacking in the work of most British art historians. Take for example Panofsky's observation of a connection between Gothic art and scholasticism which is neither mere parallelism nor a matter of the individual influence of learned advisers on painters, sculptors or architects, but rather the result of the diffusion of a mental habit, tellingly compared by him to the twentieth-century impact of the idea of evolution (Panofsky, 1957: 20–1).

This general observation is rooted by Panofsky in observation of specific connections. He cites, for example, the existence in Villard de Honnecourt's *Album* of the groundplan of an 'ideal' chevet which he and another architect, Pierre de Corbie, had devised, 'disputing between themselves', in other words following the scholastic manner of arguing out a question (ibid: 87). And he describes the world in which the High Gothic architects of France moved, the area round Paris where Scholasticism dominated education, where they were in frequent contact with its religious supporters, where they heard sermons and public debates using its style of argument, and where, in a new atmosphere of urban professionalism, they could join in such discussions as equals (ibid: 21–6).

Fritz Saxl's peculiar importance lies in his firm assertion that visual images have an independent life of their own, and therefore an independent value as historical evidence.

> think of the paraphernalia of majesty in Byzantium, the triple crown of the Popes, the ceremonial robes and objects used for the coronation of the Kings of England. Each of these objects has its history, and if it is studied in connection with historical documents and liturgical texts, it reveals facts and ideas which could not be discovered otherwise. (Saxl, 1970: 13)

Panofsky and Saxl, along with other art historians of the German and Austrian school, have subsequently been much criticised for their tendency to see art as a product determined by a Hegelian spirit-of-the-age, with no possibility of alternatives offered and little consideration given to the role of the artist's skill (Gombrich, 1969: 30–8 and 1962: 16–18; Tagg, 1975: 3–10). However the importance of their interest in the relationship between art and society has recently been recognised by a number of younger art historians, who have attempted to rework their approach, often by replacing their Hegelianism with a developed interpretation of the Marxist metaphor of base and super-structure.

T. J. Clark for example retains art history's traditional focus on the process of production involved in the making of a major artwork like Courbet's *The Burial at Ornans*, but uses it to reveal the artist's involvement with political and social developments and the way in which he both reveals and transforms them within the very structure of his work (Clark, 1973). In this analysis one of his strengths is his constant stress on the importance of what is omitted, of what cannot be said. Employing an approach developed by the French Marxist theorist, Pierre Macherey (Macherey, 1978), he shows how the cartoons by Daumier which were suppressed, the points at which the art critic falters and falls silent, are crucial indications of what current ideology will not allow.

Michael Baxandall, though not overtly committed to Marxist methodology, adopts a somewhat similar approach to Clark in his study of fifteenth-century Italian paintings, which analyses the impact on them of the artist's social role, the technical materials available to him and his involvement with the more general ways of seeing current in the society in which he lived (Baxandall, 1972). Of particular value to the analyst of the kind of visual languages to be found in Northern Ireland, is his detailed discussion of how daily visual skills and artistic skills were actually linked, while constantly setting such analyses in a wider context. For example he shows how important the gauging of volumes and quantities was in an age when containers were not manufactured in stock sizes; how an artist like Piero della Francesca was both mathematician and painter; and how his patrons, used as they were to assessing geometrical quantities, enjoyed his frequent demonstrations of this skill (ibid, 86–97). But he is careful to stress that the inter-connections were more complex and with wider implications than such direct relationships tend to imply, pointing out that in general Quattrocento Italians

> did not know more about mathematics than we do: most of them knew less than most of us. But they knew their specialized area absolutely, used it in important matters more often than we do, played games and told jokes with it, bought luxurious books about it and prided themselves on their prowess in it; it was a relatively much larger part of their formal intellectual equipment. (ibid: 101)

Baxandall argues that any society develops distinctive skills and habits which always have a visual aspect. They become part of the artist's medium; conversely the artist's pictorial style gives access the visual skills and habits through which a distinctive social experience can be ascertained.

> If we observe that Piero della Francesca tended to a gauged sort of painting, Fra Angelico to a preached sort of painting and Botticelli to a danced sort of painting, we are observing something not only about them but about their society. (ibid: 152)

In summary then the German and Austrian art historians and their more recent successors offer a number of important modes of analysing the relationship between visual imagery and social, political, economic and religious developments. They demonstrate how artists' visions are linked to the society in which they live by their involvement with a variety of conceptual and visual conventions, their dependence on the technology then available, the overt or implicit limitations on what they can say in their works, and the structure of the relationship between them and the consumers of their products. Moreover these writers make the important point that artworks are in themselves unique documentary evidence of aspects of the society in which they are produced. However, for the student of the relationship between visual images and political developments there are a number of very noticeable deficiencies in their analyses. These retain a primary emphasis on fine art works, and are almost exclusively limited to consideration of the initial process of production. The broad spectrum of visual imagery, the living function of images both at the time of their initial production and during their subsequent usage, reproduction and transformation, and the relationship between the institutional organisation of artwork and the style of imagery produced in it, are areas which remain virtually untouched in these studies. It is necessary therefore to turn to research undertaken completely outside the field of art history.

For useful material relating to the last topic one can turn to some of the most recent studies of media imagery. While in Britain there is still a tendency in media studies to relate institutional factors solely to the content of the images conditioned by them, as in the various articles in *Camerawork no. 14*, similar analyses in America, notably Barbara Rosenblum's comparative study of news, advertising, and fine arts photographs, relate the institutional organisation of media imagery to the style adopted in it (Rosenblum, 1978a and 1978b).

In seeking to establish the living function of visual images within social and political developments, much can be learnt from the work of anthropologists. Of particular interest to the analyst of political imagery is Victor Turner's stress on the multi-valency of ritual symbols, allowing different meanings to emerge in different contexts, and his emphasis on their power to condense thought and action, desire and obligation (Turner, 1967).

Clearly theories such as these, which have been developed as the result of observation of African tribal rituals, can only be used with much caution in analysing the ritual use of visual imagery in Western society, and indeed E. P. Thompson has launched a scathing attack on the misuse of anthropology in recent historical studies of religion and magic in seventeenth-century Britain (Thompson, 1972: 41–55). But when properly applied, as in M. R. Beames's studies of the use of ritual imagery by agrarian protest movements in late eighteenth-century Ireland (Beames, 1983), the kind of anthropological approach employed by Turner can assist an understanding of the way visual images can be transformed by their living ritual use, and in this process of transformation can be employed to effect an interchange between a number of meanings, derived from the political, cultural, social, economic and religious experience of their users. In a Northern Ireland context a Turnerite examination of the various ritual *uses* of the image of William III demonstrates how that image has come to fuse concepts of monarchic, local, mythical and religious leadership.

Handled with care, mass media studies and anthropological analyses of ritual imagery can supplement art historical contributions to understanding of the relationship between visual imagery and social and political developments, by their demonstration of the way the style of images is conditioned by the institutional organisation of their production, and by showing how they acquire layers of meaning in the course of their use in living rituals. However these theories and perceptions do no more than illuminate further fragments of the relationship between visual imagery and society. Their authors go no further than the art historians in offering a general view of that relationship, in which in particular the visual languages perceived as so evident in the Northern Ireland context can find adequate theoretical location. For this it is necessary to turn to recent studies of the social function of symbols and language rather than particular forms of visual imagery. In these there have been a number of attempts to determine the underlying codes and 'grammar' of myths, rituals, symbols and language, and to relate them to social structures. Of particular value is Basil Bernstein's development of the basic theory of Boas, Sapir and Whorf that people speaking different languages live in different thought-worlds (Bernstein, 1971: 121–32; Mueller, 1973: 95). It is worth spelling out Bernstein's analysis in some detail, as he ends up by proposing two socially related styles of speaking remarkably similar to the two styles of vision described as existing in Northern Ireland.

Bernstein has made particular use of Whorf's concept that languages are influenced by fashions of speaking which cut across typical grammatical classifications. In Whorf's opinion these fashions of speaking are unrelated to social structure. Bernstein has argued however that social structures generate linguistic forms or codes which transmit culture and constrain behaviour. He has suggested that there are two main codes, restricted and elaborated.

In the restricted code the form of communication is predictable, for the social relationship is based upon a conscious shared identity with no need to make intent explicit. The language is simplified and narrow, and individual differentiation is expressed by extra-verbal signals. Speech is impersonal, concrete, condensed, neither analytical nor abstract. Its major function is to define and reinforce a form of social relationship by restricting verbal signalling of individual experience.

The elaborated code on the other hand is unpredictable, with a high level of grammatical organisation and verbal selection, as the intention of the other person cannot be taken for granted. The major function of the elaborated code is the delivery of relatively explicit meaning. This form of communication facilitates the transmission and elaboration of the individual's unique experience and allows modifications to be made to suit the listener. Whereas the restricted code reinforces a particularistic social structure by the use of universalistic models, the elaborated code uses particularistic models to reinforce a universalistic society. And whereas in the restricted code the concept of self tends to be seen in terms of status arrangements, the elaborated code facilitates reflection on the concept of self.

Bernstein tends to see these codes as the product of social structures, associating the restricted code with the working class and the elaborated code with the middle class. He believes the reasons for this association lie chiefly in the family role systems and modes of social control of the two classes. In his view the restricted code arises in a social system governed by mechanical solidarity in which the family is positional while the elaborated code is found in a social system governed by organic solidarity, emphasising the personal family.

The closeness of Bernstein's restricted and elaborated linguistic codes to the loyalist and nationalist way of seeing in Northern Ireland is remarkable. Loyalist visual language, like Bernstein's restricted linguistic code, is 'impersonal, concrete, condensed', reinforcing established social and political relationships by excluding representation of individual experience. Flags and heraldic emblems dominate its wall paintings, prison imagery and political posters. Nationalist visual language, like his elaborated linguistic code is often unpredictable, drawing on an elaborate range of images, and using highly personal symbolism in an attempt to communicate to outsiders. Figures from Irish mythology, socialist movements of the twentieth century and Catholic religious tradition are constantly shuffled and blended in idiosyncratic combinations and offered in murals, badges, and posters which seek as wide a range of support as possible. In loyalist imagery as in the restricted code such universalistic models as the saviour on the white horse are turned inwards to reinforce a very exclusive socio-political enclave. Conversely nationalist imagery like the elaborated code employs such particularistic models as the victim-saviour, whether Christ or Bobby Sands's imprisoned lark, as poetic emblems of universal redemption. As in the restricted code so in Loyalist imagery strongly defined and hierarchical social structures such as the band, the lodge, the Order, the regiment, the workplace or the Church crucially affect self-representation, which manifests itself in carefully organised parades and pictures.

In strong contrast reflection on the self comes easily, not only to those employing the elaborated code but also to the nationalist image-makers. Their parades are massed, unhierarchical demonstrations and their works identify with individual sufferings and achievement. Such similarities between the linguistic codes described by Bernstein and the visual codes observable in Northern Ireland, stress both the strength of his basic theory and the weakness of the somewhat crude class-model he develops from it.

A more complex theory about the relationship between different verbal and visual codes and forms of social structure is offered by Mary Douglas, in her development of his work (Douglas, 1970). However the theories of both Bernstein and Douglas tend to imply an over-simplified, determinist production of cultural codes by social structures, leaving little room for the impact of culture on society, the role of history and change, and the contribution of individual skill.

To some extent these defects can be remedied by fusing with the theories of Bernstein and Douglas the adaptation of the generative grammar theory made by the French sociologist Pierre Bourdieu, who conceptualises cultural codes as strategies, customs or 'pre-laws', based in turn on: 'a small batch of schemes which enable agents to generate an infinity of practices adapted to endlessly changing situations, without those schemes ever being constituted as principles' (Bourdieu, 1977: 16).

These schemes he characterizes as fuzzy oppositions, such as left–right, which can be developed in much the same way as one makes play on words (ibid: 118–23).

But Bourdieu, like others employing the concept of generative grammar, leaves unanswered the tricky question of where those schemes or codes came from in the first place. This living intersection between culture and society is eloquently explored in the recent work of Norbert Elias and Janet Wolff (Elias, 1983: 214–47; Wolff, 1981).

As Philip Abrams makes clear in his *Historical Sociology* (Abrams, 1982: 228–40), Elias's strength as a sociological theorist lies in his ability to present the development of individuals and society, meaning and structure, as interrelated in a kind of game without rules, whose figurations can only be explained with the aid of history. In a similar fashion Wolff sees the relationship between society and art as a continuous process of interaction, in which social and political structures are mediated into the artwork through the technology, social situation and art conventions conditioning the individual or group actions of the producer(s), and are then modified in turn in the course of the work's manufacture and its completion and continuing production by its customers. She therefore satisfactorily avoids both the determinism and the transcendentalism between which attempts to analyse that relationship have continually vacillated.

The main drawback to Wolff's work, along with that of the majority of sociologists approaching this area, is that she confines herself to the old, limited category of 'art', instead of taking a wider and less value-structured view, by looking at 'visual imagery' or 'ways of seeing', in the fashion adopted in the insightful, if somewhat loose analyses of Walter Benjamin and John Berger (Benjamin, 1970: 221–7; Berger, 1972).

Drawing on the theories of the Austrian art historians and their successors, of media-analysts like Barbara Rosenblum, of the anthropologist Victor Turner, and of sociologists like Basil Bernstein, Mary Douglas, Norbert Elias and Janet Wolff, it is possible to construct a theory about the relationship of visual images to society which fits the present situation in Northern Ireland. It can be broken down into the following propositions:

That in order to understand the relationship of visual images to society it is necessary to abandon the traditional, hierarchical, evaluative separation of them into categories such as fine art, popular imagery and the mass media, except insofar as that evaluation and categorisation is part of those images' real, existential function;[10]

that any specific visual image is the product of a maker or group of makers whose work is conditioned, though not completely determined, by overlapping social, political, economic and religious factors, by virtue of their personal context, the technology involved in the production of their work, its location within institutional structures, and its use of existing visual conventions;

that the private and public significance of visual images are interlinked;

that an image is not static, but is further developed each time it is used or re-produced, and that in the course of these processes it both acquires additional layers of meaning and has a real impact on social, political, economic and religious developments;

that this living, developing image is not isolated, but in the various stages of its production both derives meaning from and contributes meaning to the overall visual language of its producers/users, and is appropriated by them to the specific visual language codes with which they shape their view of the world; and that those visual language codes can be seen interacting in a kind of dialogue in which opposition and overlap are both important.

What remains in question is whether this theory is relevant only to the situation in Northern Ireland, or can be deployed in relation to visual images elsewhere. As has been demonstrated at the beginning of this article, most existing analyses of visual images adhere to a hierarchical separation into fine art, popular imagery and mass media, believed to have been established in the post-Renaissance period. Implicit in this approach is a reliance on a view of society as increasingly marked by distance, whether between nation and citizen, class and class, employer and employee, producer and consumer, learned and unlearned, mass media and viewer. It is arguable however that during the past fifteen to twenty years such a view of society has rapidly gone out of date. The supposedly distancing and levelling mass media have been cute enough to realise this, with their special category programmes and magazines for groups characterised by ethnicity, gender and age rather than nationality, class, job and religion. What sociology now needs is new theoretical models which can hold in the same framework both the old and the new social categories, allowing for their constant refiguration in time, and the possibility of decreasing as well as lengthening social and conceptual distance (Cormack, 1984). In this context the theoretical model developed here for the relationship between visual images and society in Northern Ireland looks more generally useful, and less of a one-off formula than might at first appear. The world, after all, is in a constant state of chassis.

Acknowledgements

Grateful acknowledgement is made to Weidenfeld and Nicolson

for reproduction of Plate 1, to Blackstaff Press for reproduction of Plates 2–4 and to the *Irish Times* for reproduction of Plate 6.

Notes

1 Clearly there is some overlap between these two approaches. Even in the history books fine art works are often given the kind of precedence over other images to be found in the Kee illustration, and an aspiration to reflection of political realities is contained in the photographs reproduced in *Camerawork*.
2 There have been a few exceptions to these two main forms of approach to visual imagery related to the Northern Ireland troubles. Thus Frank Webster (Feb. 1977) locates the photographs of Maire Drumm's funeral carried by the Fleet Street popular papers firmly within the context of the conventions governing their production. But this kind of approach has been exceedingly rare.
3 The television series was available through the BBC in mainland Britain and Northern Ireland, and through simultaneous RTE transmission in the Republic of Ireland. The book was widely distributed in Britain, Northern Ireland and the Republic.
4 The last sentences of Kee's book, which are also incorporated in the publishers' blurb inside the front dust-jacket, are: 'History is indeed a difficult prison to escape from and the history of Ireland is as difficult as any. It is not the business of a historian – even a television historian – to propose how escape should be effected. Yet change is the business of history and the historian has a vested interest in seeing change come about. Having traced the foundations on which the prison of Irish history was built, he can only wait and hope to see British and Irish alike one day walk away.'
5 Thus in the Kee book no indication is given that the scene of the Flight of the Earls reproduced on pp. 38–9 is a recent oil-painting produced in the Republic of Ireland by the artist Thomas Ryan.
6 Kee also has a background in pictorial journalism, including a spell with *Picture Post*, and television, in which training normally consists of instruction by one's colleagues into the selection and captioning of images in such a way as to catch the eye of the reader or viewer. (For a formalised presentation of current attitudes underlying photo-journalism see Evans (1978). On the specific mode of photo-journalism employed in *Picture Post* see Hopkinson (1970).) This background may have contributed to the strongly journalistic handling of visual imagery apparent not only in Kee's television series but also in his book.
7 Mike Catto's original degree was in History of Fine Art and Modern History, but his subsequent career has been in the artworld occupations of arts-administration, art and film criticism and teaching history of art to students in the Art and Design Centre of the University of Ulster in Belfast.
8 Few discussions of art under the Nazis are prepared to admit such observable historical facts as the way in which Nazi culture fed on Expressionism, the extent to which totalitarian styles in architecture pervaded virtually the whole of the western world in the inter-war period, and the improvements in German industrial design promoted by the Nazi regime. Similarly in Ireland there have been virtually no studies of the distinctive visual culture of the country's Protestant community.
9 See for example the fairly typical assertion by Jack Lindsay (1960) that Jacques Louis David adopted the compositional ploy of placing all his figures in the same line, to express the new values of equality and democracy.
10 This does not mean that I believe debates on the value of different kinds of visual imagery are meaningless. Indeed I see them as exceedingly important. But it is my conviction that discussions of what visual images actually do are too

Belinda Loftus

often side-tracked by consideration of what they should do. On this point see
Wolff, 1981: 141. Having said this it is also important to stress that no analysis
can ever be completely free from connotations of value.

Bibliography

Abrams, P. (1982), *Historical Sociology*, Shepton Mallet, Somerset, Open Books.
Barrett, Cyril (1975), 'Irish Nationalism and Art 1800–1921', *Studies* (Dublin), 64, 256: 393–409.
Baxandall, M. (1972), *Painting and Experience in Fifteenth Century Italy*, Oxford, Oxford University Press.
Beames, M. (1983), *Peasants and power: The Whiteboy movements and their control in pre-Famine Ireland*, Brighton, Harvester Press.
Benjamin, W. (1970), 'The Work of Art in the Age of Mechanical Reproduction', *Illuminations*, London, Jonathan Cape.
Berger, J. (1972), *Ways of Seeing*, London, BBC/Penguin.
Bernstein, B. (1971), 'A socio-linguistic approach to social learning', *Class, Codes and Control*, volume one, London, Routledge & Kegan Paul, pp. 121–32.
Bigsby, C. W. E. (1976), *Approaches to Popular Culture*, London, Edward Arnold.
Bourdieu, P. (1977), *Outline of a Theory of Practice*, Oxford, Oxford University Press.
Burke, P. (1978), *Popular Culture in Early Modern Europe*, London, Temple Smith.
Camerawork, (1979), no. 14, 'Reporting Northern Ireland'.
Catto, M. (1977), *Art in Ulster: 2*, Belfast, Blackstaff Press.
Clark, T. J. (1973), *Image of the People: Gustave Courbet and the 1848 Revolution*, London, Thames & Hudson.
Clark, T. J. (1974), 'The Conditions of artistic creation', London, *Times Literary Supplement*, 24 May, pp. 561–2.
Cormack, R. (1984), Review of Richard Jenkins's, 'Lads, Citizens and Ordinary Kids: Working-Class Life-styles in Belfast', *Sociology*, 18, 1: 118–20.
Douglas, M. (1970), *Natural Symbols*, London, Barrie & Rockliff.
Downing, Taylor, (1980), *The Troubles*, London, Thames/Macdonald Futura.
Elias, N. (1983), *The Court Society*, Oxford, Blackwell.
Evans, E. E. (1957), *Irish Folk Ways*, London, Routledge & Kegan Paul.
Gombrich, E. (1962), *Art and Illusion*, London, Phaidon.
Gombrich, E. (1969), *In Search of Cultural History*, Oxford, University Press.
Hall, S. (1972), 'The Social Eye of Picture Post', *Working Papers in Cultural Studies* (Birmingham), 2: 71–120.
Honour, H. (1968), *Neo-Classicism*, London, Penguin.
Hopkinson, T. (1970), *Picture Post 1938–50*, London, Penguin.
Irish News, 2 March 1950, Belfast.
Ivins, W. M. (1969), *Prints and visual communication*, Massachusetts and London, MIT Press.
Joll, J. (1960), *Intellectuals in Politics*, London, Weidenfeld & Nicolson.
Kee, R. (1980), *Ireland a History*, London, Weidenfeld & Nicolson.
Leith, J. A. (1965), *The Idea of Art as Propaganda in France 1775–1799*, Toronto, University of Toronto Press.
Lindsay, J. (1960), *Death of the Hero: French Painting from David to Delacroix*, Studio Vista.
Loftus, B. (1983), *Images in Conflict*, Keele, Keele University Ph.D. thesis.
Loftus, B. (1986), 'Matters of Life and Death, Protestant and Catholic ways of seeing death in Northern Ireland', *CIRCA* (Belfast), 26: 14–18.

Macherey, P. (1978), *A Theory of Literary Production*, London, Routledge & Kegan Paul.

McLuhan, M. (1967), *The Mechanical Bride: Folklore of Industrial Man*, London, Routledge & Kegan Paul.

Miller, L. (1966), *Patrons & Patriotism: the encouragement of the fine arts in the United States, 1790–1860*, Chicago, University of Chicago Press.

Mueller, C. (1973), *The Politics of Communication*, New York, Oxford University Press.

Neuburg, V. E. (1977), *Popular Literature, A History and Guide*, London, Penguin.

Panofsky, E. (1957), *Gothic Architecture and Scholasticism*, London, Thames and Hudson.

Public Record Office of Northern Ireland (1976), *Robert Emmet: the insurrection of July*, Belfast, HMSO.

Rosenblum, B. (1978a), 'Style as Social Process', *American Sociological Review*, 43: 422–238.

Rosenblum, B. (1978b), *Photographers at Work, a Sociology of Photographic Styles*, New York, Holmes and Meier.

Rye, J. (1972), *Futurism*, London, Studio Vista.

Saxl, Fritz (1970), *A Heritage of Images*, London, Penguin.

Schools Council (1977), *The Irish Question*, Edinburgh, Holmes McDougall.

Sheehy, J. (1980), *The Rediscovery of Irish Art*, London, Thames & Hudson.

Swingewood, A. (1977), *The Myth of Mass Culture*, London, Macmillan, pp. 1–10.

Tagg, J. (1975), 'The Method of Max Raphael, Putting Art History on its Feet', *Radical Philosophy*, 12: 3–10.

Thompson, E. P. (1972), 'Anthropology and the Discipline of Historical Context', *Midland History*, 1, 3, (University of Birmingham).

Turner, V. (1967), *The Forest of Symbols*, New York, Cornell University Press.

Webster, F. (1977), 'Every Picture tells a lie', *Camerawork* 5: 4.

Willett, J. (1967), *Art in a City*, London, Methuen.

Willett, J. (1970), *Expressionism*, London, Weidenfeld & Nicolson.

Wolff, J. (1981), *The Social Production of Art*, London, Macmillan.

ON THE SOCIAL PRODUCTION OF VISUAL DIFFERENCE

The myth and the machine: seeing science through museum eyes

Robert Bud

Abstract

A curator explores the process of construction of a major new Chemical Industry Gallery at London's Science Museum. The Museum is found to have acted as a broker bringing together diverse interests no one of which had an overwhelming significance. The paper follows the negotiations involved in selecting objects, text and physical environment and the translation of goals during the process. An exhibit is seen as a combination of mythic form and machine, and the paper concludes that the qualities of the machine exert an ever greater demand at the expense of the myth, during the course of construction.

Introduction

When the modern genre of museum was still young, the Deutsches Museum in Munich was vividly described by a distinguished American tourist, Dean Randall of Columbia, as 'the garrison shrine of the new religion . . . a great temple erected to the gods of the new age, Science and the Machine' (Randall, 1929: 4–5). Perhaps today such a description appears overblown. Yet there is still widespread faith that the world's great science museums express profound truths about science and technology.[1] Descriptive phrases such as 'balance' and 'accuracy' indicate the parallel with the expected objectivity of science itself. It is therefore surprising that while sociologists have shown how science and technology are constructed, the same honour has not been done to the science museum.[2] The nature of the interaction between the participants and the ways in which their negotiations affect the outcome have not been documented. Here I shall explore these processes,

134

describing the experience of constructing a new Science Museum gallery dealing with the chemical industry which opened in December 1986.

Myth and machine

In describing another medium, television, Roger Silverstone has applied the description 'mythic phenomenon'. Through it 'we of the profane world have access to something which in its unmediated state and by its very distance is sacred' (Silverstone, 1981: 84). By analogy, we can recognise the mythic role of the museum in providing a specially authentic, intense, or direct contact with the 'sacred' subject, be it historical event or current development, in a sphere with the power, danger and distance of science. Just as Silverstone argues in the case of television, the museum acts to reduce fear and provide 'understanding' of the special phenomenon. Indeed the museum as a religious centre is an established metaphor. A recent official paper approvingly reports that 'the regimental museum has properly something of the nature of a shrine' (Museums and Galleries Commision, 1986: 51). The mythic function is played through the arrangement of the curators' 'holy relics'. As Walter Benjamin pointed out unique historical objects have an 'aura' (Benjamin, 1973: 223). They are enmeshed in stories or in a web of associations articulated on labels. These may indicate the sacred reference of the object by their form, as in the case of incomprehensible technicalities, or by their content, such as through reference to the 'industrial revolution'.[3] Randall's metaphor of the temple still expresses a crucial dimension of the museum.

There is another dimension: museums also resemble machines with clearly defined instrumental functions performed by an engineered system. Many exhibits take as their objectives the familiarisation of visitors with certain key facts. Even where such objectives are not codified, museums are expected to provide 'accurate' information and many children are brought in the hope that the museum as a whole will act as a friendly teaching device. The engineering of exhibits themselves is increasingly sophisticated and complex. Whatever its intentions, an exhibit must meet certain technical criteria of effectiveness. We expect it to be mechanically and electrically safe and to be designed to resist misuse, assuring the safety of objects and visitors. The process of its manufacture is, to a large degree, handled by the construction

135

industry. Characteristically, exhibits have to be designed and manufactured to a tight and inflexible time table just like many new machines.

The individual exhibit, and, indeed,the individual object combine these qualities of myth and machine.[4] There are of course tensions between the characteristics emphasised by each: the myth form requires the evocative, the authentic, the affective and the synthetic qualities of a museum while the machine tends to individual, specifiable criteria of efficiency. Analyses particularly of science museums have focused solely on the quality of performance as machines purveying knowledge. Nevertheless the great museums have managed to combine the qualities of myth and machine.

The Science Museum

London's Science Museum is one of the largest of its type, and its roots stretch back to the early days of the genre. The intentions to teach and to venerate science and technology were explicit in the arguments of its Victorian founders and were developed in the 1920s when the present building was opened.[5] Since the Second World War techniques and design methods have changed more than fundamental principles. The combination of display, instruction, history and prophecy is still generic to the Science Museum, with, by now, about three million visitors per year. Audio-visual technology and the emergence of the science centre have each increased general interest in the instructive uses of the museum. The radical industrial restructuring in Britain during the early 1980s emphasised to curators the needs and opportunities of historical record. Institutional sponsors encouraged the museum to communicate 'understanding' of technological trends to the public. Within the culture of the museum, as specialised designers and engineers have moved into the display function, the custody of collections of significant objects has provided the curator with professional identity. His or her special expertise is focused upon the recognition, acquisition and exploitation of the 'real object', the artefact which itself has historic or prophetic significance (Finn, 1965). The exhibits have continued use of such objects as the main means of fulfilling their mythic function.

The qualities of myth and machine have imposed one important requirement in common: the visitor has to be able to unquestionably assume the accuracy and rectitude of exhibits. Not only does the Science Museum have a 'sacred' subject, it is also the 'National' Museum of Science and Industry, and, as such, it is an altar of state religion. It is largely paid for by the tax payer, radical and conservative, conservationist and progressivist. With respect to each, unimpeachable truth is expected. At the same time, the museum is expected to work as an educational and entertainment machine. Because of its 'educational' role, the national responsibilities of the museum and the number of children who visit, it must not offend. And the buttons should actually operate.

A gallery devoted to a particular topic is the basic unit of the Science Museum. Although the institution as a whole displays styles developed over almost half a century, most galleries are largely constructed at one time. They represent the result of intense cooperative endeavours. No case study is 'typical', but the processes that led to the creation of the Chemical Industry Gallery are characteristic of the kind that lead to successful exhibits. The exhibit has seemed truthful, winning an accepting review by the environmentalist chemicals editor of the left-of-centre *Guardian* (Erlichman, 1986) as well as a benevolent smile from the central organ of the American chemical industry, *Chemical and Engineering News* (Layman, 1987).[6]

The gallery is built in an evocative, though not 'realistic', structure of steel girders (Figure 1). Within this are about one hundred historic and modern objects from the industry. Some are shown behind glass, many are shown in association with monochrome manikins in working positions. The labels are of two kinds. Large panels describe overall themes. They are illustrated with colourful cartoons. Small acrylic labels by individual objects describe their detailed nature. There are three interactive computers describing respectively the process by which a chemical plant may be made safer, the needs of a bacterium and the inhibition of an enzyme to prevent hypertension. Six videos showing historical films continuously, broadcast from cases or from overhead. Used in close proximity, these media are designed to complement one another in the treatment of individual topics, providing a variety of effects and stimuli.

Translation

Following the metaphor of the gallery as machine, descriptive techniques developed in the analysis of technology can be appropriated. The sociology of translation is particularly adapted

Figure 1 *The Chemical Industry Gallery*
Copyright, Trustees of the Science Museum

to the sociotechnical world of the curator (Latour, 1987). Its principles have been expressed by Michel Callon (1986) in his study of the development of scallop growing technology. He distinguishes the processes of 'problematisation', in which central actors define the problem in such a way that they are central; 'interressement' in which other spokesmen are caught; 'enrolment', in which their roles are defined; and 'mobilisation of allies' in which the effectiveness of the negotiations is tested against the constant threat of betrayal. Wherein could lie the analogy in creating a museum gallery? Continuously, one is involved in a process of selection of the best, the exemplary, the typical – the spokesmen. By analogy with Callon's account, among the participants one could count artefacts and traditions as well as human actors. Selection of spokesmen and the establishment of their interrelationships is an entirely conscious act. Having caught the actor, the process of enrolment and the location, both physical and social is again quite conscious. The gallery team member is constantly conscious of the need to mobilise allies and of the threat of betrayal. To build the gallery a series of working assumptions about the distribution of resources – space, money and time have to be shared by the whole team, to allow it to work, but they often prove incompatible with the pristine requirements of the mythic form. The participants are therefore often aware of a process of translation in which goals, and indeed objects, are displaced as a result of negotiation.

The prehistory: problematisation

The turning point in the history of the gallery was a meeting in April 1985 between two senior officers of the public affairs department of ICI, Britain's dominant chemical company, and the Science Museum Director together with myself as curator of Industrial Chemistry and the head of Museum Services who was responsible for design and technical support in the museum. Two weeks earlier, an initial discussion had raised the possibility of a Science Museum gallery answering two needs of the company: to contribute to Industry Year in 1986 and to celebrate its own sixtieth anniversary in December of that year. Originally the idea of a mobile temporary exhibit had been suggested, to which the museum had answered with the suggestion that ICI sponsor a permanent gallery in South Kensington. At the second meeting a proposal for such a gallery was to put to ICI and received with

139

evident interest. It outlined the conceptual approach a gallery would take, the objects, and the style. Through its familiarity to senior ICI management in general (many had visited exhibitions throughout their lives and the chairman was a trustee of the museum), and through this meeting in particular, the museum was accepted as the most appropriate presenter of science; and the proposal was taken as the legitimate expression of the museum's capabilities.

The document put to ICI presented the proposed exhibit in terms of groups of objects. These are the substance of any museum gallery, just as pictures are central to television and sounds to radio. The proposal had been specially drafted for the occasion, to ensure that it would fit on one side of a sheet of A4 and that it would convey our clear sense of direction and commitment to portraying the excitement of the chemical industry. Behind this was a developed conceptualisation of such a gallery based on several years of discussion. It was both a reaction against certain features of the existing gallery and an expression of evolving institutional style.

The Chemical Industry Gallery

The museum-wide tensions between historical traditions are clearly apparent in the Industrial Chemistry section which was to be the basis of the new exhibition. Artefacts, used as tools in industry have to be translated into museum objects, keeping their original physical properties. On account of size and weight most artefacts from the chemical industry are quite inappropriate for museum display. Nevertheless, particularly since the early 1970s, the museum has acquired a large number of 'important' objects compatible with the physical potential of the museum and with considerable mythic power – such as the 1938 apparatus with which the first ton of polythene had been made (Figure 2). The collection's earliest object is a model Leblanc soda plant made and donated in the 1890s. The conception of the subject was broad, as suggested by its title, covering petroleum and plastics as well as cosmetics and food canning.

In the 1970s the collection had been twice reexhibited as the Industrial Chemistry Gallery. In 1980 the display was to be found divided between a systematic portrait of the principles of chemical engineering and a variety of applications of chemistry. It was

Figure 2 The actual reactor in which the first ton of polythene was made

dominated by the full size replica section of an oil refinery column housing a large engineering model of a refinery. The evocative tower, the exhibits with both historic and current industrial significance and the long instructional labels made this an almost archetypical section. Strikingly missing, however, was the intensive use of handle-driven exhibits so familiar elsewhere in the museum. This reflected the considerable problems that any display of chemical principles entails both for the visitors trying to comprehend complex systems and for the maintenance staff trying to keep them running. It reflected too the shortage of resources that had bedevilled both exhibits.

I had joined the museum shortly after the second redisplay as curator of Industrial Chemistry. By 1985 I had come to identify anomalies in the character of the existing gallery and its predecessors, and the proposal put to ICI was intended to remedy these. It was based on experience of the sort of objects that might be available and the visions developed over my own seven year tenure as a curator. In that time separate galleries on plastics and petroleum had been built so that these complex industries could be explored in their own terms (Bud, 1987). Ways of applying new technologies which were at the time becoming more widely used throughout the museum had been developed in those galleries. No longer was the label the only means of communication – videos helped to weaken (though not entirely to resolve) the conflict between the wish to present information to the dedicated and the danger of intimidating the less curious. Working exhibits in the chemical area had, in some instances, proved practical. A style was evolving, that could be contrasted with perceived characteristics of traditional approaches, though it was the continuation of a shift that had already been occurring for more than a decade.[7] Verbal would be replaced by the pictorial, standard glass case presentation by the evocative context, the purely technical by an integration with the contextual, the conceptual by the visual, the comprehensive by the evocative. The emphasis was to be on the application of science seen as process rather than on the details of its content.

The conceptual structure had already been the outcome of extended debate. In 1981, responding to an approach by the Institution of Chemical Engineers, the museum had established an advisory committee on chemical engineering and industrial chemistry. This was chaired by Sir Frederick Warner, a leading chemical engineer, and included eminent historians of chemistry and the chemical industry as well as representatives of the major professional bodies.[8]

The committee suggested contacts, subjects for enquiry and new acquisitions but its twice yearly meetings demanded a more substantial focus. In November 1982 the committee decided to press for a gallery to open in 1987. Without knowing how support could be raised, a proposal was drafted and revised through several meetings. To transcend tensions between the chemical and the chemical engineering traditions and to narrow the topic from the diversity of industrial applications of chemistry, the 'chemical industry' was taken as the focus.

The industry has an established historiography (to which several members of the committee had made substantial contributions) that emphasises the history of the British soda industry, the competing German model of a dye industry, the development of synthetic ammonia before the First World War in Germany, and petrochemicals in America during the interwar years (Haber, 1958, 1971). There the classic histories stop and memories begin. The industry was also going through a much publicised transformation with an apparent decline in the petrochemical industry and the growth of biotechnology and pharmaceutical manufacture. From this background emerged the structure of five subject-based parts each exemplifying a certain style of the industry: chemicals from salt, synthetic ammonia, petrochemicals, biotechnology, and fine chemicals. Within the committee there were alternative views: crucial chemicals such as sulphuric acid, phenol, or solvents could be followed through several generations of manufacture. However, in the end, the industry-centred structure of the project militated against such a chemical focus. The proposal was given a realistic flavour by assuming a few practical constraints. To help us imagine the exhibit, and to prevent conflict within the museum, the location was defined to be that of the existing gallery. The objects were clearly going to be fewer in number than in previous years but possibly individually larger, so the number of sections had to be small. By late 1984 the proposal was progressing. Objectives had been articulated. Through the new gallery the visitor would have a unique opportunity to encounter the chemical industry and its impact on the individual's environment. The gallery would stimulate interest in the industry and its history, and enhance understanding of – the relation between science and technology, the changing nature of work, the relation between the industry and the environment and the nature and development of biotechnology.

These objectives reflected the wish of professionals for their world to be better understood and the museum's ability to portray the social relations of science and technology. The concept of work, for instance, would enable the portrait of the direct social context of machines, without resorting to vague and physically distinct concepts of background. Hence even before the presentation to ICI, perspectives had been determined by the museum environment as represented by the curator, interacting with the views of advisers.

The proposal put to the company was a simplification of the committee's product, emphasising glamorous presentation and exciting working demonstrations. It retained the modular structure of the laboriously negotiated longer argument and complemented it with an emphasis on large objects. The historical structure roughly matched the company's own development, since of course the history of the chemical industry in Britain has been seen in terms of ICI's development even by scholars. The company representatives were keen about the excitement that a new gallery could bring to the image of the industry. From personal experience they had a sense of the nature of a Science Museum exhibition. They seemed to value and respect its sense of authenticity and truthfulness. It was accepted without demur then and throughout the project, that the exhibit would not work if there was any hint that their sponsorship was a form of advertising.

Building the team: interressement

The company did seek a voice on the team, and Mr Ken Gee, a senior engineer who had taken early retirement was recommended. Ken was to be the principal contact with the commercial leaders and with the scientists. His function was to be the spokesman of the industry: he expressed the values and the perspective of chemical engineers, and provided valuable links that would help us mobilise other engineers. He also brought the technical skills in designing chemical plants which were not dissimilar from those required in designing the gallery itself. It was he who actually drafted the critical path analyses and the consequent time tables. In parallel, suitable designers were found by the Head of Exhibition at the museum. Ronald Green, a designer with exhibition experience and a partner in a leading firm of architects, the Casson Conder Partnership, was appointed design coordinator and proposed an association with a firm of experienced museum designers, Brennan and Whalley. This team was asked to produce initially an impression of the gallery to help ICI confirm their interest. The brief identified four fixed factors: the opening date, December 1986; the style which was to be evocative; the location and consequent space of about 400 square metres, the cost was expressed as about £300,000, and the contents which were to be broadly as in the initial proposals. The resource most in short supply was time. An outline timetable drawn up by the designers showed that they would have to begin detailed work by early December. Since they would be controlling the contractors who would actually construct the gallery, the designers' timetable dictated that of the curators. The meaning of the word 'evocative' and the kind of exhibits were now to be established. Through Ken Gee contacts at central ICI plants were established and visited. Because of the demands of the original script and the historic emphases of the company, the plants chosen were the ammonia and petrochemical works at Billingham and Wilton and the chloroalkali plants at Runcorn. These 1960s-style continuous processes generating hundreds of thousands of tons of product per annum, served as 'typical' chemical plants. It was occasionally realised through the project, that the designers could have been shown rather different works such as those used in batch process dye manufacture, sterile drug manufacture or the marketing oriented paints division. It was only towards the end that the designers were taken to a plant for compounding and packing pharmaceuticals whose style provided an alternative image of the industry.

Approval for the project's sponsorship was granted by ICI in early September 1985. Through the visits to the Teesside and Merseyside, the scientists within the company were enthused and recruited to help with the design and construction of certain individual exhibits. Meanwhile at the museum, a team was assembled. As curator of Industrial Chemistry, I was responsible overall, and in particular, for the script and the choice of objects to be displayed. In addition, to assure us that the gallery would actually happen, an experienced curator, Sue Cackett was asked to administer the complex process. She ensured that the geographically dispersed alliance between museum, designers and ICI scientists would operate. Another curator, Sue Mossman, joined the team as a research assistant, initially to find and negotiate the films and photographs used liberally in the modern gallery. Now four processes would occur more or less independently: the scientists started to develop the exhibits that had been discussed, historic objects were assembled, the designers started creating sketches, and I wrote a script listing in detail the contents of the gallery. This was the developed brief, instructing the designer what he 'must' find room for. At the same time it was part of a complex relationship which had to be acceptable to those who had already become intellectually, contractually and emotionally involved. It had to be consistent with the brief already given to the designers, and a representation of the chemical industry that would be acceptable to the advisory committee, ICI and the sceptical public. The script was a crucial element in the process of 'interressement' of the objects, the designers, the scientists, and the working exhibits they could mobilise.

The discussion will now focus on 'enrolment' and the development of two striking characteristics of the gallery – the large objects, and the panels; and on 'betrayal', with the consequential disappearance of a feature – the differentiation between the heavy chemical industry and the cleaner, smaller scale biotechnology and fine chemical industries. Diverse as these issues may appear, they are experienced together in the gallery and the final form of each depended crucially on negotiations between the participants.

Enrolment: choosing the objects

The selection of historic objects is a crucial aspect of an exhibition design. The process provides an interesting justification of Callon's emphasis on the non-distinction between animate and inanimate actors. The key objects and the overall structure were in a sense the most powerful, least flexible participants in the debates though even they were not fixed and unchangeable. Detailed data of the nature and sizes of exhibits were not yet available, when the overall structure was fixed, so the designers translated the conceptual proposal into a sketch of five sections of equal sizes. This apparently reasonable decision was the basis of discussions with a contractor and the subsequent development of the gallery. Meanwhile the objects were being chosen. Since the attention of visitors is erratic, they would have to make sense in isolation. The mythic role of the museum is however also played by the continuing story that links the objects.[9] Although the sections were each conceived historically, their message was intended to transcend particular historical moments so that they would contribute to an understanding of the industry today. To ensure intellectual coherence, and following the original objectives, each section would have exhibits illustrating history, modern developments, scientific principles, work and interaction with the environment. Thus the ammonia section was conceived to illustrate high pressure synthesis using a catalyst. It would include historic items from the museum's collection: a vial of the first synthetic ammonia made in June 1909 and given to the museum by Haber's British assistant, and, to show the subsequent engineering problems of scale-up a massive plastic replica of one of the first commercial pressure vessels which the museum had recently acquired from BASF's Ludwigshafen works (Figure 3). Established modern technology would be represented by a large model of a modern ammonia plant. Glimpses of the future would be provided by a glass cell developed by the Agricultural and Food Research Council in which using a catalyst akin to an enzyme ammonia could be produced at room pressure. This could take ammonia synthesis beyond the high pressure technology conceived at the beginning of the century and is perennially in the semi-technical news. Inclusion would emphasise our freedom from ICI even in this most central of the company's concerns. The company's scientists were keen to represent the basic principles of high pressure and catalysis. Together with Teesside Polytechnic, the head of catalyst research at Billingham made an animated film of the catalytic process. High pressure seemed a candidate for a spectacular demonstration. At first a rapid release of high pressure was envisaged, but the bang would be too loud. Instead a rising and falling ramp, driven by compressed air was conceived by Peter Burden of ICI and discussed with his own young children. He then found the appropriate contractor, Subsea Services with appropriate experience in pressurised systems, to design and build the exhibit. Finally we struggled to express the scale of this industrial enterprise. The packing line was one of the last elements to be automated and was indeed a case study on Beynon's critical analysis of Chemco in the early 1970s (Nichols and Beynon, 1977: 13–14). The use of manual labour for the arduous process of unloading was still well remembered at Billingham. It seemed possible to develop a display that would combine the imagery of a moving conveyor belt carrying an endless supply of sacks in comparison with the labour of men who had to carry them. The shapes and dimensions of these desired artefacts would determine

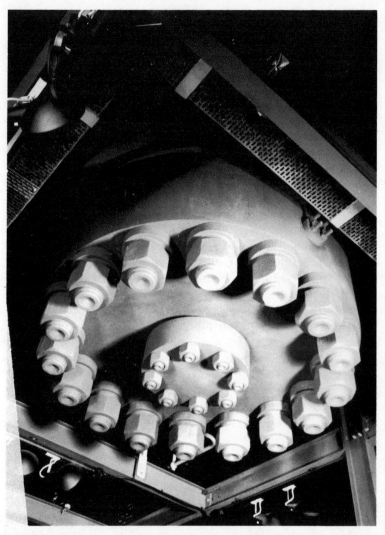

Figure 3 Replica of one of the first reactors used to make ammonia on a commercial scale
Copyright, Trustees of the Science Museum

the details of exhibit design. At the same time, only a small proportion of objects, already in the collection or collectable, could actually be used so there was always the possibility of withdrawing or negotiating an example. The instructive exhibits were drawn particularly from the imagination of ICI scientists with whom we talked. In several cases they developed their ideas talking to children and young people far removed from the museum.

A list of major objects together with their sizes was provided to the designers. They attempted to fit them to a modular structure that had been previously worked out. Generally this aspect of the project was accomplished without comment. However, in places, the translation of a list of objects into an arrangement within the space allocated became controversial. Either individual objects would have to be left out or the whole structure would have to be reformulated. But there was neither the time, nor the enthusiasm to restructure the vision. The need to preserve the fragile dynamic of the team that alone sustained the time-table took precedence over the preoccupation with individual problems.

Objects that had been originally specified in the script had to be omitted. The decision to exclude each carried with it the reconstruction of the story. There was not enough room for both a 3 metre long nineteenth-century model of a lead chamber sulphuric acid works and a similarly large model Leblanc soda plant. The Leblanc model was favoured because the Leblanc process has often been seen as the key development in the nineteenth-century heavy chemical industry. The successor technologies would also be powerfully illustrated in the gallery by real objects. A large valve weighing a ton and half and a trough encrusted with sodium bicarbonate had been saved from Wallerscote Solvay works which had closed in 1985 (Figure 4). To these we could contrast a modern electrolytic chlorine cell. Clearly the soda plant model 'had' to be included. The logic of the structure demanded therefore that the 1895 model of the lead chamber process be omitted. Sulphuric acid is a symbolic talisman of the traditional heavy chemical industry. Though there is a label about it next to the soda model and indeed a reference at the far end of the gallery, one would not be struck by its importance in a visit. Members of the advisory committee justifiably complained when the matter was raised before them. However the logic of the structure forebade it.

The conveyor belt display also had to be sacrificed. Six square

Figure 4 Valve from a soda works in an evocative context
Copyright, Trustees of the Science Museum

metres were allocated to it, several per cent of the whole gallery. However as we investigated conveyor belt technology this would not be enough, bearing in mind the need for room for the sacks to turn. We were, in Callon's terms, 'betrayed' by the reality of the conveyor belt. Another illustrative sequence that had to be abandoned included the historic objects associated with continuous fermentation. The development of continuous fermentation in the 1950s and 1960s was an elegant example of the application of chemical engineering principles to biological processing. One of the early continuous fermentation assemblies from the Centre for Applied Microbiological research at Porton Down had been acquired. So had Guinness's engineering model of their 1961 pilot continuous brewing plant. However the biotechnology section was overflowing. It had already been allowed to occupy a bay of the fine chemicals section thus breaking one convention of the design. Conceived to show the principles of biochemical engineering and particularly fermentation, it included an ICI sponsored demonstration of the process of cell growth (designed by the sixteen-year-old students at Cleveland ITEC), historic fermenters and apparatus associated with penicillin, and very modern exhibits associated with genetic engineering, plant cell culture and immobilised enzymes. Thus ingredients representing the essential categories were otherwise included. Continuous fermentation has not been a commercial success and, perhaps most telling, the objects were not attractive, translating poorly into museum exhibits. Continuous fermentation disappeared. The definition of the myth was modified by the requirements of the machine. Regrettable as this was at any moment, the process taken as a whole could not be lamented. Latour, in discussing the process of translation associated with technological innovation, has argued that the degree to which goals are translated is related to the number of participants (Latour, 1987: 117). An analogous process was at work here. The development of the project from the earliest vision could be defined in terms of the increasing specification of the machine, originally conceived only in the most broad brush terms. Even as myth the gallery would only work when encased in a successful machine.

Some objects could be included only in specified locations. A few are very heavy, weighing over a ton and the museum's building surveyor warned against a concentration of a group of these on any particular load bearing area. Thus the Leblanc model, the electrolytic cell and the heavy steam valve could not be in line. Nor could the wooden vat be placed too close to the entrance. The objects, the structural engineer, the designers and the museum negotiated and a final placement resulted. Towards the end of this process, there was little room for a fresh consideration of the visitors' interests in this over-determined situation.

Enrolment: choosing the labels

It is a truism of museum curatorship that visitors do not read the labels. Nevertheless, writing and designing labels with their texts and associated graphics are among the most time-consuming activities in the process of creating a gallery. The process of defining the contents takes an analogous path to the negotiated development of the physical structure. Since the unchallenged authority of written texts would need to be able to survive criticism from diverse angles, many outside interests were brought into alliance at an early stage. The designers with their primarily visual imagination, felt that pictorial motifs could make a decisive contribution to the comprehensibility and memorability of the main messages. At the same time, they had less interest in the detailed information about individual objects. Their concern was more to ensure that these did not obscure visitors' experience of the objects. From this dual perspective came the idea of the illustrated panel for main messages, with unobtrusive transparent labels for the detailed information about individual objects.

Generating a text that would be 'universally' acceptable was the first concern. Though the first draft was lengthy and not evocative, it did succeed in stimulating the designers to their radical concept of a typical illustration: a cartoon of a futurist giant tearing apart sodium and chlorine (Figure 5). A presentation was made to the new Director, Dr Neil Cossons, a few weeks after he had joined the Museum in March 1986. He agreed to the principle of interpreting the messages in this way, but insisted on a separate spokesperson for the ordinary visitor within the team. Sally Rousham, his nominee, was a complete layperson in terms of chemistry, though well-versed in social history. The Director also added another constraint: labels should be about thirty-five words long. Since the drafts had been of the order of a hundred words, radical rewriting would be necessary. Texts were edited; scientific jargon removed without sacrificing accuracy, and visual images multiplied. Nevertheless, when the drafts of the major panel labels

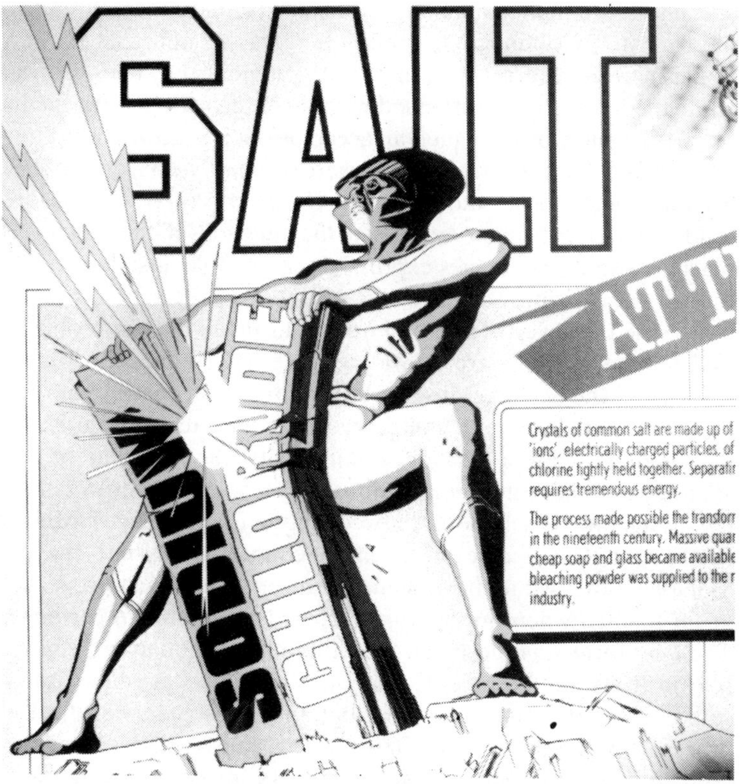
SALT
AT T
Crystals of common salt are made up of
'ions', electrically charged particles, of
chlorine tightly held together. Separatir
requires tremendous energy.
The process made possible the transforr
in the nineteenth century. Massive quar
cheap soap and glass became available
bleaching powder was supplied to the r
industry.

Figure 5 Myth expressed as cartoon
Copyright, Trustees of the Science Museum

were presented to the advisory committee they appeared to several members to be bland, without sufficient element of chemistry. In other words, there was dispute over the appropriateness of the ideal visitor and of the validity of the spokesperson. Social history for the scientifically illiterate seemed to be taking too much precedence over chemistry for the student. The labels were also sent to senior curators, to historians and to ICI specialists for their comments to ensure factual accuracy and to alert us of any offended sensibilities. It was striking that the few criticisms reflected professional, not commercial, values. Meanwhile the images were discussed with the designer. The two media of cartoon and words seemed an acceptable way of communicating with two audiences: those who were primarily concerned with accuracy and those most in search of a visual key. More fundamentally, the text expressed the function of the gallery as machine, while the images expressed the mythological dimension, though the division was never total.

The use of powerful pictorial images incurred its own problems as latent messages were considered. The ICI education officer (male) and the Science Museum education officer (male) both felt that the initial violent image would repel teenage girls. A professional science teacher familiar with the problem of the alienation of this community from science, was brought to talk to the designers. Discussions between myself, a designer, Martin Roche, and Ken Gee began to generate more appropriate images. Metaphors that would have seemed extreme and too controversial or far-fetched when put in words seemed acceptable in cartoons. The final form was the result of yet another negotiation between Martin Roche and an artist. Technically at any stage the curator could reject the entire picture, but time was pressing. As the process dragged on its function was being transformed. Of course, ultimately it would serve museum visitors for perhaps a decade. More immediately, however, the gallery with all its panels would be needed as the subject of the opening in December 1986. Meeting that deadline was becoming an ever more pressing concern, and it was undeniably intimately connected with the editorial process. The location of the large final panels, each about 1.4 by 0.7 metres, became an issue. This was conceived after the objects were arranged and the number of surfaces to which such large pieces of timber could be fixed without obscuring the view of objects was limited. Thus the story line, as portrayed by the sequence of panels became a corollary of decisions made for practical reasons. The elegant one-dimensional array expressed in the original proposal had been translated into a much more complex three-dimensional array of panels incorporating the two media of text and cartoons.

Mobilisation

For structure, services, objects and labels to be designed in parallel the project had to be the property of an unbounded network. It included staff at the two design companies, technical services at the Science Museum, various offices of the Property Services Agency of the Department of the Environment, scientists and engineers at ten ICI centres, at the Universities of Sheffield, Glasgow and Sussex and Teesside Polytechnic and Cleveland ITEC, at Brown Boveri Kent, BASF, BP Chemicals and elsewhere, suppliers of video material and photographs, specialist builders of exhibits, construction contractors and several levels of subcontractors. Following Callon, one could even include a great range of objects and demonstrations themselves within the network. Each participant had his or her own vision of the final product, which were, we hoped, the same. The extent to which this was in fact not true was seen as we worked, and argued when the vision of another seemed to inhibit the working out of personal plans. As we have seen there were many occasions in which the implications of each others' decisions were not immediately clear, for they were, of course, defined to be complementary. At the centre were five people who may be compared to Callon's spokesmen, two of the curators, two designers and Ken Gee. It was their job to anticipate the problems that could be encountered by members of the far-flung network and to bring others in, when crises beckoned.

Coping with betrayal

It was my own responsibility to assure the others that the gallery we were producing was actually a just rendition of the chemical industry. The reality of the kind of criticism that might be envisaged was proven by the press launch. In February 1986 journalists and ICI participators were invited to a buffet at the Science Museum. There Sir John Harvey-Jones, Chairman of ICI and Dame Margaret Weston, Director of the Science Museum announced the formal launch of the project. Sketches of the

155

Robert Bud

gallery and a model of the gallery were presented and a few objects held up. The magazine *New Scientist* reported in its gossip 'Feed-Back' column that some people were anxious about the treatment of environmental issues (*New Scientist*, 1986). Here was a most vivid example of what Callon has termed 'betrayal'. The alliance could counter such criticism by internal debate, persuasion of critics and by the use of appropriate exhibits (Bud, 1986a).

The alliance had to cope too with physical and commercial threats which undermined our assumptions. Throughout its construction a gallery is haunted by the problems of building a unique product, with objects not intended for a museum. Unlike the words on a page or pictures on a screen, apparently inoffensive objects can be intolerably dangerous to the visiting public and impose their own constraints. A large valve weighing a ton and a half was installed before it was surmised that the white crystals which had been assumed to be soda might be asbestos. The guess turned out to be right, and under the terms of the Health and Safety at Work Act, the Safety Officer cleared all workers off the site. In the event the asbestos was removed, and approved by the Factory Inspector, without fatally affecting the timetable.

A combination of problems within the alliance did cause a major shift in the gallery. Early conversations about the gallery had led to an emphasis on the distinction between the old heavy chemicals and the section on fine chemicals and biotechnology. This would be represented, it was thought, by a change in the environment. The floor level would change and the floor surface too. However the use of split levels took us far beyond the provisional budget allocation made to allow an early nomination of a contractor and parallel progress on a number of fronts. A distinctive plastic covering on the floor of the biotechnology and fine chemical sections did not work and it was decided to use a white painted surface there. The weekend, ten days before the opening, was allocated for curing. The day for painting came, but not the painters. It transpired that the men put on the job had resigned that day. But the work could not be delayed as wet paint would prevent access throughout the crucial week before the opening. At that time it was more important that exhibits would be checked and final cleaning completed. The painting was cancelled. In this simple decision lay the implication that the fundamental demarcation between biotechnology and petrochemicals would disappear. This had happened because of incompatibility between a succession of engineering observations and the goals which now included

156

meeting budget allocations for individual sections of the project, and the opening date. In the end the gallery opened on time and to budget. The resource limitations identified at the beginning had acted as persuasive 'facts'.

Conclusion

Here were no dead victims of cultural enrolment by anthropological curators (Stocking, 1985). Rather we see a variety of communities using the Science Museum as a means of communicating their own significance. The museum brought them together, acting as leader and as broker between sectional interests and the public. Through the processes of problematisation, interressement, enrolment and mobilisation the museum's own plans were translated into a completed gallery. Its conception began with an emphasis on the mythic functions. Increasingly during the project the needs of the machine became more distinct and more pressing. The resulting conflicts were negotiated through an unbounded network, linked as much by a faith in the value and power of such a gallery and conception of its desirable content as by money. Indeed one might conclude that the crucial role of the curator is to articulate and use the shared ideology of the museum exhibit.

Such mechanics constantly determine priorities and the resolution of decisions. Steven Brush once asked whether The History of Science should be X-rated (Brush, 1978). If a gallery really did stop developing at the point of its opening perhaps a similar question could be asked about its history. In fact, once the opening day has past, the new exhibits and the public become actors directly influencing the museum, and development begins anew.

Notes

I am grateful to Sue Cackett, Ken Gee, Ronald Green, Peter Mann, and Derek Robinson who commented upon drafts of this paper and to all the participants in the process of building the Chemical Industry Gallery who gave permission for this paper to be published.

1 The enduring belief in the duties of the medium are indicated by the attacks, during the early 1980s, on the emphases of two galleries in South Kensington, at the Natural History Museum (Halstead, 1984) and at the Science Museum (Levidow and Young, 1984).

2 It is striking that the classic works on museology, Bazin (1967) and Malraux (1953) have dealt principally with the domestication of art in the gallery rather than with the much more recent phenomenon of science museums. The critical analysis of the presentation of science has tended to be carried out in the context of the explicitly pedagogical science centre, see Screven (1984).

3 Munz (1977) shows how the concept of myth can be applied to the content of history, while Silverstone (1981) uses a complementary approach to analyse television. That lack of comprehension of the working of objects is no bar to appreciation of them is illustrated by a comment of Randall (1929: 7), 'We still peer in wonder and awe at the machines. We still gaze at the scientific instruments with dimly comprehending respect.'

4 The idea of the museum as a teaching machine is to be found in Fisher (1975), though with a slightly different connotation to that used here. The extent to which the role of the science exhibit could be divided was the subject of a debate between leading evaluators in the United States and Britain see Alt (1977) and Shettel (1978).

5 The history of the Science Museum has never been examined in depth. However the general direction of development is recounted by Follett (1978) which summarises the numerous commissions which investigated the question of a science museum during the late Victorian era as well as the detailed development of the Museum in the early twentieth century. London developments are put in context by Hudson (1987). The philosophies of the curators are still to be found only in their own writings. The underlying intent to use the museum as a means of bringing the visitor into intimate contact with Science, in terms strikingly analogous to Silverstone's, can be seen for instance in a piece written by one of the first heads of department in the present Museum, H. W. Dickinson (1926: 108):

> The idea [of development] is one that is easily grasped and he [the visitor] realizes that he is facing not the dead past but something living, something that is part of himself, something that touches his 'business and bosom'.

6 This is not to prove that the gallery was therefore 'successful', but it did fulfil the typical criteria of success used by the Museum which has relied on reviews such as these. For their shortcomings from the point of view of characterising the gallery as a machine, see Macmannus (1986). A survey of public interaction with the gallery has been commissioned in addition.

7 An 8 April 1970 proposal for a new exhibit on industrial chemistry explicitly proposed a greater emphasis on context rather than technical detail.

8 The members of the Commitee were Sir Frederick Warner (chairman), Mr Sydney Gregory, Professor Carl Hanson who passed away during the period in which the gallery was developed, Dr L. F. Haber, Dr David Pounder who replaced Professor Hanson, Professor Colin Russell, and Dr T. I. Williams.

9 The concepts of the myth in this gallery have been explored elsewhere (Bud, 1986b).

References

Alt, M. B. (1977), 'Evaluating Didactic Exhibits: A Critical Look at Shettel's Work', *Curator*, 20: 241–58.

Bazin, Germain (1967), *The Museum Age*, translated by Elisabeth Earle, Brussels, Desoer.

Benjamin, Walter (1973), 'The Work of Art in the Age of Mechanical Reproduction', pp. 219–54, in *Illuminations*, London, Fontana.

Brush, Steven (1974), 'Should the History of Science be Rated-X?' *Science*, 183: 1164–72.

Bud, R. F. (1986a), 'Ambitious Gallery', *New Scientist*, 13 March, 58.

Bud, R. F. (1986b), 'Artefacts, Stories and The Truth' presented at the joint meeting of the British Society for the History of Science and the Group for Scientific, Technical and Medical Collections, 29 November.

Bud, R. F. (1987), 'Innovation at the Science Museum: Three new galleries on Industrial Chemistry', *Chemistry and Industry*, 20 July: 479–82.

Callon, Michel (1986), 'Some Elements of a Sociology of Translation: Domestication of the Scallops and the Fishermen of St Brieuc Bay', pp. 196–233, in John Law (ed.) *Power, Action and Belief. A New Sociology of Knowledge?*, Sociological Review Monographs 32, London, Routledge and Kegan Paul.

Dickinson, H. W. (1926), 'The Science Museum, South Kensington, London', *Mechanical Engineering*, 48: 104–8.

Erlichman, James (1986), 'Museum's Chemical Exhibit Formula', *The Guardian*, 27 December.

Finn, Bernard S. (1965), 'The Science Museum Today', *Technology and Culture*, 6: 74–82.

Fisher, Phillip (1975), 'The Future's Past', *New Literary History*, Vol. 6: 587–606.

Follett, David (1978), *The Rise of the Science Museum under Sir Henry Lyons*, London, The Science Museum.

Gregory, S. A. and Bud, R. F. (1983), 'Collecting Process Engineering', *The Chemical Engineer*, April: 20–2.

Haber, L. F. (1958), *The Chemical Industry During the Nineteenth Century*, Oxford, Clarendon Press.

Haber, L. F. (1971), *The Chemical Industry 1900–1930*, Oxford, Clarendon Press.

Halstead, L. B. (1980), 'Museum of Errors', *Nature*, 288: 208.

Hudson, Kenneth (1987), *Museums of Influence*, Cambridge, Cambridge University Press.

Latour, Bruno (1987), *Science in Action. How to Follow Scientists and Engineers through Society*, Milton Keynes, Open University Press.

Layman, Pat (1987), 'London Science Museum Opens New Chemical Industry Exhibit', *Chemical and Engineering News*, 65 pt 21, 25 May: 24–5.

Levidow, Les and Young, Bob (1984), 'Exhibiting Nuclear Power: The Science Museum Cover-Up', pp. 52–79 in Radical Science Collective (ed.), *No Clear Reason: Nuclear Power Politics*, London, Free Association Books.

Macmannus, Paulette (1986), 'Reviewing the Reviewers: Towards a Critical Language for Didactic Science Exhibitions', *International Journal of Museum Management and Curatorship*, 5: 213–26.

Malraux, Andre (1954), *The Voices of Silence*, translated by Stuart Gilbert, London, Secker and Warburg.

Munz, Peter (1977), *The Shapes of Time. A New Look at the Philosophy of History*, Middletown, Wesleyan University Press.

Museums and Galleries Commission (1986), *Museums in Scotland*, London, HMSO.

New Scientist (1986), 'Feedback', 27 February: 58.

Nichols, Theo and Beynon, Huw (1972), *Living with Capitalism: Class Relations and the Modern Factory*, London, Routledge and Kegan Paul.

Randall, J. H. (1929), *Our Changing Civilisation: How Science and the Machine are Reconstructing Modern Life*, London, George Allen and Unwin.

Screven, C. G. (1984), 'Educational Evaluation and Research in Museums and Public Exhibits: A Bibliography', *Curator*, 27: 147–65.

Shettel, Harris (1978), 'A Critical Look at a Critical Look: A Response to Alt's Critique of Shettel's Work', *Curator*, 21: 329–45.

Silverstone, Roger (1981), *The Message of Television: Myth and Narrative in Contemporary Culture*, London, Heinemann.

Stocking, George (ed.) (1985), *Objects and Others. Essays on Museums and Material Culture*, History of Anthropology vol. 3, Madison, University of Wisconsin Press.

On the art of representation: notes on the politics of visualisation

John Law and John Whittaker

Abstract

This paper considers how technologies of representation are used by writers about acid rain research to re-present that research to non-scientists. The processes by which such technologies suppress what they purport to represent and replace it with novel and more docile elements which are often visual is described. Visual technologies for combining and further simplifying these elements are considered. Finally, the analogy between political and visual representation is drawn out, though the specificity of visual technologies is emphasised.

1 Introduction

There is an analysis of science which runs as follows. Scientific innovation is pragmatic, a matter-of-fact process in which bits and pieces are selected and fitted together in order to achieve an end. As in other practices, the bits and pieces are heterogeneous: chemical materials, instruments, organisms, the skills of technicians, a supply of oxygen, electronic equipment. The object is to juxtapose such objects into an array that generates a product that is somewhat less heterogeneous, somewhat simpler and somewhat more docile than what it grew from. Often this product takes the form of traces: figures, graphs or photographs replace unwieldy bodies or natural forces. They lie, on neat sheets of paper, ready to be summarised, simplified, juxtaposed, and generally rendered even more docile. They are shaped and fitted into a literary array – for the most visible end-product of much scientific work is the scientific article, the patent, or the report. At any rate, it takes the form of a document that will travel beyond the walls of the laboratory and, or so it is hoped, convince those who read it (Law, 1986).

Figures of one kind or another thus play a crucial role in the process of scientific production. They stand, in many cases, at the point where the heterogeneity of the laboratory or the field study gives way to the relative homogeneity and tractability of the two-dimensional sheet of paper. And they represent a convenient medium for economical juxtaposition and display of what might never otherwise have been put together at all. One picture, or so they say in journalism, is worth a thousand words. So it is in science. Many, perhaps most, scientific articles are built around figures, graphs and tables. Such visualisations offer a warrant for a more discursive commentary. They are, themselves, warranted by accounts of methods and citations to other literature. They are the hinge which connects the intractable world with the docility of the printed page. They are the literary lever which helps to move the readership, to persuade it that this does indeed go with that rather than the other. And they are the *representatives* of endless awkward objects and processes that are left behind in the laboratory.

Representations are not only to be found in the esoteric scientific literature. They are also common in writing *about* science. In this paper we consider some of the graphical technologies that are deployed in the latter literature. Our concern is both empirical and theoretical. Thus empirically we are interested in the strategies of representation that are to be found in writing about science. In particular, we are concerned with the range of such strategies and the way in which they generate different depictions of the world and the objects that inhabit it. In the central sections of the paper we thus consider the structure of a range of depictions that are drawn from writing about science. In addition, however, we are also concerned, more generally, with *technologies of representation*. These, we will suggest, are best understood as being constitutively political in character. That is, they represent practical solutions to the problem of representation, or how it is that one actor is able to speak on behalf of, and so silence, a range of others. If this is correct it follows that an investigation of practices of visualisation is also an investigation into topics that are more usually taken to be the subject of political philosophy. We return to this theme in the conclusion.

The methodology of literary analysis poses acute problems. Or, more exactly, the status of the findings of literary analysis poses acute problems. This is because there is uncertainty about the relationship between the findings of literary analysis on the one hand, and the processes that lead to the *generation* of that literature on the other. It is, of course, possible to analyse the rhetorical *effects* of this or that discourse without attending to the processes by which it was constructed. However, since the latter are normally in part directed by concern to achieve certain effects, it follows that to analyse documents *qua* documents, without considering the way in which they are produced (and, of course, actually received) is potentially rather constraining.

In the present paper we tackle this problem by describing the process which led to the production of a particular set of documents which were intended to depict, by primarily visual means, the conceptual and social organisation of scientific research into the acidification of the environment. This is a study that we have ourselves conducted.[1] Although there are drawbacks to such 'auto-ethnography', on this occasion we believe that it is warranted because it allows us, in its detail, to elaborate and exemplify a way of thinking about literary and in particular visual production that is generally applicable. Thus the object of this sketch is to illustrate the way in which contingent decisions taken during the production of visual depictions about science helped to determine the shape of those representations. The way in which such decisions removed the depictions from their origins in the scientific literature and translated them into quite other modes for quite different audiences is considered. In particular, we analyse the way in which complementary processes of suppression and creation led to the construction of both novel objects and of relations between those objects.

We then apply this approach to a different kind of writing about science – that of so-called popularisation. In this sphere we have chosen to look at visualisations selected from a single important and reputable semi-popular publication about the acidification of the environment. This is the Swedish Ministry of Agriculture presentation to the 1982 Stockholm Conference on the acidification of the environment: *Acidification Today and Tomorrow* (Swedish Ministry of Agriculture, 1982). We have no data on the processes that led to the production of this document, or to the many visualisations that it contains. However, by attending to the matched processes of suppression and creation that appear to have operated in the production of selected figures we are able to show the way in which a range of strategies underlie the rhetoric of representation in this report.

2 On simplification, discrimination and integration

Writing about the *practice* of science for non-scientific audiences is almost as old an art as writing about the *findings* of science for non-scientists. Recently, however, this writing has changed in character. Though there is still a stream of philosophical monographs on the character of scientific method and knowledge, this has been supplemented by a more pragmatic, policy-oriented, literature. Here the emphasis is on the distribution of scientific effort, the success or otherwise of this or that scientific collectivity, and the state of health of national scientific effort. Or, and this is what we will consider in what follows, it is concerned with the structure of scientific effort, the identification of important topics of research, and an analysis of the way in which they relate together. In short, it is concerned with mapping the dynamics of science.

There are many ways of generating topographies of scientific research. The one with which we are concerned is called co-word analysis. This rests upon a statistical and graphical treatment of the contents of the scientific literature. It is assumed (as we have suggested in the introduction) that documents form one of the major products of science and that such documents display a rhetorical structure in which concepts, problems and ideas are linked together. A persuasive document is one which convinces its readership that these links are, indeed, strong – one whose structure of concepts, problems and ideas is reproduced by other scientists in other documents. If this is correct then it follows that the received network of problems, ideas and concepts in an area of inquiry is reflected in the overall balance of the documents that are produced.

How, then, may the contents of a body of scientific literature be summarised in order to understand how concepts, problems and ideas relate together? Scientists themselves have tackled this question in several ways, for instance in the textbook and the review article. Policymakers have used peer review, and commissioned special studies, usually by high status insiders. However, co-word analysis approaches the problem by trying to poll *all* the literature in a given field of science. It attempts, that is, a 'democratic' method for identifying and assessing the relationship between the dominant concepts, problems and ideas. But how can the literature be polled? The answer is that just as an electoral system simplifies its participants by treating them as simple voters with a restricted range of options, so the co-word method simplifies the scientific literature by treating each document as a small set of keywords.

The first part of the process of producing co-word depictions is thus that of allocating keywords. This is a task on an industrial scale that is undertaken by the employees of large data-bases – for instance of the PASCAL CDST/CNRS data base in France. Every day periodicals flood into the CDST offices in eastern Paris and several hundred indexers enter details about them into a huge computer memory bank. In order to facilitate searches of the literature by user scientists the indexers not only enter the normal bibliographic details but they also read the articles and choose appropriate keywords as descriptors. They select these keywords from a detailed lexicon which is periodically updated. Most articles are allocated between ten and fifteen keywords – see Figure 1 for a typical example.

Leaving aside questions of the adequacy or otherwise of particular attempts at keywording (a matter that can only be solved pragmatically), the important point is that this is a drastic *simplification* of a subject that is otherwise intractably complex. Thus in the above example nine pages, and a series of sections ('Introduction', 'Experimental', 'Results', 'Discussion', 'Summary' as well as the usual references and synopses, and two tables, eight graphs or scatter diagrams, and three maps) are turned into eleven words or short phrases. But it is not only a matter of simplification because we are also witnessing what we will call *discrimination*. The original complex object disappears in the course of keyword-ing, to be replaced by eleven categories that are both discrete and separable. Overlap and literary confluence are replaced by discontinuity. The keywords are identifiable, easily discriminable, objects. They are also quite easily shunted around. Discrimination, then, is a process which generates discrete and coherent objects – objects that are more tractable and more easily disciplined than those that preceded them.

With the conversion of what was muddy and intractable into something that is clear and discrete a vitally important transform-ation took place. Co-word analysis became possible because *quantification was possible*. Thus it was possible to count the occurrences of keywords in a population of articles and so to measure their relative popularity. Or it was possible to count the number of articles indexed by any *pair* of keywords in order to see how often they went together. Co-word analysis followed the

F. J. Ferek, A. L. Lazrus and J. W. Winchester,
  'Elemental Composition of Aerosols Collected with Airborne
  Cascade Impactors'
Atmospheric Environment, 17 (1983): 1563–72.

Keywords:

Aerosol	Chemical composition	Cascade impactor
Measurement result	Measurement of ambient air	Sulphate
Aeroplane	X-Ray spectrometry	Air pollution
Chloride	Granulometry	

Figure 1 Article bibliographic details and key words chosen by PASCAL indexers (key words translated from French)

latter route, since the object was to see which problems, concepts and topics went with which others. The general point, however, is that by simplifying to the point where counting was possible, *a standard technology for juxtaposing, merging and summarising* could be deployed. Elaborate reviews of the scientific literature were no longer necessary. The nuances of argument did not have to be weighed against one another by means of extensive literary techniques for most had been bleached out. An obdurate stack of documents that were previously comparable only with extreme difficulty might now be arrayed on a single (if rather large) sheet of paper. They had been subjected to a process of *homogenisation* that had the effect of rendering them relatively docile.

But how should the results of this counting be presented? Though they could be exhibited in the form of a giant matrix this would be extremely difficult to assimilate. Since the object was to present an easily comprehensible depiction of the topography of an area of science to a non-scientific readership further simplification was necessary. Significant features should be highlighted while those that are thought to be unimportant were suppressed. In the case of co-word analysis suppression was done in a brutally statistical fashion. Those key-words that fell below a certain threshhold were disregarded. Low levels of co-occurrence were treated in the same way and similarly disenfranchised. The logic is similar if not identical to the rules of the West German electoral system in which a party has to achieve at least 5 per cent of the vote to obtain representation in the Bundestag.

But if small is ugly, then how should big be treated? How, indeed, should it be defined? Though the choice of different formulae for generating summary statistics created different definitions of size, the problem was not essentially statistical for there was a wealth of potential statistical tools with which to manipulate, organise and simplify the count. It concerned, rather, what should be treated as significant features of the matrix, a matter that could only be resolved with reference on the one hand to ideas about the character of science, and on the other to the concerns of those who might use the depictions that are ultimately generated. Here we cannot discuss either of these matters in detail. However, both theoretical and practical considerations suggested that the index should be capable of generating something analogous to a road map: that dense clusters of relations between keywords should (like towns) be easily identifiable, that the relations *between* those clusters should (like main roads) be detectable, and that the very largest and densest clusters should not so overshadow the others that the latter were rendered invisible.[2] The symbolic embodiment of these assumptions was a statistical formula, the index of equivalence, and a series of procedures for grouping keywords together into clusters as a function of this index. Here, then, we observe an example of a general process: the way in which the formation of discriminable objects facilitates their disappearance. By making them discrete and coherent they are rendered countable. The fact of making them countable allows them to be attached to the technology of merger represented by statistical analysis – a technology which leads to the suppression of individual cases and the formation of regularities which in turn become discriminable objects.

The various operations we have so far described (for instance the choice of index) strongly shaped, and were in turn strongly shaped by, anticipation of the production of a depiction that would be readily comprehensible to a reader. Accordingly, the last part of the process was concerned with translating figures into graphical representations. Thus it proved difficult, if not entirely impossible, to produce a visual representation that depicted the quantitative results of calculating the index of equivalence. It was, in other words, difficult to find a topographical convention in which those clusters that were closely related were physically close to one another in the figure. Accordingly, a decision was made to reduce the level of quantitative detail and detach this from the topography of any possible figure: strong, medium and weak links between clusters were to be roughly distinguished by thickness of connecting lines (as was the strength of relations within each cluster) but no figures were to be included, and neither were these to be represented by graphical means in a two-dimensional space.

Once the decision was made to suppress individual keywords and quantities it became necessary to find a technique for representing clusters and highlighting the way in which they related to one another. The convention adopted was simple: clusters should take the form of boxes, while their links should take the form of lines linking those boxes. It will be seen that these are, respectively, visual instances of the processes of discrimination and interrelation. Discrimination was further strengthened by a decision to label each cluster. Thus each of the boxes representing a cluster of keywords was given a name which was intended to point to its dominant question, topic, problem or concern. The object-ness of clusters was further strengthened in this way.

However, the effect of discriminating the clusters in this way raised a further problem – the fact that some represented a much larger body of work than others. In order to reflect this fact in an immediately assimilable manner, it was decided to vary the size of the boxes as a function of the number of documents contributing to each. In this way a further form of metric was introduced.

At this point it was necessary to devise a set of conventions in order to draw the depictions. These were created both in order to overcome graphical indeterminacy and to cope with a series of quite severe constraints. The indeterminacy arose because there were, as we have seen, no graphical constraints on the length of links between different boxes. Since the length of such links did not 'mean' anything any box could, in principle, be placed anywhere in the space covered by the figure. This, however, was only the case in principle because there were a range of constraints. First, there was the question of assimilability, the requirement that it should be possible to read the depictions with relative ease. This suggested, *inter alia*, that the number of overlaps between lines linking themes of research should be minimised. A second constraint posed severe problems. This was that it should be reasonably easy for the reader to compare different depictions of acidification-relevant research at different periods of time. This suggested that clusters from different time periods that were similar should appear in roughly the same place in their respective figures. A third constraint was that the depictions should, so far as possible, make some qualitative sense – that they should, as it were, 'tell a story'. Here there were various possibilities. In fact, however, the drafting was strongly influenced by a conventional casual-visual schema for depicting acidification-relevant processes that is widespread in the exoteric literature. In these depictions sources of emissions (factories, vehicles, etc.) are drawn on the left, emissions rise up the figure and move across to the right during which various chemical and meteorological phenomena are depicted. They then descend onto the biosphere where various effects on aquatic systems, soils or forests are visualised.[3] Thus, though there was no causal imputation in the case of the co-word visualisations (for research on vehicle exhausts does not cause research on atmospheric chemistry or on tree damage), the adoption of this convention made the figures somewhat easier to read than would otherwise have been the case.

Finally, the figures were placed in a textual context where they were labelled, some details of their provenance were offered, and a key was provided to the visual convention for line thickness and equivalence values on the one hand, and the relationship between box size and number of papers of the other. In addition, they were used as a point of departure for commentary in the accompanying text: the latter simultaneously used the figures as a warrant for discovering certain findings, and offered itself as a resource for simplifying and discriminating the objects in the figures still further.

Though parts of the process of transformation that led to the generation of these visualisations are not yet completely stabilised it is not the details of the process nor their practical warrant that are important here. The object, rather, is to illustrate a set of general processes. Thus we have tried to describe the way in which much was suppressed and lost. Rules of selection were elaborated and deployed in order to impose simplicity on material that would otherwise be intractably complex. This was necessary if what had previously been distributed across time and space was to be concentrated at one point and treated as a whole. In this process most of the original richness of the material was lost – a matter that is more or less problematic according to the standpoint of the critic.

However, the imposition of contingent simplicity was paralleled, as we have suggested, by a process of production. New objects were brought into being. Those objects – in the present example keywords, statistical calculations and clusters – which were relatively homogeneous and simple, replaced their more complex and distributed cousins. They were the tools that made it possible to gather many places and times into one location. They were the resources that helped to bring a 'centre of calculation' into being, a place which operated not upon disparate and intractable hetero-geneity but rather on homogenised and discriminable represen-tatives of the heterogeneous. Here docile, vaccinated, versions of the intractable were juxtaposed, manipulated, merged and interrelated.

3 Rhetorical technologies in popular visualisation

In the last section we considered the way in which a particular visualisation was generated, and outlined the way in which processes of simplification, discrimination and integration operated to generate a new universe of objects and sets of links between those objects. In this section we consider other ways in which simplification, discrimination and integration may be achieved. As

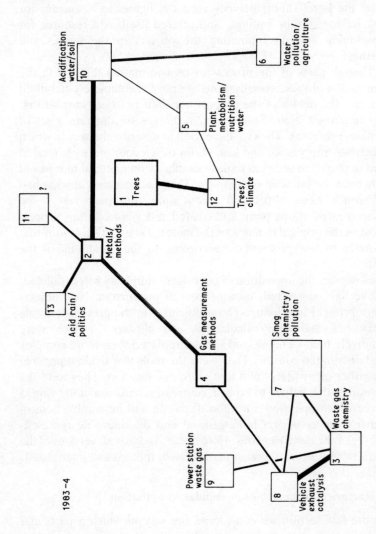

Figure 2 Depiction of research on acidification of the environment, 1983–4

1983–4

Acidification water/soil 10

Water pollution/agriculture 6

Plant metabolism/nutrition water 5

Trees 1

Trees/climate 12

11 ?

Metals/methods 2

Acid rain/politics 13

Gas measurement methods 4

Smog chemistry/pollution 7

Waste gas chemistry 3

Power station waste gas 9

Vehicle exhaust catalysis 8

we indicated in the introduction, our examples are drawn from *Acidification Today and Tomorrow*, a reputable, semi-popular publication produced by the Swedish Ministry of Agriculture, that was produced for the 1982 Stockholm Conference on the acidification of the environment. The aim of *Acidification Today and Tomorrow* is explicitly political: it is intended to persuade its readers that Scandinavia, and in particular Sweden, are large net importers of such pollutants as sulphur dioxide that are produced by the combustion of fossil fuels, and that this is causing widespread damage to the environment as a result of consequent acidification. Speaking abstractly, then, it brings a set of politico-scientific objects into being, and argues that they are related to one another in a particular way.

The figures that we discuss in this section form a very small part of a book length argument, and their rhetorical effect, like that of the co-word maps we have already discussed, cannot be understood unless this is taken into account. In addition, unlike the co-word maps, we are in this case only able to guess at the processes of production that led them to take their actual shape. Nevertheless, in each case the finished product reveals much about its organising principles and the rhetorical technologies of simplification, discrimination and interrelation that shaped it.

(a) Photography, spatial organisation and the creation of the sacred
In *Acidification Today and Tomorrow* the photographs are mostly in colour, and are mostly of breathtakingly beautiful countryside scenes: of ponds surrounded by trees; of meadows and lakes with flowers and grazing cattle; of upland rivers and waterfalls; of forest scenes; of growing wheat. And, interestingly, in most cases they are not related to the text except by proximity – and even then they never share a page with text or even with a caption. Instead, they seem to play a celebratory role: they are selected and bound into the book because they are 'about' what the book would like to happen if all went well, but otherwise they have nothing to do with the argument explicitly at all.

The precise argumentative role of these photographs is thus not, at first sight, very clear. They do not, as do the figures we will discuss below, play an explicit part in the argument of the book. They are just there. But, of course, they are not just there. The key to understanding their rhetorical organisation is to note that they stand in contrast to the text that surrounds them. They are untouched by all the talk of pollution. They are untouched by

171

Figure 3 Page 17, *Acidification Today and Tomorrow*
Swedish Ministry of Agriculture, 1982

pollution itself. *They represent the purity of the natural world.* Waterfalls, trees, mountains, blue skies, melting snows: in most cases the appeal is to the non human. Where the human intervenes it does so beneficially and harmoniously: small, red-painted barns and rowing boats, fields of ripening wheat. In the pictures there is a natural order, an order entirely apart from the human, or there is a natural order in which sensitive humans may harmoniously participate. The timelessness and rhythms of the seasons set their own pace. All is reversible. By contrast, the text is quite unlike this. It is filled with scientific detail which spells out the damage, possibly irreversible, that is being done to the environment as a result of human activities, and in particular the combustion of fossil fuel. The effect, then, is essentially Durkheimian: a distinction is being erected between the sacred and the profane. *Within* the photographs unchanging, transcendent values are being celebrated. And they are celebrated by setting them apart from the profanity of the text and its polluting human messages. And the message comes to us all the more clearly for being unspoken: the unarticulable mysteries of the sacred are in danger of pollution; the barriers are being broken down.

This effect is achieved by photographic and spatial means. First nature is simplified and it is re-presented as pure. This is not so easy, for those who actually venture into the wilderness know that it is full of biting flies, carcasses, dead trees and land-slips, and they also know that power lines, roads and quarries abound. The pictures have thus been carefully selected and framed, for the production of a sacred representation of nature requires a technology of purification.[4] Second, nature is spatially distinguished from the profane. It is, as we have noted, physically removed from the text. Occupying its own page, it becomes a bounded and unitary object which may then (third part of the process) be counterposed with the profanity of the text. The technology of deletion, discrimination and interrelation is thus graphic. The rhetoric rests upon a background of conventions about the world, the character of photographs, and the organisation of texts. And it is, of course, like all rhetorics, defeasible.

(b) Semi-naturalistic causality

Acidification Today and Tomorrow also makes use of a number of semi-naturalistic sketches. Unlike the photographs, these are captioned and labelled and most relate rather directly to the main argument. For instance, the first figure in the book depicts a scene, drawn in a somewhat primitivist mode, in which factories, houses and cars are seen to be producing smoky emissions. These move up and across the picture converting themselves in the process into little balloons which are labelled, using chemical conventional notation, with the names of chemical species and reactions. These pass the sun and enter into clouds, and are then deposited upon an idealised terrain of woods, hills and lakes to which labels such as 'leaching', 'transport' and 'effects on vegetation' are attached. The caption is very long, and it authorises a causal story that is illustrated by the drawing.

That this figure is greatly simplified is self-evident. Much is omitted from it. There is, for instance, no depiction of the chemistry of fossil fuel combustion despite the fact that these are important to an understanding of processes of acidification. In addition, however, simplification and discrimination are both achieved by techniques of *scaling*: molecules of sulphur dioxide and other chemical species which are normally invisible are rendered visible, as we have noted above, and move across the sky, only to disappear again when they reach the ground. Again, the factories, people and fish are disproportionately small – though not as small as the diminutive mountains and forests. As in medieval scenes of the crucifixion, size, and in particular departures in size from the conventions of perspectival representation, are thus used as an indicator of importance. Discrimination is also, however, achieved by the use of conventional or *stylised represen-tation*. The plumes of grey and black smoke from the factories, and in particular from the houses and a single car, bear only a slight resemblance to the emissions from such sources viewed under most conditions. And, as we have already indicated, invisible molecules are rendered visible by conventional means. Finally, discrimination is also assisted by labelling: tags such as 'NO_x' and 'H^+' are attached to the chemical balloons so the reader is left in no doubt that they are to be distinguished from one another.

So far, then, visual conventions of suppression, scaling, stylis-ation and labelling have been deployed to generate a space filled with selected and discriminable objects. Now, however, the objects, like those in co-word analysis and the photographs we have already discussed, are interrelated. Here the technologies of linkage are mixed: spatial proximity is, perhaps, the most important of these, but it is supplemented by conventional indicators such as arrows, a series of labels that depict relations or processes rather than unitary objects, and a caption and a text that

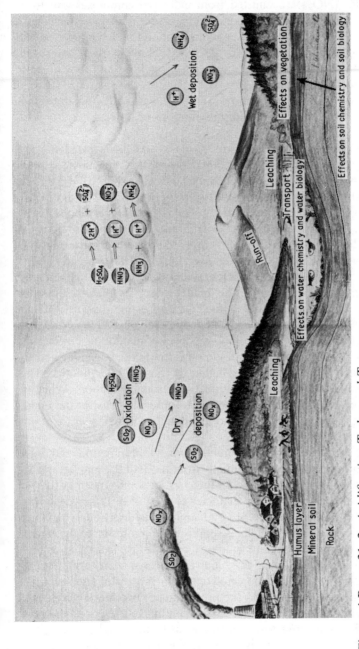

Figure 4 Pages 31–2, *Acidification Today and Tomorrow* Swedish Ministry of Agriculture, 1982

175

authorise specific connections: 'Sulphur dioxide (SO_2) and nitrogen oxides (NO_x) are emitted from industrial complexes and towns . . .'. The effect of these connections is thus to propose much more than a correlation (as in co-word analysis) or a contrast (as with the photographic realism discussed above): they assert and illustrate a strong claim about causal relations and they do so by mixed means that rest, in particular, on the use of a range of seminaturalistic conventions. These depart, but also draw their force from, perspectival representations of objects.

(c) Graphical representation

The book contains many *graphs*. One of these concerns the pH of lakewater and the level of animal life (See Fig. 5). In this the x axis represents time – the years between 1977 and 1981 are arrayed along it. The y axis has two scales. One represents the level of occurrence of planktonic crustaceans, and the other pH (acidity) values. In 1977 and early 1978 the latter varies between 4.5 and 5.5: the water is relatively acidic. Then, in early 1977 it rises to 6.5 (i.e. it becomes less acidic) and does not fall below 5.5 again until early 1981. The reader observes that this increase coincides with the liming of the lake in question, because the time when this occurred is indicated by a labelled arrow, and then observes the curve describing the level of planktonic crustaceans. This varies greatly in value. Thus it is low at the beginning and end of each year, and much higher in the middle months. This, however, is noise in the form of seasonal variation. What the reader is, in particular, expected to observe is that in the middle months of the year it rises to much higher values *after* the liming than it did before.

The technologies of simplification, discrimination and inter-relation here differ substantially from those of the photograph and the semi-naturalistic sketch. Much has, of course, been lost. While we can only guess at the character of most of this suppression, the way in which objects (pH and number of individuals per litre) appear in the graph as lines representing figures strongly suggests that quantification and methods of statistical summary entered early in the process: that individual cases were arithmetically merged having been subjected to a prior process of discrimination. At any rate, the result is the production of two new objects which are able to take their place on a graph but re-present an unknown number of heterogeneous and intractable objects and measurements.

Interrelation is achieved by graphical means: there are, as we

pH and occurrence of planktonic crustaceans after liming

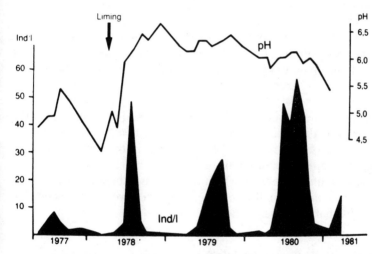

Figure 5 Page 128, *Acidification Today and Tomorrow*
Swedish Ministry of Agriculture, 1982

177

have noted, three sets of metrics: level of planktonic crustaceans, pH and time. The juxtaposition of the first and the second is managed by means of the third. Time is arrayed metrically on the horizontal axis. A linear progression of befores and afters is achieved, in part by labelling. And the scale is not simply ordinal, but cardinal. It is possible to locate the middle of each succeeding year and compare the crustacean levels, and in turn to compare these with pH. Time has been converted into a spatial dimension as have, in a second dimension, crustacean levels and pH: again, labelling is essential here. The graphical character of the space that has been projected is thus crucial to its capacity to interrelate discriminated objects. Horizontal proximity and relative vertical position are the keys to understanding the relationship between the two objects in question. And, because the scales are all cardinal, the relationship between the two objects is very precisely defined.

Finally, the relationship between the graph and its surrounding text is important in at least two ways. First, there is a reflexive relationship between the caption and the graph. Thus the former, which reads 'Trend of pH and planktonic crustaceans after the liming of lake Blanksjon in Tiveden (southern Central Sweden)', instructs the reader about what may be found in the latter. However, the latter can conversely be treated as evidence for the existence of the trend that is mentioned in the caption. Second, and perhaps more important, there is reference to an article in the scientific literature from which the data have been drawn. For the first time in our analysis of visual depiction we find a warrant for claims that lies outside the text itself.

4 On the art of representation

We have argued that representations may be treated as the end-product of technologies for simplifying, discriminating and inter-relating objects. In the creation of representations much is suppressed. Such suppression is necessary if heterogeneous objects distributed through time and space are to be brought together in a conformable space at a particular time. But alongside simplification there is another process that we have called discrimination: new classes of objects are brought into being, objects whose boundaries and properties are clearer than those they have replaced, objects that may more easily be interrelated with one another. These new and relatively docile objects replace their savage cousins, but they also speak on their behalf – they are their representatives for no depiction is able to represent unless it also speaks for something else. Finally processes of interrelation take place: relationships between the newly constituted objects are defined and they are allocated a place, a significance, within the representation as a whole.

The creation of representations is thus a delicate balancing act. The need for tractability and assimilability suggests that the discriminated objects should be docile. This, however, is likely to mean that they should be quite unlike those whom they represent – which in turn means that their representativeness is always questionable. This is thus, in a somewhat unusual guise, a version of the problem of political representation and indeed, the parallels between visual and political representation are far from superficial. In both, representatives of far-flung subjects are gathered in one place. In both, the heterogeneity of those subjects is reduced to homogeneity and it is necessary to ensure their silence, to prevent them from speaking in other ways. In both, then, there are whole technologies for simplifying, discriminating and interrelating in order to ensure the creation of a tractable order and the silence on which this depends. And in both there are constant disagreements about the legitimacy of those technologies and about the proper application of their rules.

It is in this sense, then, that we want to say that the technologies of visual representation are political in character. In the case of writing about science it is not just that they present politically relevant material, narrowly defined – though in both the empirical cases that we have considered this is indeed the case. It is also that they speak for others that have been deprived of a voice, that have been transformed from objects that spoke for themselves into mere shadows of their former selves. And the fact that this is not, in general, seen as a political act reveals the extent to which these processes of transformation are successful: not only are the voices taken away, but the memory that they might have spoken other-wise has been lost. Of course, we exaggerate: there are many disputes in science, just as there are disputes about popularisation and, in our own area about the validity or otherwise of co-word analysis. But, characteristically, these are disputes *within* rather than *about* technologies of representation. The essentially political character of the network of such technologies within which we live is grasped only with difficulty.

Bruno Latour (1983) tells us that science is politics, but it is politics by other means. Science is politics, he says, because scientifically created objects such as microbes may come to dominate the national political stage and alter the relationship between social actors. He draws on the case of Pasteur to illustrate his point, and it is clear that a similar argument could be mounted about the acid rain depictions and their mixed social and natural objects that we have discussed in this paper. However, the point, as Latour has elsewhere argued (1987; 1988), goes much deeper than that. Science is constitutively political because, like visualisation, it marshalls, organises and purports to speak on behalf of objects that are rendered silent. And, as we have suggested in this paper, in this respect what is true for science is also true for the visualisations that are to be found in writing about science.

But the other half of Latour's argument is equally important: science is politics, but it is politics *by other means*. Here he is telling us that science represents a specific set of methods for representing and operating on others – that science, though it is political in the double sense mentioned above, cannot be *reduced* to politics. Or, to put it in another way, our current conceptions of what are to count as political are impoverished. So it is with visual representation. We have argued that visualisations can be treated as processes of production in which voices are taken away and docile objects are constituted and interrelated. This, however, is simply a general way of asserting the political character of visualisation or, better, a way of claiming that current definitions of what is to count as political are unduly restrictive.

If, following Latour and less directly Foucault, we argue that it is the specificity of the methods by which politics is pursued that most deserves study, then, in the present context, it is on the various techniques of visual representation and the way in which they become legitimated that we should concentrate. In the present paper we have only touched upon the surface of this problem. Nevertheless, in the small sample that we have considered we can identify no less than five such technologies (though several are deployed simultaneously in most cases). Each of these bases its appeal to represent on different grounds.

Some of these are well known. There is, for instance, first the technique of reference to another publication. This is an appeal to individual authority, though individuals are not necessarily people but may take the form of journals or institutions. This form of appeal was deployed in the last of the empirical cases which we discussed though it is, of course, widely used in areas where visualisation is absent. Second, there are appeals to textual argument. These, which form the subject of a large literature on rhetoric, have not been considered in any detail in the present paper, though we have several times noted the way in which text and visualisation stand in reflexive, mutually warranting relationship to each other. And third, there are the technologies of quantification. These, which are, of course, no more specifically visual in character than the first two, represent an immensely powerful set of techniques for suppressing and merging objects into forms that are docile and easily manipulated. The results of such manipulation which are susceptible to visual depiction in terms of a limited number of conventions of which tables and graphs are the most obvious examples, obtain their warrant in part at least from their 'democratic' character: many discriminable objects are able to find (a very specific kind of) voice in the form of a statistical summary. Everyone gets a vote.

Turning to methods that are more specifically visual, there is a fourth technology, that of photographic realism. This takes the form of a set of artful practices which have the effect of concealing themselves (Lynch, 1985; Law and Lynch, 1988). Thus the finished product, the photograph, presents itself as simply recording what was actually there when it was taken. The camera, or so it is conventionally believed, cannot lie, so the photograph is able to stand as a naive representative for the object that it depicts – the object is transformed, without apparent distortion, from its original lumpy and awkward state into a two-dimensional docile form.

The final set of conventions that we have encountered in the present paper are also specifically visual: these represent the technology of semi-naturalistic depiction. The processes involved in the production of such depictions are complex and we have done no more than touch upon them. Nevertheless, the basis for claiming representativeness appears to lie in the way in which they combine a version of perspectival recognisability with quite deliberate conventional departures from that recognisability. The recognisability provides a general warrant – 'everyone knows' that trees or factories 'look like this' – so the viewer understands that it is not a particular tree or factory that is being depicted, but rather all trees and factories. And then the departures from perspectival expectations (assisted by appropriate labelling and textual glossing) make it possible for the viewer to detect the typical relations that link the objects that have been so discriminated.

We are not, of course, suggesting that this list is either definitive or complete. Thus Bud's analysis (op. cit.) of the considerations that led to the mounting of a museum display on the chemical industry, or Lynch's and Edgerton's (op. cit.) analysis of the conventions that generate computer depictions of astronomical phenomena consider several further technologies for visual depiction which solve the problem of representation in yet other ways. Our basic point, however, is that these technologies are political in character because they speak on behalf of others. Until we understand the specificities of representative practices, whether these are located within or outside what we conventionally think of as politics, we shall not understand how it is that some find themselves able to silence and so wield power on behalf of others.

Acknowledgements

We are grateful to Michel Callon and Gordon Fyfe who commented on an earlier version of this paper.

Notes

1 We are grateful to the ESRC for financial support within its Science Studies and Science Policy Programme.
2 Theoretically these suggestions correspond to the notion that scientists tend to form smallish groups that work together on related topics or themes of research, that there are, however, no firm boundaries between either groups or topics, and that both are liable to change, sometimes quite radically and rapidly. Practically, they correspond to a policy concern to identify important, strategic, or up-and-coming themes of research even if these do not coincide with disciplinary boundaries or the received wisdom.
3 One such depiction is discussed in the next section.
4 For discussion of the art of photography in the similarly 'popular' medium of amateur bird-watching see Law and Lynch (1988).

References

Knorr-Cetina, Karin D. and Mulkay, Michael (eds.) (1983), *Science Observed: Perspectives on the Social Study of Science*, Sage, London, Beverly Hills and New Delhi.
Latour, Bruno (1983), 'Give Me a Laboratory and I will Raise the World', in Knorr-Cetina and Mulkay, pp. 141–70.
Latour, Bruno (1987), *Science in Action: How to Follow Scientists and Engineers Through Society*, Milton Keynes, Open University Press.
Latour, Bruno (1988), *War and Peace among the Microbes*, Cambridge, Harvard University Press.
Law, John (1986), 'On Power and its Tactics: a View from the Sociology of Science', *Sociological Review*, 34: 1–37.

Law, John and Lynch, Michael (1988), 'Lists, Fields Guides and the Descriptive
   Organisation of Seeing: Birdwatching as an Exemplary Observational Activity',
   Human Studies, forthcoming.
Lynch, Michael (1985), *Art and Artifact in Laboratory Science: a Study of Shop
   Work and Shop Talk in a Research Laboratory*, London, Boston, Melbourne and
   Henley, Routledge and Kegan Paul.
Swedish Ministry of Agriculture Environment '82 Committee (1982), *Acidification
   Today and Tomorrow*, translated from Swedish by Simon Harper.

Aesthetics and digital image processing: representational craft in contemporary astronomy

Michael Lynch and Samuel Y. Edgerton Jr

Abstract

This paper examines whether 'aesthetic' considerations play a part in contemporary scientific work, and focuses on a scientific field undergoing rapid transformation through the introduction of digital imaging and image processing technologies. Interviews with astronomers at two image processing laboratories indicate that they orient explicitly to the 'aesthetic' judgments of their audiences when preparing images to promote and popularize their research. Although they acknowledge no such 'aesthetic' pretensions for their 'scientific' work, further analysis shows that a more ancient aesthetic, that of perfecting nature through a crafting of resemblances, is deeply a part of routine image processing work.

Introduction: on the distinction between art and science

The relationship between art and science continues to provoke discussion among historians and philosophers of science. A widely shared view of this relation is summarized by Graubard (1986: ix): 'The correspondences that may once have existed between art and science, that were certainly evident during the Renaissance, that may have continued well into the eighteenth century, have been dissipated.'

According to this view, modern science and modern art have both diverged from a common foundation in *techne*: with artistic innovation no longer limited by a single representational standard, and scientific technique being subordinated to independent standards of rationality. While modern artists may mimic, parody, or metaphorically appropriate scientific innovations, we are told, scientists do not correspondingly borrow from art.

184

An artist at work may want for his or her own purposes an image from science, or its sound; a scientist on holiday may be pleased to think of himself or herself as having an aesthetic sensibility. But the places the sciences inhabit do not on the whole have or need the arts in them. (Cavell, 1986: 171–2)

Some scholars (Kuhn, 1974; Steinberg, 1986) remind us that it may be more fruitful to consider the profound differences between art and science, than to invoke shared *Zeitgeist* or to define broad aesthetic criteria like symmetry, harmony, and parsimony, supposedly guiding scientists' theoretical preferences.

We agree with advocates of the 'two cultures' view that science and art have diverged professionally and institutionally, and that if it makes any sense to speak of 'aesthetics' in contemporary science, such 'aesthetics' may have only vague or occasional relation to the stylistic innovations associated with modern art. The figure of the Renaissance man, proficient as artist as well as scientist and engineer, largely vanished from the scene after the seventeenth century. Nevertheless, we will argue here that modern science includes 'artistic' practices and 'aesthetic' judgements. These may not be informed directly by developments in the professionalized art world, but they nevertheless are to be found *within* scientific practice.

Prior to the dissociation of art from science, 'aesthetics' delimited a common basis in craft, where available materials were used to render realistic images. Renaissance scientists appropriated artistic conventions, since these conventions facilitated the tasks of mapping and measuring the sensual manifold, and they made use of newly developed print technology to construct, reproduce, and circulate visual images of phenomena and apparatus (Ivins, 1953; Edgerton, 1976). Such innovations enabled scientists and engineers to identify phenomenal properties, perform measurements, and document claims by working with two-dimensional drawings. Linear perspective, chiaroscuro, cut-away and exploded views (Edgerton, 1984; 1986a), and the integration of visual and Cartesian space (Tilling, 1975) enabled scientists to make use of a kind of 'virtual witnessing' (Shapin, 1984), where discoverable relations were disclosed not through direct inspection of 'things-in-themselves' but through the construction and analysis of graphemes.

After the eighteenth century it becomes more difficult to discern direct borrowings by scientists of techniques and conventions developed first by artists, but scientists continued to innovate with visual representation (Rudwick, 1976; Edgerton, 1986b; Gooding, 1986). Nineteenth-century scientists appropriated, for specialized disciplinary use, new engraving techniques, tints and dyes, and photographic and graphical means for documenting order and movement (Giedion, 1948). These connections between practical and technological innovation, artistic convention, and scientific change are complex and overlapping, but for our purposes they suffice to demonstrate that innovation with visual display and documentation continued to have a significant impact in science.

A growing recognition among historians of the significance of pictorial and graphic innovation in science is complemented by recent developments in the sociology of science. In the past decade a number of sociologists and anthropologists conducted detailed ethnographies of scientific laboratories (Collins, 1985; Knorr-Cetina, 1981; Latour and Woolgar, 1979; Lynch, 1985a). Influenced by developments in ethnomethodology (Garfinkel, 1967) and the sociology of knowledge (Barnes, 1974; Bloor, 1976; Mulkay, 1979), ethnographies of science investigate the real-time performance of experiments and the practical discourse of scientists. They document the importance of laboratory 'craft' for making experiments work, and they suggest that scientists' work with visual renderings, models or inscriptions can be treated as artisans' shop practices (Garfinkel et al., 1981). Such 'craft' includes practices for composing and analyzing graphic and pictorial exhibits of the phenomena under study, and cannot be described simply as a by-product of verbal 'ideas' or experimental logic.[1]

In this study we contend that a 'craft' of visual representation is hidden within the ordinary details of scientific practice. To document this contention we arranged to ethnographically study a contemporary scientific field where new means of visual representation are being developed and adapted. We chose to investigate the field of astronomy, since we understood that new modes of detection and visual representation, relying on digital representation of data and digital image processing, were rapidly transforming this ancient science. Our study, which is still underway, focuses on astronomers' methods for preparing images for various purposes. We aim to discover whether scientists attribute 'aesthetic' properties to their work, and to explicate what 'aesthetics' might mean in the context of that work. In exploring the relations between aesthetics and science we raised the following questions: to what extent are scientists apprised of developments in professional or commercial art?; in what sense are their representational technologies and conventions like those used by contemporary artists?; and, most importantly, aside from any connections to an 'external' world of art, to what extent do the local practices of scientists consist of a craft of representation?

Background: digital image processing in astronomy

With the development of ground-based and satellite detectors for radio, X-ray, and infra-red radiation, and the use of charge-coupled devices (CCD) in optical astronomy, digital image processing has become a major part of astronomical research. Image processing laboratories, consisting of assemblies of digital computers, specialized software packages, keyboards, TV monitors, and specialists who know how to use and program such equipment, complement the great observatories as significant technological facilities for astrophysical research.[2] Many astronomers conduct much, if not most, of their research at such facilities; displaying images on monitors, combining and superimposing separate images, trying out different ways of visualizing or mapping data, and converting the data into numerical readings and graphic displays.[3]

Interview and observational materials discussed in this paper were collected in the summers of 1986 and 1987 during an ongoing study of image processing in astronomy.[4] We selected two image processing laboratories for study: one was part of a major national centre for astrophysical research, and the other was a university laboratory which performed NASA sponsored research on the geophysics of the ionosphere. Both facilities include 'state of the art'[5] computers, image processors, and software packages. Through interviews with practitioners, observations of their routine work, analysis of tape-recorded discussions between collaborators, and photographic documentation of image processing, we aim to investigate whether and to what extent, 'aesthetic' considerations enter into the way astronomers compose, transform, and select images for various audiences and purposes.

At both facilities, astronomical data are initially collected from orbiting detectors or ground based observatories. In many cases incident electromagnetic radiation, presumably emanating from the source, is translated by the detector instrumentation into digital electronic signals. These are then stored on tape at the observatory site, or are beamed to earth from space-based detectors. In some cases, conventional photographs taken at an observatory are later digitized at image processing facilities. When transferred to a computer disk and displayed on a video monitor at an image processing laboratory, an image is reconstructed as, in one astronomer's words, an 'array of numbers'. Typical monitors display an array of 512 × 320 pixels (picture elements), each of which, in an 8-bit binary system, can encode up to 256 discrete values. Each pixel value can, for instance, represent the 'intensity' of incident radiation at a particular site on the detector, so that the entire array constitutes a two-dimensional map of intensity gradient. Pixels can also be used to encode other 'dimensions' such as spectral frequency and red-shift.

Despite the relatively gross resolution compared to photography, digital image processing is reputed to have numerous advantages: much greater quantum efficiency for detecting incident radiation, greater dynamic range for representing contrast, linear response of detection systems to incident light, and the ability to easily transform the configuration of any image. Image processing enables a particular 'array of numbers' to be represented as a contour map, black-and-white or colour picture, or numerical matrix. Separate images taken of a particular field can be added to each other, to increase signal-noise contrast, or to superimpose images taken at different wavelengths. Available software can be used to generate graphic indices of flux, polarization, and relative distributions of energy at different wavelengths from individual images and series of images. While photography and related imaging techniques are far from inflexible in their ability to selectively expose relevant details (see Lynch, 1985b; Yoxen, 1987; and Amann and Knorr-Cetina, 1988), digital imaging, with its access to geometric arrays of pixels, enables the constituent 'elements' of a picture to be directly handled at the computer console.

Software packages[6] enable numerous operations to be performed to enhance the visibility and analyzability of data. Contours can be 'smoothed' through the use of Gaussean and other functions to average the values of each pixel with those in a surrounding region; contrasts can be 'sharpened' through a variety of methods for subtracting 'noise' and consolidating 'signal'.[7]

Among the more evident visual modalities used in image processing is colour. Images can be represented in terms of gradients of grey-levels, or series of contour lines, but hardware and software have been developed which enable colour to be used as an index for specified measures. Colour 'palettes' or 'look-up tables' translate the numbers in a digital image into a combination of 'true', 'enhanced', or 'false' colours. For instance, a simplified palette might have the following key:

Intensity		*Colour*
0–50	=	Black
51–100	=	Blue
101–150	=	Green
151–200	=	Yellow
201–250	=	Red
250–256	=	White

The equipment allows for these and other colours to be arranged in numerous other combinations. Each 'bin' (the range of numbers represented by any colour) can be broadened or narrowed, gradients between colours can be shaded, and an entire field can be represented in varying monochromatic shades.

Colour combinations can be used to 'bring out' thematic features in a field, or to suppress backgrounds. For instance, expanding the lowest intensity bin to 0–150, colouring it black, and concentrating the remaining colours in the palette within the interval 151–256, will tend to contract the visible figure, since visual differentiation will be limited to only the highest intensities, and variations in the lower intensities will be suppressed into a uniform dark background (see Figure 1). Using the technology to slide the scale of colours through the numerical range, or varying the dynamic range of the numbers recorded in the data, enables practitioners to actively play with gestalt properties of the field. Such properties include figure-ground contrast, figural closure and continuity, and regional homogeneity and differentiation. These perceptual themes, usually attributed to a complicity between eye and brain (Gregory 1966), are directly achieved through hands-on manipulation of the computer console in reference to local features on the visible surface of the figure.[8]

A members' distinction between 'aesthetics' and 'science'

From the outset of the interviews,[9] we mentioned that we were interested in aesthetic aspects of astronomical images. We were relieved to find that rather than treating such an interest as alien or irrelevant to their work, the astronomers we interviewed did not

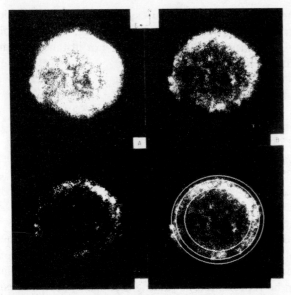

Figure 1 Four exposures of Tycho's supernova remnant

Black and white exposures of X-ray image of Tycho's supernova remnant (first seen from earth in 1572). Exposures A, B, and C, of digital data from the orbiting Einstein Observatory, selectively 'bring out' details of the emissions and/or suppress background. A is digitally processed to expose relatively low intensity levels as well as the higher intensities, while B, and especially C, expose only the higher intensity pixels. C exposes only the highest intensity pixels, so that the background is uniformly dark, while in A the background is speckled (presumably as a result of background radiation and electronic noise). B exposes both the brightest emissions, believed to result from hot stellar ejecta from the supernova explosion, and fainter emissions, believed to result from swept-up interstellar gas. Emissions are especially bright in the north-west outer region of the shell, and in selected 'knots' exposed elsewhere in the shell. Fainter emissions are at the outermost edge of the shell. Concentric circles in section D of the Figure are drawn (on exposure from B) with image processing equipment and used to assess the symmetry and regional distribution of intense emissions. With the use of colour palettes, regions of different intensity can be differentiated into distinct bands of colour, 'knots' can be set off with bright colours against darker backgrounds. (Figure courtesy of Fred Seward, Harvard-Smithsonian Astrophysical Observatory.)

hesitate to talk about aesthetics or to explicate what they considered 'nice' or 'beautiful' about particular images.

We did not define 'aesthetics' when we talked to our informants, nor did there seem to be any need to do so. Instead, our questions (indeed, our very presence at the facility) placed the topic in circulation, and further conversations and observations enabled us to begin to grasp how astronomers understood its reference to their work.

Mention of aesthetics often led to discussions of what some astronomers called 'pretty pictures'. Such pictures were arrayed on office walls and in the hallways of research facilities. Each astronomer we interviewed had collections of pictures to show us. These included loose-leaf binders of glossy prints, graphs, and contour maps of astronomical phenomena; collections of colour slides for showing at conferences and public lectures; and images stored in computer files. Some of these were prepared specifically for 'public' consumption. For instance, during a tour by a group of visitors to an image processing facility, one of the researchers demonstrated a 'dog and pony show' – a series of images kept on file for the specific purpose of entertaining visitors. Other researchers also kept such files, and were eager to show them on appropriate occasions.

Some of the astronomers had gained reputations for their 'pretty pictures'. They were noted for, and took pride in, their innovative use of false colour and other graphic effects. Several of them had published, or were currently working on, semi-popular books and articles. Readerships were said to consist of amateur astronomers and/or 'educated laymen'. Suitable illustrations were prepared and selected (both by authors and editors) specifically for such publications, and were distinguished from those produced for 'scientific' projects. One astronomer, for instance, had developed special techniques for preparing slightly enhanced true-colour pictures of astronomical objects. His pictures routinely appear in *Sky and Telescope* and other semi-popular magazines, and one of his pictures appeared a few years ago on the cover of the *New York Times Magazine*. Another astronomer spent a considerable amount of time making motion picture films. The films were made for public educational programmes, and utilized advanced image processing technology to create mobile displays of galaxies, galaxy clusters, and gravitational lenses which would rotate in three dimensional perspective to demonstrate theoretical effects such as the gravitational bending of light. Although such films were prepared as popularized artistic renderings, efforts were made to create realistic, though speculative, effects.

Two of the researchers we interviewed mentioned that they had an active interest in pictorial art, and that they in fact exhibited artistic works. One of them used computer programs to systematically 'distort' astronomical images to compose abstract and colourful patterns. The other produced computer art for occasional exhibition, although his pictures were not based on astronomical images. While they were reticent to acknowledge any specific relationship between their artistic and scientific projects, they did allow for the possibility that their scientific imagination was affected by artistic insight. The informants provided very little detail on just how such a connection might be made, however, and they maintained a firm distinction between 'scientific' and 'artistic' uses of image processing technology.

Pretty pictures were said to be important, not simply for personal diversion and popularized display, but for *promoting* astronomical research. For instance, one scientist mentioned that spectacular false-coloured images can come in handy as cover-illustrations for grant proposals reviewed by NASA and other government bodies. Another researcher amassed a large collection of slides, and developed captions for them, to be packaged as a promotional programme for a series of astronomical satellites proposed for launching by NASA. Images were selected and prepared specifically for these purposes, using false colour schemes believed to appeal to lay audiences.

The production of pretty pictures was time consuming, requiring a great deal of care, and we were shown that such work required a distinct order of tasks and techniques. For the most part pretty pictures were prepared as such, rather than simply being taken from collections of images produced in the course of specialized projects. For instance, an astronomer stated that when conducting research at the observatory (on a remote mountain in Arizona) he sometimes will use an evening for 'taking pretty pictures' when high cirrus clouds interfere with more sensitive measurements. While the clouds interfere with photometry, they do not prevent pictures to be taken of, for example, galaxies, star forming areas and supernova remnants, which later can be processed into colourful photographic slides. At image processing facilities, pictures were processed differently, depending upon whether they were to be displayed for 'the public' or for 'science'. Stylistic 'orientations' to these different audiences were explicated primarily in terms of (1) the uses of colour, and (2) a quantitative/qualitative distinction.

(1) The uses of colour
As mentioned above, image processing technology enables practitioners to use colour as an index for intensity gradients and other numerically represented properties. Endless variations are possible for selecting particular colours, arranging them in a palette, and correlating them to numerical 'bins'. Nevertheless, false colour renderings are rarely published in professional journals such as the *Journal of Astrophysics*, partly due to cost (over $2,000 per page assessed to authors for colour plates). Semi-popular magazines like *Scientific American* and *Sky and Telescope* include numerous false-colour illustrations, while the vast majority of illustrations in research journals are graphs, contour maps, and black-and-white photographs. Aside from questions of cost, several astronomers told us that they prefer to analyze images in black-and-white, using a continuous gray scale rather than a colour palette to represent intensities. They noted that gray scale renderings are more easily interpreted. A graded scale from black to white more readily translates the quantitative gradient of intensity levels than does a set of discrete colour contours. A monochromatic field, according to this reasoning, more readily shows the substantive continuities of a nebular object, avoiding any implications of bounded segments along the contours of adjacent colours. According to one informant:

Colour has been oversold by the computer industry itself. The industry has told many people that the eye is sensitive to fewer levels of gray than colour. But the eye gets confused. You still do the best by showing the most subtle detail by using gradients of gray than any but the most disciplined use of false colour. (13 August 1987)

Although they associate colour primarily with promotion and popularization, astronomers do sometimes make use of colour for analyzing their data, and they present colour slides when reporting on research to disciplinary colleagues. But, we were told, they do not aim for the same sorts of colour effects as they might when composing a picture for a poster or popularized article. When commenting on a false-colour image in a semi-popular magazine, in which an object was displayed against a magenta sky, an astronomer stated that false colour:

> is really a cheap way of dressing up the presentation. It doesn't really convey much information, but it's something editors like. An editor will often say, 'I like that picture, because of the reds,' where to me it's outrageous because it has nothing to do with the science, the astronomy. It's a distraction. (13 August 1987)

We were given the impression that colours were used more freely, even gratuitously, for popularized images. Given a less discriminating audience, the entire composition of a picture was less constrained by demands for precise astronomical reference for any conspicuous contrast, formal aggregation, or discriminable detail.

(2) A quantitative/qualitative distinction

With the exception of images produced specifically as non-representative 'art', popularized pretty pictures were said to show definite astronomical content. To differentiate them from 'the science', astronomers often used a quantitative/qualitative distinction:

> the pictures [in a promotional slide set] give you a very qualitative feeling. With these, and its true in the slide set that we try to get a concept across or an idea across, but we don't particularly use it to measure a real physical quantity. (7 August 1987)

At times, astronomers spoke of pictures as epiphenomenal appearances, of secondary interest to the numerical measures developed through analysis from the 'same' digitized data. When discussing a false-colour x-ray image of a supernova remnant reproduced in a *Scientific American* article, an astronomer mentioned:

> You can't do any numerical analysis with this. These [colour pictures] are all made with digital arrays. You can very precisely measure the intensity at any point. But you do that with the digital data, not with these. (21 August 1987)

Another expression of this qualitative/quantitative distinction was less explicit. After initial interviews we asked to observe how our informants used the image processing equipment. We were interested in the day-to-day research, and not just the production of popularized images, but the astronomers often assumed that because we were interested in 'aesthetics' we would only be interested in work with false colours and 'pretty pictures'. The following passages are taken from one of the authors' field notes:

> When I asked if it was OK if I sat in and observed him at work, he warned me that he was only doing 'robot' tasks that had little aesthetic value. I assured him that I would find them interesting. (24 July 1987)

> C. was in one of the image processing labs. I approached her and asked if it would be OK if I sat by as she went about her work. She said it was fine with her, but that she would be 'doing science' today, and would not be doing much with colourful images. (3 August 1987)

In another instance, after we had observed two astronomers trying to work out a new program for 'sharpening' images, one of them addressed us and stated:

> You know what, I have a feeling we're going to be pretty boring for you guys this afternoon, 'cause Andy [a pseudonym] and I are kind of struggling with this program. It's not in as nice a state as I had thought . . . I have a feeling that you're just going to hear me and Andy talk back and forth about, um, 'That's as good a value as any.' . . . I think that watching two people here, trying to struggle through real state of the art software where nobody quite knows what's going on won't be much fun. (7 August 1987)

Since our research was associated with 'aesthetics', the astronomers apparently distinguished what in their work would be of interest to us. They seemed to assume that we would be most interested in their uses of colour and other manipulations of the visible surfaces of images, but not with the work of calculating values, plugging readings into computer programs, and other quantitative data processing routines. Only with difficulty were we able to assure our informants that we were very much interested in such 'uninteresting' technical routines.

In sum, we were given a number of indications that practitioners believed that aesthetics had important, but limited, relevance to their practices. For the most part they associated it with the popularization and promotion of astronomy. While promotion was obviously important for sustaining support for astronomical research, it was separated from the work of doing professional astronomy *as a science*. Aesthetics was a sidelight, in some contexts like a hobby, and was treated as a means for engaging the attention, enhancing the amazement, and enlisting the support of popular audiences. The apparent constrast between 'aesthetics' and 'science' is summarized in the schema below.

Rendering:	Context	Format	Analytic content
'Aesthetics':	Promotion	Colour picture	Qualitative
'Science':	Profession	Map/Graph	Quantitative

Re-examining the distinction

From the above, it would be easy to conclude that aesthetics plays a part in science, but one that is restricted to a limited domain, that of the promotion of science to audiences of non-practitioners. The distinction between 'pretty pictures' and 'the science' supports the widespread view of an historical divorce between art and science, since 'aesthetic' renderings of digitized data are demarcated from the practices, audiences, and products associated with specialized scientific research. (In one respect, the divorce is not complete, since practising astronomers, and not professional artists, produce 'aesthetic' astronomical images.)

Despite what the initial interviews suggested, further inquiry on how astronomers spoke of 'aesthetic properties of astronomical images and how they went about preparing visual data for 'scientific' analysis belied any notion of a binary opposition between two domains of discourse and practice. We were able to appreciate that what astronomers attribute to aesthetics is inseparable from their science, and what they call science includes aesthetics (although, perhaps, in a more ancient sense of the term than conveyed in quotations above). Without denying the validity of the distinction's reference to separate markets for scientific products, we can note that it is misleading to suppose that, (1) the sense of what is nice or beautiful about popularized, colourful renderings has nothing to do with substantive astronomical properties, and (2) doing 'real' science excludes any notion of art or aesthetics., *Hidden within the dichotomy between 'aesthetics' and 'science' is a specification of each member of the pair contained within the explication of the other.*

(1) The astronomical reference of 'aesthetic' appreciations

On several occasions during interviews, informants showed us pictures which they said they liked 'for aesthetic reasons'. We pursued such mentions, in hopes of receiving more detailed explications of just what about any picture was held to be 'aesthetic':

S. is showing M.L. a series of slides of radio and x-ray images of supernova remnants (see Figures 1 and 2):

S.: This is one that starts out red and goes through yellow and white. One of these – here's one that has some green in it. Here's some radio data, that's a multi-colour. This is radio with purple and this is radio with blue. I thought that aesthetically I like these maps that have sort of one colour, they start out dim, then go brighter, and then go white.

M.L.: Okay, why is that?

S.: I just think those are prettier than these that have many different colours in them.

M.L.: Is it strictly a matter of liking one colour –

S.: The reasons are artistic rather than scientific.

M.L.: I was wondering. Other people told me that they like the more uniform thing because they think it doesn't give a misleading picture. You see a gradient of structure rather than a series of discrete –

S.: Yes, yes, there's that too.

M.L.: Okay, but that's not just what you're talking about when you say you like the aesthetics.

S.: Well, I don't know, maybe it is. You show this picture to someone and you say, here this is what it looks like. Now, this is a – you can't see it, so you [inaudible] it really doesn't look like anything, I mean you can't see it with your eyes. But, this does seem to be more realistic than that.

M.L.: Imagining it as an optical object it would look more like that.

S.: Yes.

M.L.: I guess even the choice of colour would have some

197

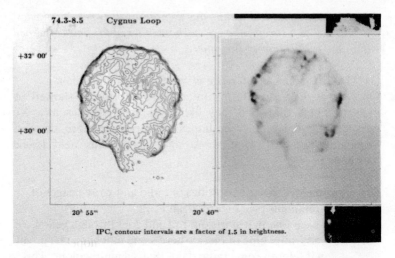

Figure 2 *Two images of Cygnus Loop supernova remnant*
Since we are unable to use colour figures in this paper, we are
using this black and white figure to provide an approximate sense
of the difference between a colour map using contrasting colour
bins and one using a monochromatic palette. Contour map on left
and black and white exposure on right demonstrate two visual
representations of digital X-ray data of a supernova remnant taken
from orbiting Einstein Observatory. Frame around the images
provides celestial coordinates. The contour map shows discrete
levels of intensity. In a colour map, bright contrasting colours can
be used for each contour interval (or 'bin' of intensity levels). With
a 'conventional' palette, the background would be dark blue or
black, and successive contours would be coloured with lighter
shades of blue, one or more shades of green, yellow, red, and
then, perhaps, white for peak intensities. A monochromatic scale
would more closely resemble the image on the right (a negative
exposure, where highest intensity values are exposed as darkest).
If, for instance, purple was used as the monochromatic shade,
bright saturated purple would be used for the regions showing
dark in this black and white exposure. Backgrounds would be
black or darker shades of purple. The monochromatic exposure
provides more of a sense of continuity between 'dark' and 'light'
regions. (Figure courtesy of Fred Seward, Harvard-Smithsonian
Astrophysical Observatory.

relation if it were an extension of the spectrum, or an
extension of that end of it.

S.:   Right. At one time I thought I wanted to make the x-ray
purple and the radio red, because it gives you an idea
that this is a higher energy photon.

The astronomer, S., initially expresses a preference for a
relatively uniform gradient of colour (different shades of blue, or
purple in the case shown), compared to one using several contrasting colour contours (see Figure 2 for black-and-white facsimile of
this difference). He accounts for this preference as an 'aesthetic'
one, but when pushed with leading questions, he states that the
composition he prefers is more realistic than the other. 'Realism' is
problematic in this instance since, as he notes, the radio objects
are invisible, so any visual representation is hopelessly non-
realistic. But, he prefers the relatively continuous gradient since it
provides a sense of very slight variations in the faint nebular
emissions, instead of distinct regions of bright contrasting colour.
He goes on to mention how colours like red (for a low energy
source, beyond the red end of the optical spectrum) and purple
(for a high energy source) have some representational significance.
Shortly thereafter, he mentions about the same, preferred,
composition:

S.:   You can see more structure in that than in this.

In another instance, two researchers (a post-doctoral researcher
and an image processing technician) were interviewed as they
examined different renderings of an x-ray image of a galaxy.
Palettes for both renderings used blue for low intensities, and
yellow and then red for high intensities, but one included a dark
brown bin between the blue and the yellow.

(30 July 1987)
C.:   There's a different one which is, I don't think, as pretty
as that one.
M.L.: Why's that?
C.:   Uh, (pause), I think it doesn't show as many levels? I
think that it just goes red, yellow, blue, and the things,
say, in between the yellow and blue just sort of look
brown or something, it's not –
J.:   It's something of a question of aesthetics because there's

> this dark, this dark area in between the colours, whereas
> – it doesn't, you see like there's this dark band between
> the colours. And that area where it's dark there is not
> really dark in the image in the sense of being *faint*, it's
> very bright there in the image, but because of this
> particular set of colours, there's these dark rings between
> . . . the bands of very bright colours, the blue and the
> yellow, there's dark bands.

As these instances illustrate, 'aesthetic' preferences for particular compositions were initially stated without definite explication; but, when pushed, astronomers defended such choices on a naturalistic basis. Although colour composition, contrast, exposure, and scale were said to be arbitrary ways of presenting an invisible phenomenon to given audiences, their use was explicated in terms of a representational realism. Such realism was not, and could not be, justified as a direct mirroring of otherwise visible properties, since visible colour and form acted as *indices* of invisible, but arguably objective, properties. Nevertheless, such indices were justified (and apparently selected) with an orientation to their 'natural' connotations.

False-colour palettes are a case in point. In principle, image processing technology enables users to translate a given array of numbers into an endless variety of colour combinations. Some colours, and some combinations, are easier to 'make' than others, and most astronomy software packages offer relatively few palettes. Even within the limitations of a single, pre-packaged palette, users can easily 'roll' the sequence of colours across the numerical values represented in a digitized picture; they can 'squeeze' colours into a specified interval, or expand the dynamic range of a configuration of numbers to expose greater degrees of contrast. Further effort can modify the program to create further colours and different sequences of colours. Some colours are more difficult to create than others, requiring greater expertise and more expenditure of time to make the necessary program changes.

Given the freedom with which colour can be used, we were intrigued as to whether any conventions for using false colour had emerged in astronomy. Some of our informants told us that definite conventions had not emerged, and one mentioned that the absence of conventions for false-colour and colour enhanced images was a source of confusion for readers of semi-popular books and articles.[10] Despite such testimonies, and despite the fact that a glance through issues of, for instance, *Sky and Telescope* will reveal a variety of false-colour compositions, a particular colour palette does seem to predominate. This 'conventional' palette uses a dark blue or black for low intensity 'background' sky, one or more lighter shades of blue for slightly higher intensities, and then proceeds through yellow, red, and sometimes white for highest (saturated) intensities. Occasionally, shades of green, orange, and beige will separate light blue from the yellow. When we raised the possibility that this was a 'conventional' palette, our informants seemed indifferent to the existence of such a convention and unaware of how it may have emerged, perhaps because, for them, this palette seemed so 'natural' as not to be worthy of interest.[11]

The 'conventional' palette makes iconic use of colour, with black and dark blue indicating a dark featureless sky, and contrastive and saturated reds, yellows, and whites indicating intense sources. An alternative palette, which is also naturalistic though in a different way, arranges colours in a spectral sequence of red, orange, yellow, green, blue, indigo, and violet for progressively higher numerical values. This latter sequence is used, selectively, when colour is treated as an index for wavelength (red for long wavelength radio sources, and purple or blue for short wavelength x-ray sources) or in 'velocitygrams' where colour indicates red-shift. Both conventions selectively evoke 'natural interpretations' of colour in a local orientation to the phenomena under study.

Colour choices were said to respond to practical considerations. Despite his preference for palettes using different shades of purple, an astronomer informed us that purple 'looks nauseous' when developed on commercial slide film, so he does not use it.[12] Some colours are hard to 'make' with available equipment and software, and, as stated before, a limited number of palettes are 'given' with the software packages. However, these constraints do not alone account for a convergence upon the 'conventional' palette, since this palette is only one of the palettes readily accessed with the technology.

The 'conventional' palette by no means holds rigidly; local indexical designs and even the preferences of magazine editors provide occasion for alternative treatments. Nevertheless, it was commonly used, and its use was readily explained in terms of 'natural' considerations.[13]

(2) Pictures as narrative accounts

Astronomers do not simply show pictures; they juxtapose pictures with spoken and written text. 'Headers' are written for images, and stored in digital memory. They include names or numerical indices for sources, celestial coordinates, types of emission, filters, time, and observatory site.[14] In most cases, pictures are presented along with captions, and/or are discussed within the text of an article. Consistent with the quantitative/qualitative distinction discussed above, popularized captions make minimal use of numerical information, and consist largely of narratives. Although practitioners distinguish such narratives from the way the data are presented to disciplinary colleagues, they tell an evidently 'scientific' story.

Captions do not simply tell what is 'in' a picture: they orient viewers to similarities, contrasts, and other relevancies; they supply substantive identities for distinguishable features; and they supply metaphors, extrinsic connections, and genealogies which instruct viewers' understanding of what they are being shown. As suggested by the cliche, 'a picture is worth a thousand words,' it is common place to view captions as working off of information supplied in pictures, but digital image processing demonstrates that the opposite can just as readily obtain. The features of a picture can be adjusted to fit a caption. Note the following interchange between a researcher (A) preparing a series of slides and captions for a promotional exhibition, and her research assistant (B).

A: I'm actually playing around with Eta Carinae downstairs [where image processing equipment is located].
B: The uh – x-ray.
A: Yeah.
B: You don't like the x-ray.
A: Well, my caption says the x-ray looks a lot like the optical.
[B and A both laugh]
B: So, you're going to change the picture rather than change the caption.
A: Yeah.

It intrigued us how 'adjusting a picture to a caption' could be done. Researcher A showed us at the image processing equipment how she did this with X-ray data of Eta Carinae (a bright star associated with an emission nebula visible from the southern hemisphere). By adjusting the relationship between intensity and 'background' colouration (the range of intensities construed as dark in an image), she was able to contract or expand the apparently luminous shape of the emission nebula on the screen, so that its contours roughly approximated those shown in a separate optical image. This assimilated the picture to the caption, which asserted that the X-ray emissions resembled the optical (something that is not always the case):

> The X-ray image of the Carinae nebula is remarkably similar to that in optical light. The optically prominent nebula also is bright in X-rays and the major optically obscuring lanes also shadow the X-ray emission as well.

In colour palettes using contrasting colour contours, boundaries between adjacent colours can be adjusted across the range of intensities to selectively expose features. During a discussion of a specific illustration of a supernova remnant in an article he published in *Scientific American*,[15] an astronomer explains how he selected the candidate image (transcript, 21 August 1987):

M.L.: When you select a picture here, there's usually a caption and a bit of text that goes along with it. Do you, like with these sheets of possibilities that you have [a sheet of colour slides of differently processed images from the same data], do you ever look to what it is that you'll be talking about with this object for selecting the picture? For instance, the knots [relatively intense regions of emission within the supernova remnant] in this x-ray thing, so you'll want to have a picture where the knots show up in a very distinct colour.

S.: Yes, that picture was tailored to show all of the features we talked about. And we did talk about the fact that there are knots in it, and that it has a certain lumpiness that's important. We talked about this faint emission coming from the outermost region, and we talked about the very bright emission from within the ring here, and it turns out that this picture almost shows these things too well. By accident, the boundary between the blue and the yellow is the boundary between two different regions we were talking about. We were talking about this blue out here and we were talking about the region – the

emissions that come from this bright red. So, when the
editor read it he said, 'Aha, I see, one – the debris from
the star is yellow and the interstellar medium that's been
heated is blue.' And in fact they drew this picture here [a
diagram in the same article] showing that. And, we had to
say, 'Well, we didn't uh – Yes, that's what we're saying,
those yellow regions are probably stuff from the star, and
the blue is not.' But we didn't mean to make the picture
that way.

M.L.: When you say it shows it almost too well, are you saying
that in this picture not everything that's yellow or blue
corresponds to this theoretical –

S.: That's correct. It's not – If you look at this picture, you
say, 'Okay, there's a knot, this is ejected from the star,
and that's something else.' And that's not the case.

The editor had *seen* the boundary between contrasting colours
as marking a substantive division within the object, rather than as
a contour line on a map of gradually varying regions of brightness.
For this editor, colour contrast marked a substantive division
within the object's emissions. According to S., this bit of
misplaced concreteness was a productive misunderstanding, providing readers with at least *some* grasp of the astronomical issues:

S.: And actually, for this article and in the context of that
article, that's not bad. You could think about it that way
if you wanted to, but it's not what the picture actually
represents.

The ease with which digital image processing enables the
constitution of a picture to be flexibly manipulated allows pictures
of an object to be *made to refer* to narratives, as well as vice versa.
Pictures are sequentially developed, elaborated, and modified,
and their visible constituents are manipulated as elements of a
language referring to 'something else'. The tailoring of a picture is
not necessarily a mark against the integrity of its reference, since,
like any language, the indexical constituents of the image may be
used to *lead* as well as *mislead* the viewer's understanding, so that
the flexibility of the language's use is not inevitably linked to
deception.

The aesthetic basis of scientific images

An astronomer (D.) and his image processing assistant (E.) explain how they dealt with a troublesome problem, while reconstructing a sequence of image processing operations performed on a series of pictures of an 'artificial comet'. The comet was launched into the upper atmosphere in a study on the diffusion of emissions from its combustion and disintegration. The problem was that a series of vertical lines showed up in each image from the series. These were attributed to an unknown source of periodic noise, and proved recalcitrant to routine noise-suppression procedures (transcript, 8 July 1987):

E.: The noise is periodic.

D.: Ultimately we want to characterize the size of this [artificial comet] in terms of how many kilometers it was, how did it move, put an absolute grid in [celestial] coordinates on that. Fancy – there's a big long tail there – some fancy processing, to show up – to show up the features. Uh, we could almost do all of that with the lines there.

M.L.: Uh huh.

D.: But, the lines are distracting and its – we – we uh – don't want to show poor quality data. . . . We don't know why that happened, and it (hasn't happened) since then.

D. and E. explain a series of efforts to remove the alleged artifact. They encountered a variety of troubles with incomplete software documentation, including difficulties getting the software company to supply missing documentation on a Fourier transform package. M.L. then asks whether other astronomers would question their results if they were to publish the data without removing the lines.

D.: Probably not question the data but it's a . . . I'm watching my words, but it's an implicit sign, I think, of your competence.

M.L.: Uh huh.

D.: That if you publish those noisy pictures (   ) a crummy picture, (we'll know) what a crummy system that is. . . . Whether or not that carries over to your science, I don't know. We have a reputation here of publishing very high

205

> quality of pictures and graphics in colour. And we like those compliments and we like that reputation, so we worry about that. . . .
> I think the signal of the artificial comet is unmistakably there. And, we could probably do most of our science without that.

M.L.: Uh huh.

D.: But obviously we're spending a (considerable amount of time – several man months of effort simply cleaning up the data set into a more visually attractive one. Uh, not just the visual, say alone, but because it implies competence.

Note that D. maintains a distinction between efforts to 'clean up' the data to make the set of pictures more 'visually attractive', as opposed to what is required for 'doing the science'. But, in the case the 'aesthetic' work is oriented to a community of practitioners (as well as NASA administrators who sponsored the project), who are held to be capable of assessing the competence of the astronomer's work in reference to the appearance of published data.[16] Although distinguished in principle from 'the science,' the work of removing (in another astronomer's words) 'cosmetic defects' from the data was integrated with the totality of efforts to prepare the data for presentation to a professional audience.

'Cleaning the data' prepares the field for analysis. Astronomers do not normally view this work as 'aesthetic', since it includes some of the more routine operations they perform when working with digitized data. Typically, a few such operations are programmed into software functions which are called upon when digitized data are displayed on a monitor and rendered into analyzable and/or publishable data. A relatively simple sequence of such procedures, which we observed and documented, consisted of the following operations with optical data from a 24 inch telescope using a CCD detector (see Figures 3–6):[17]

(1) Subtracting bias-frame and flat field image. Whenever he makes a series of images with the detector, the astronomer takes a picture at zero exposure (bias-frame) and another out-of-focus picture of a uniform white patch inside the walls of the observatory (flat field). These are stored on tape and then subtracted from subsequent images in the series to correct for electronic noise and variations between sensitivities of different pixels on the detector. (See Figure 3.)

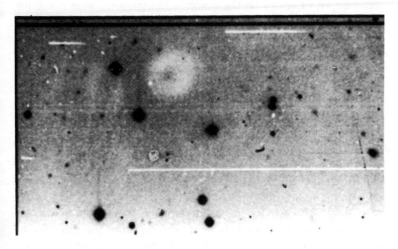

Figure 3 'Noisy' CCD Image

This figure shows 'raw data' from a CCD detector on a 24 inch optical telescope. The figure is a negative exposure, showing bright sources as dark against a light background. The image shows numerous 'cosmetic defects' attributed to various sources. These include electronic 'bias' (resulting in selective overexposure of pixels toward the lower part of the image), rows of 'burnt out' pixels (horizontal bright and dark lines), a spot of epoxy left on the detector from the manufacturing process (small light patch in right-centre of image, just above the bright horizontal line), and cosmic ray traces (small dark spots; larger, relatively circular dark spots are said to be stars). A sequence of procedures is used to 'clean up' these defects, resulting in image shown in Figure 4. (Figures 3, 4, 5, and 6 courtesy of Rudolph Schild, Harvard-Smithsonian Astrophysical Observatory.)

(2) 'Bootstrapping around cosmetic defects.' The astronomer has used the particular detector for the past six or seven years, and he has developed a routine sequence of procedures to deal with familiar artifacts arising from imperfections in the detector. These include horizontal lines attributed to rows of pixels that fail to activate, a spot of epoxy on the detector left from the manufacturing process which dampens the sensitivity of the pixels below it, and impacts of cosmic rays on the plate while it was exposed. Some of these exhibit characteristic profiles which are detected by pre-programmed software functions and then automatically replaced with background values. Others are 'painted out' by hand by copying an area of background sky over the profile of the cosmetic defect. (See Figure 4.)

(3) Image sharpening program. This works to consolidate a signal[18] in selected regions of the field and 'bring out' previously invisible detail. It is one of several methods through which images can be enhanced and restored. In theory (although the assumptions and mathematics remain controversial), it should improve the resolution of an astronomical source beyond that of the particular telescope used to detect it. It aims to compensate for atmospheric diffusion of signal, imperfect telescope optics, and tracking errors. (See Figures 5 and 6.)

The procedure works on the assumption that a bright star should, ideally, be visible from earth as a discrete, high intensity, point. The image sharpening program develops a point-spread function for a profile of a bright star the user selects within the field of the image. Assuming that this function represents diffusion and distortion of incident light throughout the field, the program can then use that function as a template for de-convolving images of other sources; in effect, extracting aspects of the local observational situation from selected sites in the field observed. Diffuse sources should become brighter and more sharply bounded as scattered emissions are, in theory, restored to their proper sites in the array of pixels.

Practical Cartesianism
While some of these procedures were described as 'cosmetic' in effect, and some of the steps (such as removing cosmic rays) are occasionally omitted when photometric readings are taken, they can also enhance the observable and measurable properties of the data. Signal is progressively discriminated from background, illumination is spatially consolidated (especially with the image

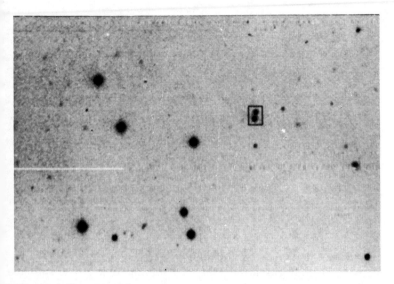

Figure 4 Processed image
Many of the 'defects' shown in Figure 2 have been removed
through a sequence of operations, including subtraction of 'bias
frame' and 'flat field' images, removal of cosmic ray traces,
replacement of horizontal lines and other 'burnt out' pixels with
background 'sky' values. A box cursor is drawn around image (in
upper right), believed to be that of the twin QSO 0957+561, first
discovered in 1979. The double image is believed to result from
a 'gravitational lensing' effect, where a point source (a distant
quasi-stellar object) is 'lensed' by an intervening galaxy whose
gravitation bends the light from QSO, resulting in a double
image. The sector of the image framed by the box cursor is shown
enlarged in Figures 5 and 6.

209

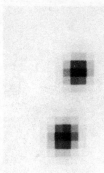

Figure 5 Twin QSO before image sharpening
This is an enlargement of the sector of Figure 4 framed by the box
cursor. The image shows that each of the two bright sources
(believed to be the double-image of the twin QSO resulting from
gravitational lensing) cover an area of several pixels, and that
the intensities are diffused. This is the condition of the image
prior to the running of an 'image sharpening' procedure. This
procedure utilizes a program for consolidating intensities around
the presumed point source, thus enhancing the resolution of the
image. The program is based on assumptions about the difference
between the point-spread function of a hypothetical point source
and that of a bright star represented in the particular image. It is a
way of 'subtracting' presumed distortions arising from atmospheric
diffusion and telescope optics.

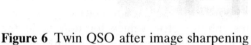

Figure 6 Twin QSO after image sharpening
This picture shows the result of several iterations of the image
sharpening procedure. Although the procedure is controversial,
explication of the resulting image can provide documentary
support for its presumed enhancement of resolution. The uppermost (or northern) image of the twin QSO is compacted into four
pixels, while the lower (or southern) image appears more diffused.
This is consistent with previous observations with more powerful
telescopes and with astrophysical analysis of the particular object,
where the southern component is believed to pass through the
galaxy. The more diffuse appearance could result from a combination of scattering effects and superimposition of radiation from
the galaxy on the QSO image. Other diffuse structure near
the southern component was said to be background 'noise'
consolidated by the image sharpening procedure.

sharpening procedure) and assigned to thematic profiles. Meanwhile, visually intrusive projections from the detection system are 'subtracted' from the field. A *practical* Cartesian operation takes place, aiming to establish, and visually articulate, a *cut* between objective sources of radiation, and transient conditions of the observing situation.[19] The procedures amount to an externalized, technically accomplished, 'perceptual' process, which, in the words of one astronomer, constitute a program for 'seeing the physics'.

Does it make sense to speak of these practices as having an 'aesthetic' orientation? Such an orientation is manifest in the concerns with 'cosmetic defects', but is it fair to say that the various manipulations of signal-noise ratios and of image sharpening involve 'aesthetics'? These procedures are systematically designed, carefully operated, and justified by good reasons, such as: a knowledge of detector electronics and of the peculiarities of the observational instrumentation; an assessment of astronomical entities and of their characteristic profiles; a reliance on previously established coordinates, photometric values for objects in the field; and various other local applications of physics, mathematics, and computer science.

Without denying any of these rationales for routine image processing, we nevertheless can speak of the progressive reconstitution of a 'noisy picture' into a visually coherent and naturally interpreted astronomical display as an aesthetic project. But, what aesthetics means here is not a domain of beauty or expression which is detached from representational realism. Instead, it is the very fabric of realism: the work of composing visible coherences, discriminating differences, consolidating entities, and establishing evident relations. These perceptual relations take place through a *crafting* of gestalt contextures, where relational elements in any configuration are manipulated through image processing machinery and software. This hands-on process of 'interpretation' can be treated as an *art* situated within the performance of scientific practice.

Conclusion

What does our study, at this point, suggest about the relations between science and art? When we began this project, we were intrigued by the blocky form and contrastive colours in false-colour digitized images, and these features recalled the abstraction of colour and form in expressionist and related modernist art.[20] Could it be the case that, as in earlier epochs (Edgerton, 1986b: 184), modern scientists are 'packaging' their representations in terms of currently fashionable formats and colour schemes in order to entice readers (both other scientists, and members of other publics) to appreciate their achievements?[21] We aimed to discover whether astronomers explicitly or implicitly relied upon aesthetic sensibilities and representational conventions developed earlier in the art world, and we figured that we might shed light on this by interviewing astronomers and observing how they compose and interpret astronomical images.

As yet, we have not found much evidence on biographical or cultural linkages between 'artistic' experiences and 'scientific' accomplishment. While it may very well be the case that particular astronomers borrow from their experience with artistic training, or from their exposure to gallery exhibitions and popular art, more complex relations between modern art and science also seem to prevail. Such relations are suggested in astronomers' use and explication of a distinction between 'aesthetics' and 'science'. Our analysis of this distinction is summarized as follows:

(1) When speaking in the abstract, astronomers use the term 'aesthetics' in a modern sense, where aesthetics is abstracted from practical realism and dissociated from efforts to make a picture *show* its astrophysical content.

(2) A division of labour between 'the science' and making 'pretty pictures' for public display reproduces the modern dissociation between art and science.[22]

(3) While the distinction between 'the science' and 'pretty pictures' seems at first to suggest that arrangements of colour and form in popularized illustrations are made simply to 'please the eye', when expressing their own 'aesthetic' preferences[23] astronomers explicate visible detail in substantive astrophysical terms. Rather than expressing something *other* than an aesthetic understanding of a picture, such narrative explications of compositional detail reveal an intimate association between science and a *particular* version of aesthetics emphasizing the simplicity, 'graphical elegance', and representational utility of compositional detail.[24]

(4) Ethno-methodologically,[25] routine preparations of images, bootstrapping around cosmetic defects, and 'seeing the physics' fulfil the traditional purpose of art, which, as Gadamer (1984: 74) describes it, is a perfecting of nature, removing sources of obscurity:

[Kantian aesthetics] had far-reaching consequences. For now art, as the art of beautiful appearance, was contrasted with practical reality and understood in terms of this contrast. Instead of art and nature complementing each other, as had always seemed to be the case, they were contrasted as appearance and reality. Traditionally it is the purpose of 'art', which also embraces all the conscious transformation of nature for use by humans, to complete its supplementing and fulfilling activity within the areas given and left free by nature. And 'les beaux arts', as long as they are seen in this framework, are a perfecting of reality and not an external masking, veiling or transfiguration of it. But if the contrast between reality and appearance determines the concept of art, this breaks up the inclusive framework of nature. Art becomes a standpoint of its own and establishes its own autonomous claim to supremacy.

The members' distinction has pragmatic value in the sense that it marks a division between organizational contexts; a separation between works and the audiences for which they are designed. At the same time, we recommend, on ethnographic grounds, that the distinction be treated as a division between modern and traditional modes of aesthetics.[26] What we now call science sustains an ancient art: a crafting of natural resemblances; an 'art' which is practised as *mere technique* without 'aesthetic' pretensions (in the modern sense). To call it *art* is to belie modern usage, and (within modern usage) to misleadingly abstract it from its ordinary practical utility.

Astronomers do not take up the modern artistic challenge, as they have no interest in completely abstracting art from natural representation. If, indeed, astronomers make use of colour and other elements of composition as abstractable representational media, rather than as mirrored properties of objects,[27] they do so as committed realists, aiming to endow their compositions with naturalistic adequacy.

Scientists are unlikely to understand their ordinary practice as deeply 'aesthetic' in orientation, since this would require a profound change not only in *their* understanding of aesthetics, but in the modern conception as well. To do so would require that they (and we) no longer associate aesthetics exclusively with subjectivity, so that 'aesthetics' would now draw attention to how the materials through which a craft is embodied lend form and substance to the objects revealed. This also requires a re-understanding of art, where art consists of placing things in a form and on a scale fitted to human practice and social interaction. Nevertheless, examination of the detailed production of visual displays in science suggests to us that science may have taken over the original sense of *techne*, while professional art has become dissociated from traditional representational concerns.

Acknowledgement

We are grateful to Professors Michael Mendillo and Jeff Baum-gartner, and image processing specialist Bin Chuang of the Boston University Astronomy Department; and Professors Matthew Schneps, Rudy Schild, Fred Seward, Christine Jones and Dan Harris of the Harvard-Smithsonian Astrophysics Laboratory. Their cooperation, patient explanations of their projects, and generous offers of their visual materials for our documentary purposes, made this study possible. We also would like to thank the National Endowment for Humanities for awarding a summer stipend to one of the authors in 1987.

Notes

1 See Latour (1986) for a general discussion of social studies of scientific 'visualisation'. Also see edited collections by Latour and De Noblet (1985), and Lynch and Woolgar (1988).
2 According to one of our informants, development of image processing capabilities offers strategic advantages. A CCD detector mounted on a small telescope, when used in conjunction with state-of-the-art image processing equipment and software, enables an astronomer to upgrade images to be comparable to those taken at a much larger observatory. Observing time is scarce and highly competitive at the largest optical observatories, and it is difficult to gain extended observing time without considerable 'political' clout. Much freer access to a smaller observatory enables the particular astronomer to pursue a project requiring repeated observation of a single source on successive clear nights for several weeks at a time. Investment in image processing provided an alternative pathway for technological development to the building of larger ground-based detectors and orbiting observatories.
3 Accounts of the transformation of astronomy in recent decades include Edge and Mulkay (1976) and Hirsh (1983). Articles on the development of CCDs and the impact of digital image processing on astronomy include Amelio (1974), Sulentic and Lorre (1984); and Janesik and Blouke (1987).
4 Research in summer 1987 was funded by a National Endowment for the Humanities Summer Stipend (awarded to Michael Lynch, Ref: FT-29556-87). We are grateful to NEH for this support.
5 Such equipment was 'state of the art' for astronomy, though not necessarily for e.g., the military, where advances in image processing technology are supported by much larger budgets. Although astronomers tailor the equipment and software to their own specialized purposes, some of the technologies were

    originally developed for use in spy satellites. Image processing is also used in telecommunications, and medicine.

6 Some software packages are pre-packaged. Frequently used packages are the Astronomical Image Processing System (AIPS), developed by The National Radio Astronomy Observatory, and The IRAF Data Reduction and Analysis System. Adaptations of these software packages, as well as more specialized programs are developed on site by astronomers and their technical assistants.

7 For our purposes, the signal-noise distinction is a practical accomplishment, not a given. Digital image processing enables practitioners to discriminate and suppress features believed to be artefacts. Numerous software functions are used with a local orientation to gestalt properties of the data at hand. Numerous practical guides to image processing are available. See Baxes (1984) for an introduction to some general image processing functions.

8 Rosenfeld and Kak (1982, Ch. 3) relate image processing functions to gestalt 'laws' of visual perception. See Lynch, Livingston and Garfinkel (1983) for discussion of the gestalt themes as technical achievements of embodied scientific work. In further research, we intend to develop our account of how astronomers compose gestalt properties through image processing.

9 The interviews included repeated discussions with two researchers and an image processing specialist at one facility; and five researchers and two assistants at the other facility. These astronomers specialized in different areas. Some mainly worked in the optical spectrum, while others specialized in radio, X-ray, and infra-red astronomy. Some studied characteristics of the earth's ionosphere while others performed astrophysical research on objects in deep space, such as supernova remnants, quasi-stellar objects, and galaxy clusters. Interviews and conversations were tape recorded, and transcribed portions quoted in this paper are indexed by the interview date.

10 One astronomer remarked to us during summer 1986 that the current generation's experience of Halley's comet (which had recently 'visited' the night sky) was dominated by the many false colour and colour enhanced versions that were published in the popular press (the naked-eye view was notably unremarkable). Similarly, Young (1985) notes that the highly publicized pictures of Jupiter, Saturn, and their moons reconstructed from the Voyageur probe signals were colour enhanced, and that these enhanced colours are now widely thought by the public to be the 'real' colours of the planets. Young tries to redress what he sees to be a problem by publishing reconstructed 'true colour' versions of the Voyageur pictures, so that Jupiter's moon Io (the famous actively volcanic moon) no longer is pizza coloured, taking on a more subdued yellowish hue.

11 We do not yet have a clear impression on how the 'conventional palette' became established. It is possible that designers of software packages had a hand in establishing it, but we have yet to determine if this is the case.

12 In this remark, the astronomer distinguishes the 'appeal' of a colour separate from its representational function. Although, as we have argued, most stated preferences for colours or colour schemes were explained in reference to what could be said or shown with the picture, astronomers did sometimes mention other considerations. Another astronomer mentioned that she preferred bright contrasting colours for false-colour slides, in part because they remain vivid when projected in lecture halls where lights cannot always be completely dimmed.

13 Magazine editors were said to prefer bright 'flashy' colours, without regard to their naturalistic interpretation, while astronomers expressed preferences for the 'conventional' palette and/or monochromatic schemes. Some astronomers expressed distaste for flash for its own sake, associating it with vulgar tastes. This distinction reminds us of Gombrich's (1963: 17) discussion of the renunciation of glitter in Renaissance art:

Boccaccio celebrates Giotto as the painter who 'had brought back to light that art that had been buried for centuries under the errors of those *who painted rather to delight the eyes of the ignorant than to please the intellect of the wise.*' This contrast between a low kind of art that appeals to the eyes of the simple-minded and a 'higher' form that can be appreciated only by the cultured, becomes a commonplace of criticism in the sixteenth and seventeenth centuries. (Quotation from G. Boccaccio, *Decamerone, Giornata, VI Novella, 5.*) (Emph. in orig.)

Astronomers distinguish 'aesthetics' from 'the science' in a re-assertion of this classic polarity between high and low art, except that they identify 'art' only with the 'low' or popularized form, and they place the 'higher' form entirely outside the domain of art.

14 One practical problem for designing headers is to select colours in a palette for the text and graphic overlay which do not grade into those representing the constituents in the visible field. A numerical range (within 0–256) is reserved for the graphics, while the remainder is assigned to intensities within the field. This problem of the colour of graphic lines and labels emerges, since digitization places text and visual object on the same ground, so that a separation between text, indices, and visible thing need to be explicitly designed rather than taken for granted.

15 Since, interestingly enough, we are precluded from publishing colour pictures in this journal, we refer readers to the colour illustrations in the *Scientific American* article discussed in this transcript (Seward, Gorenstein and Tucker, 1985). Colour images discussed in the transcript are on pp. 90 and 91 of the article, and the editor's hand-drawn 'model' is on p. 92.

16 Lynch (1985a: 94ff.) in a study of laboratory practices describes how neuroscientists spoke of 'lookers' and 'users' when distinguishing publicly presentable electron micrographs from artefact-ridden micrographs which nonetheless could be used for research purposes.

17 This sequence of procedures is far more complicated than we have presented it here. In further work, we intend to analyze the sequential organization of such preparatory procedures.

18 As stated earlier (note 7) 'signal' is members' usage, implying a coherent source, discriminable from other possible sources. Such usage does not guarantee that in any case such discrimination can be made with certainty; indeed, the image sharpening procedure was quite controversial, and the astronomer using it stated that some of his colleagues consider it to be 'black magic'.

19 The 'cut' does not negotiate a boundary between objectivity and subjectivity in the usual sense, since evidently 'objective' sources are removed. These include cosmic rays, diffused light in the atmosphere, and optical and electronic effects from the instrumentation, all of which are provisionally and thematically placed on the proximal side of the 'cut'.

20 Some of the art associated with the Bauhaus movement (Whitford, 1984) seemed formally akin to digital images. For discussions on resemblances between modern science and art see Waddington, 1970 and Vitz and Glimcher, 1984. These are discussed in Edgerton, 1985: 28, and Lynch, 1985c.

21 It is widely believed that scientists work exclusively for their peers. For instance, Cavell (1986: 172) notes that while artists make their works available to a public:

Scientists, on the other hand, do not work for a public but exclusively for their peers. (I leave aside the question of their clientele or patronage.) Science can be said to have no public, only beneficiaries or victims.

In contrast, our study indicates that scientists view colleagues in their fields as one sort of 'public', and also devote a great deal of effort to producing work for 'patrons' (like NASA) and other general audiences.

22 As we view it, this dissociation is not so much between different professional cultures as it is between aesthetic standards associated with different audiences.
23 The tie between visible features and astrophysical 'content' is also revealed when astronomers denigrate others' pictures as exhibiting unnecessary features.
24 As stated above (note 13), the members' distinction between science and aesthetics may be viewed as a version of a distinction between 'high' and 'low' art, where 'mere sensory appeal' is associated with the 'low' or vulgar. Emblematic expression of such an 'aesthetic' preference is found in Tufte's (1983: 177ff.) discussion of the aesthetics of data graphical design. Tufte states a clear injunction to 'avoid content-free decoration', including what he calls 'chartjunk' – gratuitous design elements which dress up a chart. Note, that for him, 'non-decorative' design expresses an aesthetic, and not an absence of aesthetics.
25 The term ethnomethodology was coined by Garfinkel (1967) to refer to the 'methodologies' inherent in ordinary practices. The term is now associated with a sub-discipline of sociology, but in this passage, we wish to invoke the original motive for the term, with its orientation to methodology as a discoverable phenomenon. In this case, we are not speaking of scientific methodology as it might be formulated in astronomy, but to a larger totality of order-productive practices in ordinary scientific work.
26 Gadamer (1984: 75) attributes the division to science's hegemony:
    The shift of the ontological definition of the aesthetic to the sphere of aesthetic appearance has its theoretical basis in the fact that the domination of the scientific epistemological model leads to the discrediting of all the possibilities of knowing that lie outside this new method.
    To this we can add that science, at the same time, embodies the traditional aesthetic, leaving art with the residue.
27 Alpers (1983: 27ff.) argues for a connection between the descriptivist realism of seventeenth century Dutch painting and the development of optical instruments, particularly the camera obscura. The camera obscura framed and projected an image as a complete scene whose visible details could be copied on a canvas. Today we see a decomposition of scenes into atomic pixels, and a treatment of such elements as manipulable graphemes. The image can neither be viewed as a copy not a simulation, but as a realist narrative produced through contextures of graphemes.

Bibliography

Alpers, Svetlana (1983), *The Art of Describing: Dutch Art in the 17th Century*, University of Chicago Press.
Amann, Klaus and Knorr-Cetina, K. (1988), 'The fixation of visual evidence,' *Human Studies*, *11*(2–3).
Amelio, Gilbert F. (1974), 'Charge-coupled devices', *Scientific American*, *230*(2): 399.
Barnes, S. B. (1974), *Scientific Knowledge and Sociological Theory*, London, Routledge and Kegan Paul.
Baxes, Gregory (1984), *Digital Image Processing: A Practical Primer*, Englewood Cliffs, N.J., Prentice Hall.
Bloor, David (1976), *Knowledge and Social Imagery*, London, Routledge and Kegan Paul.
Cavell, Stanley (1986), 'Observations on art and science', *Daedalus*, *115*(3): 171–7.
Collins, Harry (1985), *Changing Order: Replication and Induction in Scientific Practice*, London, Sage.

Edge, David and Mulkay, Michael (1976), *Astronomy Transformed: The Emergence of Radio Astronomy in Britain*, New York, Wiley.

Edgerton, Samuel (1976), *The Renaissance Rediscovery of Linear Perspective*, New York, Harper & Row.

Edgerton, Samuel (1984), 'Galileo, Florentine *disegno*, and the 'Strange Spotted-nesse' of the moon', *Art Journal*, *44*, 3.

Edgerton, Samuel (1985), 'The function of artistic form in the study of the stars', *Celestial Images: Astronomical Charts from 1500 to 1900*, Catalogue of an Exhibition, Boston University Art Gallery, January 23–March 25.

Edgerton, Samuel (1986a), 'The Renaissance development of the scientific illustration', in J. Shirley and D. Hoeniger, (eds), *Science and the Arts in the Renaissance: A Symposium at the Folger Shakespeare Library*, Washington D.C.

Edgerton, Samuel (1986b), 'Observations on art and science', *Daedalus*, *115*(3): 182–6.

Gadamer, Hans-Georg (1984), *Truth and Method*, New York, Crossroad Publishing Company.

Garfinkel, Harold (1967), *Studies in Ethnomethodology*, Englewood Cliffs, N.J., Prentice Hall.

Garfinkel, Harold, Lynch, Michael and Livingston, Eric (1981), 'The work of a discovering science construed with materials from the optically discovered pulsar', *Philosophy of the Social Sciences*, *11*: 131–58.

Giedion, Sigfried (1948), *Mechanization Takes Command*, Oxford, Oxford University Press.

Gombrich, E H. (1963), *Meditations on a Hobby Horse and Other Essays on the Theory of Art*, Chicago, University of Chicago Press.

Gooding, David (1986), 'How do scientists reach agreement about novel observations?', *Studies in the History and Philosophy of Science*, *17*.

Graubard, S. R. (1986), 'Preface' to *Art and Science*, special issue of *Daedalus*, *115*(3), v–xvii.

Gregory, R. L. (1966), *Eye and Brain*. London: World University Library.

Henderson, Linda Dalrymple (1983), *The Fourth Dimension and Non-Euclidian Geometry in Modern Art*, Princeton, N. J., Princeton University Press.

Hirsh, Richard F. (1983), *Glimpsing the Invisible Universe;* Cambridge, Cambridge University Press.

Ivins, William (1953), *Prints and Visual Communication*, London, Routledge and Kegan Paul.

Jamesick, J. and Blouke, B. (1987), 'Sky on a chip: the fabulous CCD', *Sky and Telescope*, *74*(3): 238–42.

Knorr-Cetina, Karin (1981), *The Manufacture of Knowledge*, Oxford, Pergamon Press.

Kuhn, Thomas (1977), 'Comment on the relation of science and art', pp. 340–51 of *The Essential Tension: Selected Studies in Scientific Tradition and Change*. Chicago: University of Chicago Press.

Latour, Bruno and Woolgar, Steve (1979), *Laboratory Life: The Social Construction of Scientific Facts*, London, Sage.

Latour, Bruno (1986), 'Visualisation and cognition', *Knowledge and Society*, *6*: 1–40.

Latour, Bruno, and De Noblette, J. (eds) (1985), *Les Vues de L'Esprit*, special issue of *Culture Technique*, *14*.

Lynch, Michael (1985a), *Art and Artifact in Laboratory Science: A Study of Shop Work and Shop Talk in a Research Laboratory*, London, Routledge and Kegan Paul.

Lynch, Michael (1985b), 'Discipline and the material form of images: An analysis of scientific visibility', *Social Studies of Science*, *15* (1).

Lynch, Michael (1985c), 'Aesthetic horizons of scientific observation,' paper presented at *The Uses of Experiment: A Conference on Experimentation in the Natural Sciences*, Newton Park, Bath, England (Aug. 31–Sept. 2).

Lynch, Michael, Livingston, Eric and Garfinkel, Harold (1983), 'Temporal order in laboratory work', in K. Knorr Cetina and M. Mulkay (eds), *Science Observed*, London, Sage.

Lynch, Michael and Woolgar, Steve (eds) (1988), *Representation in Scientific Work*, special issue of *Human Studies*, *11*(2–3).

Mulkay, Michael (1979), *Science and the Sociology of Knowledge*. London, George Allen and Unwin.

Rosenfeld, Azriel and Kak, A. C. (1982), *Digital Picture Processing, Volume One*, New York, Academic Press.

Rudwick, Martin J. S. (1976), 'The emergence of a visual language for geological science 1760–1840', *History of Science*, *14*: 149–95.

Seward, Frederick, Gorenstein, Paul and Tucker, W. H. (1985), 'Young Supernova Remnants', *Scientific American*, *252*(2): 88–96.

Shapin, Steven (1984), 'Pump and Circumstance: Robert Boyle's literary technology', *Social Studies of Science*, *14*: 481–521.

Steinberg, Leo (1986), 'Art and science: do they need to be yoked?' *Daedalus*, *115*(3): 1–16.

Sulentic, Jack W. and Lorre, J. J. (1984), 'The magic of image processing', *Sky and Telescope* (May): 407–11.

Tilling, Laura (1975), 'Early experimental graphs', *The British Journal for the History of Science*, *8*.

Tufte, Edward R. (1983), *The Visual Display of Quantitative Information*, Cheshire, Conn., Graphics Press.

Vitz, Paul and Glimcher, Arnold (1984), *Modern Art and Modern Science A Parallel Analysis of Vision*, New York, Praeger.

Waddington, C. H. (1970), *Behind Appearance*, Cambridge, MIT Press.

Whitford, Frank (1984), *Bauhaus*, London, Thames & Hudson.

Young, Andrew T. (1985), 'What color is the solar system?' *Sky and Telescope* (May): 399.

Yoxen, Edward (1987), 'Seeing with sound: a study of the development of medical images', in W. E. Bijker, T. P. Hughes, and T. J. Pinch (eds), *The Social Construction of Technological Systems: New Directions in the Sociology and History of Technology*, Cambridge, MA, the MIT Press.

Pictures from the subsoil, 1939

Geof Bowker

Abstract

In this paper, an anatomy is given of the ambiguous representations of the subsoil produced by the Schlumberger Company during the 1930s. In 'normal' scientific work, ambiguities are carefully concealed so that the visual depictions that accompany a text lend it authority and give it the appearance of clarity. However, in a patent trial instigated by Schlumberger over electrical methods of picturing the subsoil adjacent to oil wells, sharp relief is thrown on the shading of information. In particular, we see that it was in the interests of Schlumberger and their rivals to produce graphics open to multiple interpretation, and that the juggling and control of these was a conscious part of their work – and indeed necessary to their survival.

Introduction

Anyone who has ever dug a hole in a piece of muddy ground knows that what comes out on the other end of the spade is messy, inhomogeneous and – assuming you would want to – pretty difficult to describe. As you dig, the sides of the hole start caving in and as your spade comes up it often scrapes the side of the hole – so that what you get is not a pure sample of the level you are excavating but includes an indeterminate amount of other stuff. Those who drill oil wells are faced with an aggravated version of this. For them, it is no idle exercise to try to describe the dig inch by inch; the location of oil-bearing strata and the optimal exploitation of an oil field hang on the result. However, the holes they dig are deep: in 1939 in America they would frequently reach 6,000 feet. Further, a 'driller's mud' is kept circulating through them so as to prevent blowouts and clear away the cuttings just made. Early attempts to physically take samples of the strata the drill bit was passing stumbled against the problem that this turbulent fluid would often leach the very oil you were interested in from the specimen.

During the 1930s 'electrical logging', a means of picturing the subsoil in terms of the electrical activity around the drill bit, came increasingly to replace attempts to take samples. In fact, it led to a curious reversal whereby getting your hands dirty by sampling the oil sand was seen as providing useful psychological reassurance and getting an electrical log was the real material evidence. A consulting petroleum engineer brought this out in 1939:

> It is a very peculiar situation. Many of these people have a feeling that they want to look at it, and to the so-called practical oil man that maybe was a driller and now is an independent operator, a lot of wiggly lines don't mean so much to him as seeing something taken out of the ground. So it is quite frequent that they take cores that I don't particularly care about their taking. Q. Why do they want to look at the mechanical cores that they take? A. To make them feel better, to see the oil sand, I guess. Q. And that is the only reason that they take them, so that they can feel better when they see the oil sand? A. I try to talk them out of it quite frequently, and often they say 'Well I will feel better if I look at it'. (*Trial* 7: 87)

The electrical logs that were the new material baseline produced kicks in a graph that were arguably easier to interpret than shovelfulls of mud (compare Figure 1 and Figure 2). Yet we have a recursion problem here. What the logs did better than sample-takers was picture the subsoil, yet how could you check the reality of this assessment without introducing a third, objective, method of picturing (welcome to the hall of mirrors)? In this paper, we will look at how differing claims about what was actually being pictured by the electrical logs were adjudicated in the courtroom by looking at a case for patent infringement brought by *Schlumberger*, pioneers of electrical logging, against *Halliburton*, who entered the field later using methods that may or may not have been the same.

The theoretical interest for the sociologist of science of describing the anatomy of a courtroom controversy about visualisation procedures is twofold. First, we will get a way of analysing visualisation problems that is the actors' own – though not of course theirs only. The advantages of using the actors' own terms have been enumerated in work by Latour (1987) and Callon (1986) among others. These come down largely to the observation that if we start applying our own descriptive categories to scientific controversies, we are ineluctably drawn into judging the controversy.

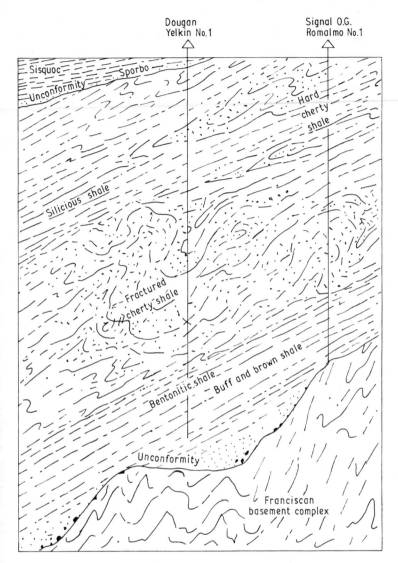

Figure 1 Detail diagram of oil-bearing layer

Some reasons for this will come out in the course of this paper: the general problem is that our own categories have an implicit or explicit way of dividing-up reality, of deciding what truth is, and thus enter directly into the dispute we are attempting to give an account of. They lead us directly or tortuously – depending on how

223

relativist we are trying to be – into prejudging the issue. One way of suspending our own categories is to 'follow the actors' (Latour 1987) and use their language alone. As we follow them into the courtroom we will see them render explicit a whole range of factors – social, scientific, political – that inevitably escape analyses of scientific papers and normally escape laboratory

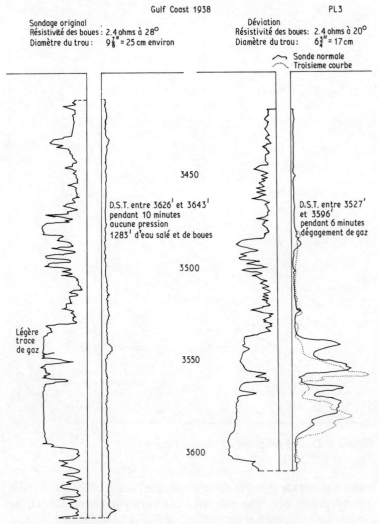

Figure 2 Schlumberger demonstration that electrical logging can be more precise than sample-taking

studies with their emphasis more on the 'black-boxing' of facts (how scientific facts get to seem so much more objective than aesthetic taste) than on attempts to re-open boxes that seem black. The second theoretical interest stems from the fact that we will get accounts that span the oil industry of what the actors thought that the 'curves' (the electrical logs) in front of them measured. In general, studies of science have an implicit belief that what really counts is what the scientists ultimately conclude and then reify into scientific discovery – a single, unproblematic fact or a single, unproblematic black box depending on one's point of view. We will see that there was a variety of possible interpretations of the curves that *Schlumberger*, sold and that part of the work that *Schlumberger* did was precisely to maintain that variety in place. They did not seek to hold a mirror to nature, they sought to create a sufficiently ambiguous visual representation of the subsoil to hold in place the network of often conflicting interests that they dealt with.

The naming of the curve

The counsels for neither the plaintiff nor the defence in the case *Schlumberger* vs *Halliburton* would have been happy with the idea of holding a mirror to nature. Indeed, they spent a deal of time discoursing on the meaning of the word 'nature'. *Schlumberger* was bringing a suit against *Halliburton* for the infringement of the two patents used in their electrical well-logging activities. These patents described configurations of electrodes that gave rise, through a series of intermediaries, to a moving shadow which an operator followed with a pencil as a scroll of paper unfurled to the rhythm of the sinking of the electrodes in an oil well. The title of the first patent contained the fateful word: 'Electrical Process and Apparatus for the Determination of the Nature of the Geological Formations Traversed by Drill Holes' (US Patent 1, 819, 923).

Commenting on the title for the prosecution, Campbell tells us that we cannot expect too much from the 'resistivity curve' (or 'log') described by one of the patents:

> One of the things I want to comment on there is the word 'nature'. The word 'nature' in that title does not mean and could not mean, at all events, that this man by this method was going to get a signal up on his recording sheet, the log, which would spell o-i-l, oil, or s-a-n-d, sand. He knew that. (*Trial*, 10: 23)[1]

225

Drawing on the authority of Webster's Universal Dictionary (the 1935 edition), Campbell took 'nature' as 'distinguishing qualities', and 'to determine' as 'to mark the boundaries of' – so that the damning phrase 'determination of the nature of' became 'demarcation of the boundaries of some distinguishing qualities' (*Trial*, 10: 24–5). The defence, trying to drive a wedge claim and curve, argued (also using Webster's) that 'nature' meant 'kind' (*Trial*, 15: 2019–20). You could only get 'nature' in a homogeneous medium untroubled by a drill hole – viz in the laboratory (*Trial*, 15: 1840–8). Homogeneous media did not exist in the real world, and the act of drilling was sufficiently intrusive as to constitute an exacerbated case of what we might call the observer paradox:

> when you drill the well you are doing considerable violence to the earth. For one thing, the strata have been in place for many years; and have had time to become rigid and have a stable equilibrium, as nature always tries to do, and when a well is drilled through this strata there is extreme disturbance. It is analogous to sticking a knife or a sword through a person's flesh. You do a lot of things. You tear out some of the formation, and you put in for the time being a fluid, a drilling mud, which is quite different in temperature from the formation! (*Trial*, 13: 1098–9)

Thus for *Halliburton*, the curves could possibly tell you about the unacceptable face of drilling but they could not be tracing out the noble features of nature, which existed either in a laboratory or beyond the pale of civilisation – but nowhere in between. For *Schlumberger*, the measuring device occupied precisely the middle ground between the two:

> Some people . . . think of it as a news reporter who travels in strange lands. Certainly these lands are strange down the drill hole. That reporter sends back cable messages as to what he observes. . . . So this little reporter goes down that drill hole on that unpleasant journey and reports back constantly each strange land that it traverses in terms of its electrical characteristics, which we call 'resistivity' here. (*Trial*, 10: 18)

Thus where nature was and what it had to do with the curves under consideration had to do with who was asking the question.

So we cannot simply say what the curves pictured. Let us see in

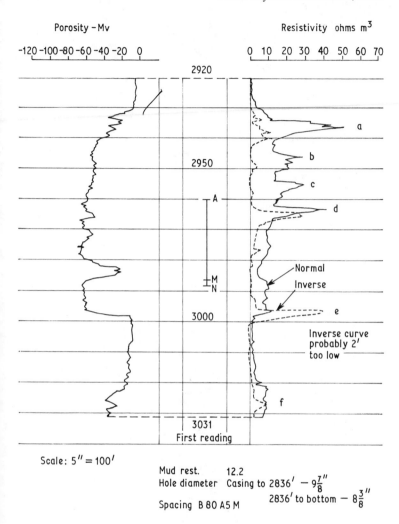

Figure 3 Porosity curve, normal curve and inverse curve

more detail how they were taken and what they were claimed to picture. Here I will be giving a popular science account from *Schlumberger*'s angle: it will itself come under criticism later by the protagonists in the trial. The first curve, the resistivity curve, worked on the principle that measurements of the resistance of a given volume of soil to having current passed through it give an indication of whether there are highly conductive layers (for example strata containing salt water or various metals) or resistant

227

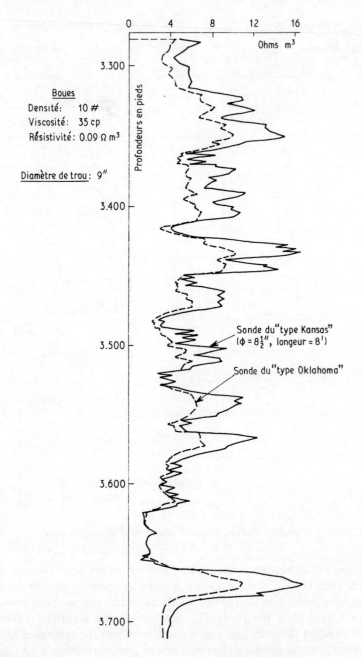

Figure 4 Typical resistivity curve – different measuring devices give different curves

228

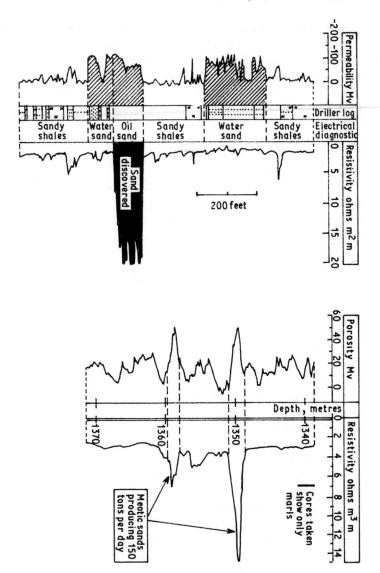

Figure 5 Changes in resistivity and spontaneous potential

layers (for example those bearing oil, which is highly resistant). It was obtained by throwing an electrode into the driller's mud to the side of the well-hole in order to ground it, and lowering a second electrode into the well to be logged. An electrical current was then

229

sent between the two electrodes, which were known as 'B' and 'A' respectively in all of *Schlumberger*'s literature. Two subsidiary electrodes, christened 'M' and 'N', were lowered with A into the well – M and N were fairly close to each other and above A in the case of the normal log and below it in the case of the inverse (Figure 3 and Figure 4). A potentiometer at the surface of the well measured the difference in potential between M and N as they descended the well, and the resultant log was a tracing of the quivering of this potentiometer's needle. A kick in the curve was interpreted to mean a change in the resistivity of the strata traversed by M and N (Figure 5).[2] The greatest difficulty with recording this first curve came in part from the fact that, as Dr Rust pointed out, great violence had been done unto the earth, and consequently a series of stray electrical currents were created by the interaction between the driller's mud and the immediate environs of the well caused by electrochemical reactions and electrofiltration (*Proselec*, Nov. 1936). These had to be countered – as did telluric currents caused by a range of factors including magnetic disturbances, sunspots, cosmic rays and trolley buses (Bowker, 1987). The method employed was that as the electrodes were lowered, an operator would hover over the potentiometer; and bring it regularly back to an artificial base line (called zero) in between surges of current.

This first curve stood on its own for several years. For some terrains, the resistivity curve was useful for the discovery of oil sands, which had a much higher resistivity than sands bearing salt water for example. For others it could not serve this purpose – if, for example, there were too many other highly resistive strata near the oil-bearing sands. In these latter cases it could still be used for the purposes of the correlation of the wells of a given field. Here the curves provided electrical 'horizons', which were like signatures of a particular stratum that could be traced from well to well, allowing a three-dimensional map of the field to be built up (Figure 6). In yet other fields, the resistivity curve was useless – if the field was too complex (too many faults and not enough horizons) or too simple (the geologists did not need any external assistance) and so on.

Schlumberger engineers were, however, years ahead of the behaviourists' maxim 'if it moves, measure it'. By the late 1920s, several engineers had noticed that it was sometimes really difficult to bring the potentiometer's needle back to zero so that a measurement could be made. As one engineer expressed it, they even sort

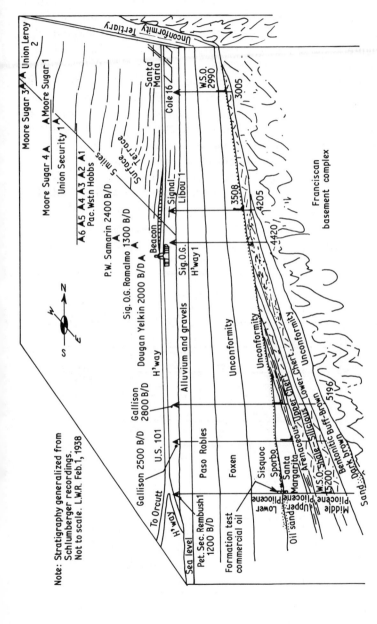

Figure 6 Block diagram based on Schlumberger electrical logs

231

of knew that this happened when the electrodes passed porous strata. So one day, Henri Doll decided to turn off the current and measure the kicks that had been ignored (Doll, 1972). Thus was born the second curve, known diversely as the porosity curve, the permeability curve, the self potential curve, the streaming potential curve and the left-hand curve. It worked on the general principle that there is for whatever reason more electrical activity surrounding permeable than surrounding impermeable strata. Each of its names refers to a theory as to why this should be the case – only the difference between left and right was to remain unchallenged in the course of the trial. This second curve looked different from the first one. It produced strong kicks opposite oil sands as did the resistivity curve, but it did not in general react to highly resistant non-permeable strata (Figure 7) – and thus overcame the latter's major flaw. Even if the two combined could not spell o-i-l oil, they seemed to yield oil's signature as no other method could.[3]

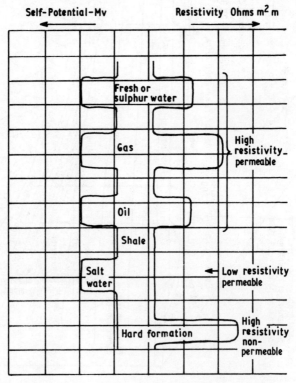

Figure 7 'Typical' or 'Ideal' curve for training and advertising purposes

Let us look a little closer at the act of measurement of the two curves. There was a roll of paper attached to the winch that lowered the electrodes into the well in such a way that:

> The paper moved in synchronism with the electrode as it went down the hole. Every time the electrode moved, say, 10 feet the paper would move a given distance, maybe half an inch, so that it was in perfect synchronism with the electrode as it went down the hole and the operator moved the slidable arm backwards and forwards so as to make a continuous curve. He was the man that moved the slidable arm and the slidable arm moved the pencil across the paper and the potentiometer enabled him to determine by means of a little shadow that it cast on the paper just where he should move the pencil from moment to moment and he followed that shadow across the paper' (*Trial*, 17: 2864)

Moving from the era of the first curve to that of the second, we move from the time when a single operator battled a parasite, to one where two operators battled two parasites. The description of the two curves brings out this formal feature, whereby each curve became a parasite of the other, a quiver in its needle:

> In these conditions, the operator charged with the control of one of the potentiometers turns the knobs of that potentiometer so as to bring the needle of the galvanometer to zero. This operation has the effect at the same time of reducing the extent of the oscillations of the other potentiometer. And reciprocally the operator charged with controlling the second potentiometer, in the act of bringing the needle of his galvanometer to zero, makes the oscillations of the first potentiometer disappear. As a consequence, if these compensations are constantly made, the two needles stay at zero and are rigorously immobile, then one can read off from the potentiometers C and D the differences of potential delta V_1 and delta V_2 that one is after, that is to say the S.P. and the delta V of resistivity. (Notes on the Semi-Automatic Recorder, 1938)

Thus the electrodes descend in the drill hole, two operators fight to keep their respective needles at zero, and the pencil traces the curve of their struggle.

What to call the resultant composition? You would scarcely sell a great many of these curves by titling them: 'The Struggle of the

Lone Engineer for a Null Quiver'. Yet neither could you be too
precise scientifically about your title, for often you did not really
know *what* was measured. The first curve was and remained the
'resistivity' curve. The second curve started life as the porosity or
permeability curve (the thing out there that the parameter served
to identify) and became the SP curve (the name of the parameter).
'S.P.' was a vague title, that meant at different periods 'streaming
potential', 'self potential' and 'spontaneous potential'. Leonardon,
director of the Schlumberger Well Surveying Company, was asked
about the naming of the curve during the *Halliburton* trial:

> Q. Why did you write 'Streaming Potential' on this exhibit L-4?
> A. Because that is the way we call it. We call it porosity. We
> have given awful names to it. We call it permeability. It doesn't
> mean anything. When you have a daughter, when she is born
> you have to give her a name, and that is the way I would call it.
> In other words, I have been put on the spot by geologists and by
> so many people asking me, what do you mean by that, and I
> have always answered, well, this is what is measured, and this is
> what you interpret. (*Trial*, 2: 543)

The third curve was known once and for all as the third curve
(Figure 8). Stender Sweeney of the Richfield Oil Corporation gave
a nice account, which concentrated on the curve as a thing-in-
itself, and left the parameter measured and the configuration of
electrodes out of the issue:

> There was the permeability and the porosity curve, and then later
> there was a more sensitive curve, which was developed, which
> was commonly referred to as a third curve, the purpose of which
> was to give a clue as to the fluid contents of the formation.
> (*Trial*, 7: 44)

I won't even talk about the fourth and the fifth curves: though
these were sufficiently well-defined that a log could give a
resistivity curve and a fourth curve without passing through the
third curve (the title 'second' was an honorific held by the SP curve
but never used). These, be it noted, were names for the oil
companies – internally *Schlumberger* used names that described
the configuration of electrodes, this being information they wanted
to keep from their competitors (Figure 3 – the 'inverse' is the third
curve).

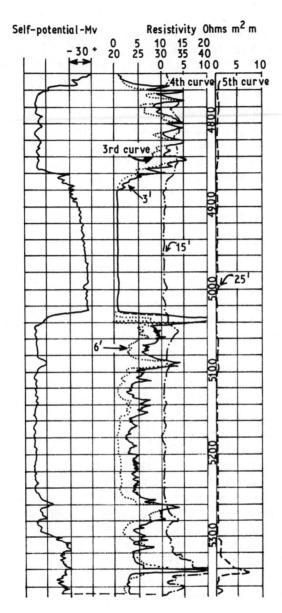

Figure 8 Third, fourth and fifth curves

235

The curves took on a life of their own, such that any attempt to get beyond them and hook them up to nature led quickly, in the context of the trial, to redundancy. Thus Eby the geophysicist would not allow himself to be put on the spot by the defence counsel: 'Q. What do you mean by an electrical log? A. An electrical log is the product or result of what you obtain in taking an electrical log. In other words, it is the result of electrical logging' (*Trial*, 10: 100). I am not mocking his clumsiness, I am underlining his insight: the curves were *sui generis*. How and why they were is the question we will now treat.

The framing of the curve

We just want the truth. Let us try to work out who was right in the court case *Schlumberger* vs *Halliburton*. It is quite simple, really. Take a curve, any curve, from a *Schlumberger* log, and compare it with a curve from a *Halliburton* log of the same well. If the two are equivalent then we have established a prima facie case that the two methods used are the same. We will then look at the *Schlumberger* patent. If it describes the way to draw the curves, and if it has priority over any other methods used, then *Schlumberger* was in the right. This is a game for high stakes, though, so we will have to go slowly. Whatever *Schlumberger* were doing, they were doing a lot of it. From June 1932 to October 1940 they logged 108 million feet, the equivalent of some 2.5 times the diameter of the earth, or some 400 times the round trip between the judge's home town and the court room (*Trial*, 17: 2947). They had over 95 per cent of the business going in the field (*Trial*, 17: 2948).

So let us start the trial by taking a curve, any curve. Easily said. The first problem was that the curves to be used in the trial were in general the property of the oil companies, and these did not necessarily want to broadcast valuable information about their wells. Thus Ennis of the Oil Well Water Locating Company, used by *Halliburton* to prove prior art (the common existence of a method before its patenting), said that he could only produce in evidence published logs, and

> anything that we have published was records that we were allowed to publish, and any changing in the formations in the records were suggestions made by whoever was in authority to allow us to publish those records, so when I make the statement as to the accuracy as to the depth of the well, I couldn't actually

say that was the depth of the well. . . . Q. And you couldn't say
that the so-called open hole was the correct footage on that
factor, could you? A. Well, within possibly 25, 30, 40 or 50 feet.
(*Trial*, 4: 424)

So we can start with a curve, but we can't be sure it's a real one.
And nobody necessarily knew what the real one was – to the
extent that Dr Rust had to admit that it turned out that the curves
attached to the original Blau and Gemmer patent were in fact
Schlumberger logs (*Trial*, 13: 1173).

So there is a bit of confusion about reality, but let us not
exaggerate the problem. Both parties could and did go to the oil
companies that were supporting them, and get permission to use
real logs. However, we have not yet exhausted the problem. Take
a curve, any curve. But what do we mean 'any curve'? All curves
are not the same. The defence asked the prosecution expert
witness, Dr Aiken, to read an imaginary log:

Q. Suppose I told you that the resistivity of a formation was four
ohm meters. Would you deduct the nature of that formation
without any other information? A. In Texas here? Q. Without
any other information. A. You always have other information,
Mr Martin. You cannot use any physical method utterly
divorced from everything else. That just doesn't happen. The
user of anything always knows something. (*Trial*, 12: 848)

The curve only exists within a context. We cannot just take any
curve: if we did we would be prejudging the outcome, lining up for
Halliburton against *Schlumberger*.[4]

For *Halliburton*, if the patents described a valid method, then
they should be universally applicable, without differentiation by
area. For *Schlumberger*, context was prime – for the interpretation
of both curves and patents. Thus Aiken, having made his point
about the specificity of curves, does the same for words. He is
asked to define the word 'parameter':

what we mean by parameter would depend on what we are
talking about. Here we are talking about geophysical
exploration. . . . So when we consider a word we must consider
it in connection with its context, and not arbitrarily make it
mean something the patent obviously did not intend it to mean.
(*Trial*, 12:853–4).

The same problem of the context-dependence of words and drawings appeared in *Halliburton*'s attempt to prove that the *Schlumberger* method had in fact first been used by Fox in the tin mines of Cornwall in 1830. The expert witness for the defence drew a sketch of the Fox equipment, as described in his articles, and compared it with the *Schlumberger* drawing attached to the patent. Mr Cole, counsel for the prosecution, complained about 1830s electrical equipment looking so like 1940s productions:

> Mr Cole: Of course all of us are entirely human in our approach towards matters of this kind and I guess it is altogether human for Dr MacKeown to prepare a drawing that looks very much like the drawings of some of the patents in suit when he comes to reconstruct one in 1940. The Court: Well, your suggestion reminds me of why old man Bob Harris quit the Baptist Church. Mr Cole: Why did he do it, Judge? The Court: Well, somebody showed him a picture in the Bible of Jesus being baptized in the River Jordan and John the Baptist pouring water on his head, and he said it should not be in the Bible. (*Trial*, 14: 1340)

Some few weeks later, the Judge returned to the point: 'You take the Bible and read it. You don't have to adopt those pictures that are in the Bible unless you want to, and if they meet your views of what the Bible says it helps' (*Trial*, 14: 1727).

These hermeneutic stances by *Schlumberger* and *Halliburton* also need to be put into context. For both plaintiff and defendant, reality and its interpretation attract different modalities in the courtroom, in scientific literature and in advertising literature.[5] And this introduces us to another problem of taking a curve, any curve. The courtroom itself is no isolated arena. There are competitors in the back rows taking notes, picking up ideas. Worthington Campbell, who represented *Schlumberger* on a case against *Geoanalyzer* (which was settled out of court) made the point when summarizing the strategy used in this earlier case:

> It was also decided to include the porosity patent in the belief that we might later obtain more convincing evidence of clear infringement. In the absence of such clear and convincing evidence we always feared that a judge might be confused by a composite curve in which self potentials and resistivity values were mixed, since the same curve would be the basis for the

charge of infringement of both porosity and resistivity patents. Geoanalyzer in its answers to interrogatories admitted the resistivity or resistance curve but denied the influence of self potentials. . . . the Court might have said some things that would have told others how to obtain a mixed curve which would not infringe, although to a skilled man it might well serve for porosity indications. (Campbell to Leonardon, 4 April 1938; Box USA)[6]

Schlumberger might indeed want to talk about and defend their curves, but there were things best left unsaid. Thus Leonardon, managing director of *Schlumberger* in the United States, refused to go too far in describing optimal electrode spacings for an ideal cubic meter: 'Now it is by a long and costly experience that we determined which are the best spacings in different areas so I am not inclined to give you all the details' (*Trial*, 1: 268–9). A later interview suggests that an unpatented new idea did slip out at the trial, and was taken up by the *Halliburton*, so that in the end *Schlumberger* had to buy back the use of their own invention (Doll, 1972). The counsel for the Oil Well Water Locating Company was quite explicit about the need for a secret space:

I have cautioned the witness against furnishing you anything; in fact, when you first requested the drawings or anything like that I told you 'No', and it was only after you took depositions here the other day that I finally consented to permit Mr Ennis to see if he had any advertising literature or the like which might show what he was doing at a certain period of time so far as his public operations were concerned. (*Trial*, 4: 445)

In the context of the trial we cannot just 'take any curve'. Neither the oil companies nor *Schlumberger* nor the defendants will allow us to, and, if we believe *Schlumberger*, no one curve is just any curve. Tracing the difference between a 'typical' curve (Figure 7) and an actual curve (for example, Figure 9), we will now see to what extent each curve was in turn constitutively local, decorative, and open to radically different interpretations from the actors who dealt in it – the well surveyors and the oil companies. The typical curve in question was produced by the Houston Geological Society Study Group on Electrical Logging, and was entitled 'Typical SP and Resistivity Diagram' (Figure 7). This diagram is indeed typical of a whole range of representations of

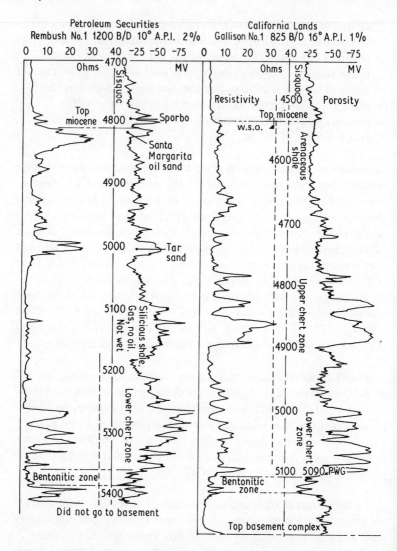

Figure 9 Example of commercial resistivity and porosity curves

electrical logging, giving as it does a clear picture of the ideal effect (cf the presentation in Allaud and Martin, 1976).

There are concessions to realism, in that the gas is on top of the oil, is on top of the water, and there is a hard bedrock. But just looking at the curves themselves, we know immediately that something is wrong. Any curve, as opposed to the typical curve, is saw-toothed (Figure 9). This is due to several factors, an important one being the phenomenon known as 'measurement hiccups' (H. Renault, 1931). The electrodes A, M and N encounter the different strata in turn. Imagine that A and M are in a very resistant layer, and N encounters a conductive layer. There is a kick on the curve. Then either M and N come together in the conductive layer, or N has already passed through by the time that M arrives. In the meantime, A itself may or may not have passed through a conductive layer higher up. At each boundary (and the boundaries are not necessarily well-defined) there is a kick in the curve, so that instead of having an effect opposite a given layer, there are a series of effects. The curve is a composite reading of these variations; and *Schlumberger* engineers had a subset of reference curves to show them which possible sequence they might be dealing with (Figure 10). In principle, the result was unreadable if you had: 'configurations of electrodes whose length was of the order of the thickness of the layers traversed', but 'this clearly supposes that we know what kind of terrain we are dealing with and what magnitude of effect we will get' (Renault, 1931: 24). This is a first paradox that stresses the importance of local knowledge.[7] A Texas sonde was not the same as an Oklahoma sonde (Figure 4), you needed different configurations to get the same curve. The left hand curve was also a composite curve. There were two effects at least determining its shape: electrochemical and electrofiltration. Both separately were indications of what was called porosity, but they could have opposite signs and so cancel each other out (SPE to Léonardon, 11 March 1937, Box USA). Further, spontaneous potential increased relatively uniformly with depth as the temperature of the drilling fluid went up – another local factor that varied from field to field, from well to well. To make matters worse, salt layers could dissolve locally in the drilling mud, so that the effect range of both curves was limited to the mud itself (Figure 11). Thus in both cases, we are dealing with composite curves that had to be interpreted by the engineer, or the geologist, on the spot. The actual curve – the tailored, local curve – was sufficiently fine-tuned that *Halliburton* charged that in fact: 'the plaintiff in this action, the Schlumberger Well Surveying Corporation, has concealed from the American public and has preserved in secrecy the methods and apparatuses it has actually successfully used in the field' (*Trial*, 10: 62–3). Far from there being an obvious kick in the right places in accordance with mutually agreed theory, there was actually suspicion in the early years that the curves were a

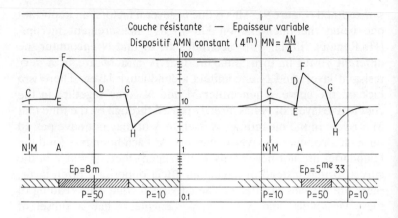

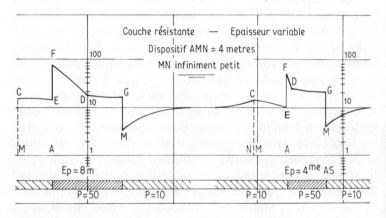

Figure 10 Reference curves

decorative blind covering the actual garnering of information elsewhere:

> When the Schlumberger was first introduced, part of our duties was to go out on the truck, regardless of the clemency of the weather, and sit there while they ran their log, to see whether the Frenchmen were trying to put something over on us. (*Trial*, 7: 61)[8]

In the context of the oil field, however, it was not appropriate to argue the infinite interpretability of the curve and the skill of the individual interpreter. The rhetoric of the time and the impulsion of the oil companies was to exclude the human – thus J. Boyd Best claimed of the Schlumberger: 'It is an accurate log, without any personal element involved, and as such we use it to find sands not located by the driller's log, and use it to map faults and structures, and for correlation'. And this impersonal effect was enhanced by the lay-out of the logs given to the companies. This comes out particularly clearly in the case of another element lacking from the typical curve – the scales appended to the top of every log (Figure 3). The SP curve was given in millivolts, and the resistivity curve in ohms per cubic meter by *Schlumberger*, in impedance ohms by *Halliburton*. The scales at the top gave the impression that specific parameters were being measured; so that the judge got quite confused by Blau's testimony that

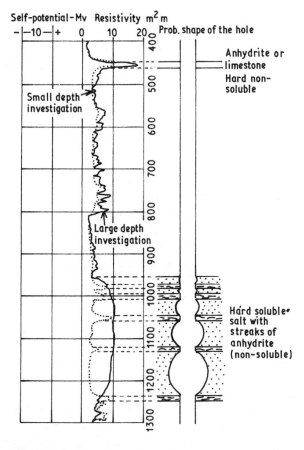

Figure 11 Dissolution of salt smoothes curves

those things which are measured are not specific resistivities or the contact potentials. The Court: You mean by that then that the plaintiff measures something, and the defendant measures something, but you are not willing to name them?' (*Trial*, 13: 1248)

Thus Turner, a Halliburton engineer was asked about his relationship with the curves:

Q. And you help the customer interpret them? A. In interpreting what the different curves mean. Q. And what purposes do these numbers at the top of the two scales serve, under potential, on this exhibit 124, graduated in millivolts, minus 50, minus 150, minus 200, what is the purpose of that, so far as you are concerned? A. So far as I am concerned, that on the potential side is of no value. Q. On the impedance side on this Exhibit 124, under 'Impedance Ohms', appear the figures 75, 150, 225, 300. A. To me that represents the scale on which the log was run. Q. I understand'. (*Trial*, 16: 2469–70)

Turner was pushed on the question as to why there were different numbers for dry and for wet holes:

Q. Well now, I don't believe I still quite understand the difference between those two scales there. What is your explanation for that? A. I think that plainly shows you that the scale really doesn't have any value as far as the scale is concerned. It is just run on that scale so as to bring out the magnitude of the kick'. (*Trial*. 16: 2476–7)

The numbers on the top of the logs were decorative, then, in the sense that they were non-essential to the interpretation of the logs. What they did serve to do was to send a message that the curves were a scientific production and not some French person's artistic impressions. They also served to distinguish a particular opus, to mark it as original, to sign the oeuvre. One of *Schlumberger*'s best coups during the trial was to scale down one of their logs to match a *Halliburton* log taken of the same well on the same day – the tracings were sufficiently identical that *Halliburton* did not challenge the similarity. This raised a question of the scales used, put by the defence attorney to *Schlumberger*'s expert witness:

Q. In view of your last statement then, if the scale the defendant puts on suggests he is measuring something else than resistivity then the scale does not indicate the value of the resistivity, does it, the specific resistivity? A. We have been over that before. This is a resistivity curve. The only reason I could see for putting such an arbitrary scale on it might be the hope that it would suggest that the defendant was measuring something else. (*Trial*, 12: 837)

A second decorative dimension of the curves was attached to the process of habituation. The loggers' strategy was to get the oil companies used to seeing the curves, whether or not they got useful information from them. Thus the director of *Schlumberger* operations in Venezuela wrote in 1934 to the central office in Paris that:

I propose to leave the prices for this style of operation [logs of holes being repaired] as they are. As it turns out, the results furnished by such runs are sometimes influenced by the presence of pieces of 'liners' or other 'fish'. But it is in my opinion good politics to help and encourage companies such as Gulf, who are having us log systematically all the holes that they repair, despite the risk of obtaining distorted diagrams which therefore yield incomplete information. (Bayle to SPE, 11 April 1934, Box Venezuela)

This habituation factor – get them used to it and give them what they are familiar with – went back to the original form of the curves: 'A set of *Schlumberger* logs (Resistivity and SP) is similar to a normal lithological log "translated into an electrical code" which, with proper experience, can easily be read' (Thomeer, 1937). The logging companies did not want to continually change the curves, even if this would bring improvements. For example, there was a certain configuration of electrodes for which, when fresh-water mud was used by the drillers in the well-hole, there was: 'an increase in the size of the kicks opposite water-layers and a diminution opposite oil-bearing layers. You can easily see that this singularly complicates the fundamental problem of the distinguishing of oil-bearing layers'. And yet the configuration in question was good for correlation purposes, used little current and 'In the end, we need to keep using it for reasons of continuity, because a lot of diagrams have been made with it in the past and

Geof Bowker

the geologists are used to it' (SPE to Léonardon, 16 March 1937, Box USA). Given the often precarious relationship between geologist and geophysicist – the former feeling threatened by the latter – it was worth some sacrifices to keep the geologists happy, to give them a feeling of control. The solution was to *add* another curve which did not have the same problems, and to leave the vestigial curve in place. Sometimes the need to keep the curves the same could determine the measuring equipment used, as H. G. Doll recalled in 1972 when talking about the difficulties of going over to film in the recording devices:

> Now the first reaction was a fight, in effect, between the people on the ground and the company people. . . . The curve with a logarithmic scale didn't look at all like the one on a linear scale, whence the desire of the companies to have linear scales. But in places where there was a wide variation in resistivity, we had to have up to three galvanometers – one which started to go over the edge of the film when we reached 10 . . . [and so on]. Of course if you wanted to draw these 2 curves indicating different quantities on the same piece of film, all this mixture of scales and things made a frightful mess. . . . it was a long fight. (Doll, 1972; see Figure 12)

So the 'typical curve' has failed us by its exclusion of local and decorative factors integral to the log. The final untypical thing about it is that it is extremely easy to interpret. For a variety of reasons, there was always in fact quite a liberty of interpretation with respect to the curves provided by the oil companies. We will now follow two examples of a two-tier difficulty in interpreting the logging process: at the level of circuit diagrams depicting the equipment and at the level of the resultant curves.

The 'Stratagraph' equipment was used by Lane Wells to 'determine the nature [that fateful phrase] of formations behind the casing' (*Proselec*, 1937: 1) – the casing being the concrete tubing put round the sides of a completed well to prevent its collapse. The method constituted a threat to *Schlumberger*'s dominance in the field of logging, for they had no sure method for logging completed holes. It thus became the object of a critical study in *Schlumberger*'s internal technical magazine, *Proselec*. The first problem for the author was to get hold of any information at all about the method, which Lane Wells wanted at once to keep secret so as to steal a march on the competition and to reveal so as

246

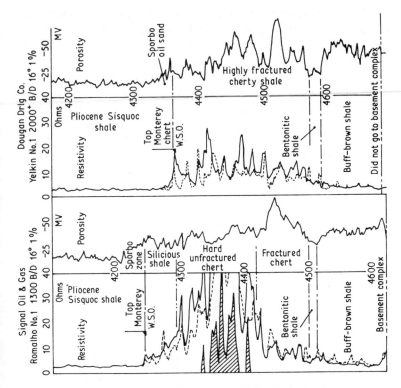

Figure 12 Scale changes render curves difficult to read

to establish scientific credibility. The tension between these conflicting desires is drawn into the only circuit diagram *Schlumberger* could get hold of:

> the stratagraph circuit diagram reproduced in Plate 1, is a copy of the plate attached to the conference given on 22 September 1936 by Mr Joseph Jensen to the A.I.M.E. [American Institute of Mining Engineers] meeting at Los Angeles. (Figures 13 and 14 are the original and the interpretation)

This diagram, according to the author of the article was patently false:

> If you look at the circuits represented in Plate 1, you see straight away that the right hand circuit could not in any way influence the left hand one, because the current given off by the zinc-steel

battery on the right hand circuit is clearly much too small to be able to modify the potentials of the casing at different depths in any way at all. (*Proselec*, 1937: 1)

Drawing on some remarks made during the conference, and on the use of the word 'balance' in an advertising booklet produced by Lane Wells, the author proceeded to redraw the circuit diagram in such a way that it might work. The original Lane Wells diagram, then, was not a depiction of a workable device as much as a representation of the conflict between competition and credibility.

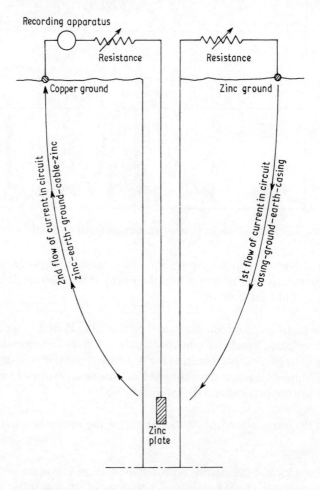

Figure 13 Ennis presents the stratagraph

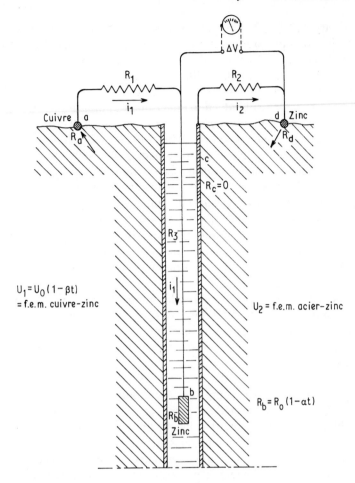

Figure 14 Schlumberger interprets Ennis' stratagraph

At this same level of circuit diagrams, a similar difficulty arose with the *Schlumberger* resistivity patent (the right hand curve) during the trial. In the Patent drawing, the source of the electric current was marked 'E'. There was much deliberation about whether 'E' meant direct current or any source of electricity – the significance of this being that *Halliburton* used alternating current (e.g. *Trial*, 2: 456–7). As Leonardon let out when he let fly, it was partly a case of knowing where to stop: 'Why don't you include the power plant if it were electrical circuits that take juice from the city, why don't you include that on the diagram, the power plant of

249

the city?' (*Trial*, 2: 433). The *Schlumberger* lawyers constructed a reader for the patent, whom they called an 'intelligent electrical man' (*Trial*, 15: 1870–7). This latter would know that AC or DC could be used, and that although there was no switch on the diagram allowing for the regular cutting of the current – this being necessary to control induction effects in DC applications and being a feature of all *Schlumberger* devices – it was pretty obvious that you needed such a switch. This difficulty dovetails into the Stratagraph dilemma: if the patent diagram were too precise it would render public useful secret information like optimal electrode spacings and voltages, if not precise enough it would not convince patent lawyers and oil companies.

Yet it is not only the circuit diagrams that are the outcome of a tension between secrecy and openness: the curves themselves also were. To continue with the *Schlumberger* case, we have just seen that one issue was whether alternating current produced different results to direct current – did the two additional parameters of impedance and capitance effect the curve? At the time of the trial, *Schlumberger* was absolutely sure that they did not. Their certainty came from experiments that they had run on some curves without the companies who bought them being aware of the stakes:

> So as not worry the companies, we suppressed one of the two SP curves at one time, without going into the question of what the PP [provoked potential] which the first trials had brought out meant. Now that the companies are used to seeing our oscillograph diagrams, don't you think it would be possible to start recording the two SP curves again, so as to carry out systematic PP tests? We should be able to do this without troubling the companies too much, because we just need to explain to them that one of the SP curves is the real SP (which is not so untrue), and that the distance between the two curves represents the capacity of the terrain. We see quite an advantage to carrying out such tests. Given the systematic nature we can give to these trials – since they are so easy to do – the number of experiments will be very high, and as a consequence we can generate significant statistical samples. If by any chance the tests produce interesting results with respect to PP, their value is evident. If on the other hand these tests show that capacity effects are of no interest, because for example they are as close as may be proportional to resistivity,

we will get the companies used to thinking that capacity is not at all interesting and as a result we will have cut the grass from under the feet of our competition, who would like to rise up against us one day waving the banner of capacity (or phase difference, which is the same thing). (SPE to Léonardon, 1 April 1936, Box USA)

Thus the two curves produced were constructed to mean different things to the companies that bought and to the geophysicists who drew them. Patent diagrams, advertising material and curves were coded both for opacity and for openness.

In leaving the typical curve behind, we have encountered a number of varieties – vestigial curves, decorative curves, local curves and opaque curves. All these varieties contribute to the framing of the curve, to creating that cross between a drawing designed to please a viewer and a mechanical tracing of some given parameter. The uniting thread of this play of bluff and counter-bluff was that what you sought to represent was not 'nature' in the sense of painting a true picture of that thing out there, but 'nature' in the sense of difference – as we saw above *Schlumberger* said as much at the trial. An oil-bearing layer was defined by the fact that it gave a kick to a curve – if there was no kick then as far as drillers, and thus the annals of human history, were concerned there was no oil. There were two discourses – a practical one on similarity and difference that regulated the development of curves and incorporated aesthetic and strategical considerations, and a theoretical one about the parameters that were being measured. *Schlumberger*'s analysis of Stratagraph shows just how independent these discourses could be, and why they were kept apart:

It seems very likely that the 'Stratagraph' people have misinterpreted the origin of their measures. They have landed by chance on a device that gives differentiations opposite porous layers but for reasons completely other than what they suppose. . . . However, we should not launch into an overly precise technical discussion with the Companies of the reasons why 'Stratagraph' in fact measures temperatures, for this might give the latter the means of improving their methods – by using alternating current for example. On the other hand we should clearly indicate to the Companies that we can resolve the problem of logging in cased wells by using thermometry. (*Proselec*, 1937: 6)

Science was not some baseline to which all else referred, but one weapon among others to attack the curves of others and one terrain on which to defend your own. It was internal to the geophysical company, often secret. What was really sold was not a picture of nature, it was just curves.

The taming of the curve

It is clear from the above account that there is no such thing as a 'picture' of the subsoil produced by *Schlumberger*. The curves were perceived differently by the different actors involved: the practical man who sought 'scientific' proof of a field whether this were needed or not, the geologist who was used to certain curves and the geophysicist who used certain others and so on. Moreover, this was not some regrettable state of affairs that *Schlumberger* would have liked to clear up: on the contrary, they worked very hard to maintain the ambiguity in the possible readings. We saw this most clearly in the case of the continuing provision of a curve known to be of little value: there was one curve for the customers, who might otherwise be led to doubt more generally the value of *Schlumberger* measurements, and one for the geophysicists.

Two sets of factors gave rise to the representational ambiguity that *Schlumberger* strove to maintain. The first set stems from the need to keep their methods relatively opaque to their employers and their competitors (often one and the same). This set worked across the board, from the design of equipment (adding dummy knobs, removing manufacturers' name plates and so on) to the writing of scientific papers (discussing general problems without providing the expertise necessary to solving any particular one) to the mixing of useful and useless curves. What mattered here was creating a space within which *Schlumberger* could work: one into which flowed equipment and resources and out of which flowed curves and their interpretation – but within which things were kept murky so that none could understand the full process, so that they could retain control of the process of interpretation.[9] The second set of factors is that they wanted to do many different things with the same curves. Under the guise of normal readings, they could test hypotheses and thus use the oil fields as their laboratory. To do this they needed to be able to introduce variety into the curves. They could get companies habituated to a product, so that it would seem odd to have a well without a logging even if no new information were provided. To this end it was better to provide a regular, uniform product. They wanted to be able to both impress company geologists with the simplicity of their work and mystify them with its complexity – for the large companies were their major consumers and competitors (*Halliburton* was financed by Humble for its electrical logging work). Any firm decision – in favour of total mystification or total transparence – would have disastrous consequences. *Schlumberger*, then, retained ambiguity in its visual representations as part of its overall survival strategy.[10]

On the surface it would seem that there is nothing more technical and unproblematically scientific than the representation of the readings of a resistivity meter. Yet in looking at these we have discovered a site of social conflict no less intense and fraught than we would find in an analysis of tea-room conversation in a university department. Indeed, through such case studies as the above, the general result that the 'harder' a scientific fact, the more 'social' it is[11] comes ever closer to its (social) proof. The pictures from the subsoil that we have analysed provide a graphic representation of work on two fronts – the taming of the curve through the use of the oil field as laboratory and the domestication of the user.

Acknowledgements

This essay has been made possible by generous funding from the Fondation Les Treilles. I would like to thank Patrick Gillet, keeper of the musem at Crèvecoeur for his help and hospitality, and I am indebted to Bruno Latour for his human (and inhuman) insight.

Notes

1 I refer here to the Proceedings of the Trial *Schlumberger vs Halliburton*. These consist of some 18 volumes of typescript proceedings – depositions and the trial itself, and eight volumes of exhibits. They are held at the Schlumberger museum at Crèvecoeur en Auge. I give volume number followed by page number.

2 See Allaud and Martin, 1976 for a good, simple description of the act of logging.

3 Campbell, for the prosecution, compared it to an eye and the engineer interpreting it to a bank teller verifying signatures (*Trial*, 10: 15–17).

4 Here we see being played out in the courtroom a contemporary philosophical debate about relativism. Cf. the approach of Latour in Latour, 1987 and of Callon with respect to the foreshadowing/reproduction of sociological debates among engineers in the non-development of the electrical car.

5 Latour and Woolgar, 1986 has the classic statement of this theme.

6 References to correspondence in the Schlumberger archives currently tempor-

arily held at the Ecole des Mines de Paris will give first details of the letter – author, recipient, date and then the Box in which the letter is to be found).

7 Cf. Collins, 1985, on experimenters' regress.

8 This is not such a strange idea – there have been a series of stories, up to the present, of geophysical measuring devices that seemed only to measure the credulity of the oil companies.

9 Cf. Callon and Law, 1988 on areas of relative space and time autonomy.

10 Cf. Eckhardt, 1940: 1208: 'The normal conduct of geophysical operations involves a complex series of compromises between considerations of geology, geography, geophysics; finance, law, and related management policies'.

11 Cf. Latour, 1987.

References

Allaud, Louis and Martin, Maurice (1976), *Schlumberger: Histoire d'une Technique*, Paris, Berger-Levrault.

Anonymous (1937), 'Etude Critique du Procédé Stratagraph', *Proselec*, 22: 1–6.

Anonymous (1936), 'Les Potentiels Spontanés dans les Sondages', *Proselec*, 21: 1–21.

Anonymous (1938), *Notes on the Semi-Automatic Recorder*, Roneo.

Bowker, Geof (1987), 'A Well-Ordered Reality: Aspects of the Development of Schlumberger, 1920–1939', *Social Studies of Science*, 17: 611–55.

Callon, Michel (1986), 'The Sociology of an Actor-Network: the Case of the Electric Vehicle', in Michel Callon, John Law and Arie Rip (eds), *Mapping the Dynamics of Science and Technology: Sociology of Science in the Real World*, Basingstoke, Macmillan.

Callon, Michel and Law, John (1988), 'On the Construction of Sociotechnical Networks: Content and Context Revisited', *Knowledge and Society*, forthcoming.

Collins, H. M. (1985), *Changing Order: Replication and Induction in Scientific Practice*, London, Sage.

Culture Technique (1985), 'Les Vues de l'Esprit', Neuilly sur Seine, CRCT.

Eckhardt, A. E. (1940), 'Partnership between Geology and Geophysics – Prospecting for Oil', *Bulletin of the American Association of Petroleum Geologists*, 24: 1204–8.

The Houston Geological Society Study Group (1940), 'Electrical Well Logging', *Bulletin of the American Association of Petroleum Geologists*, 24: 1287–313.

Latour, Bruno (1987), *Science in Action*, Milton Keynes, Open University Press.

Latour, Bruno and Woolgar, Steve (1986), *Laboratory Life: the Construction of Scientific Facts*, Princeton, New Jersey, Princeton University Press.

Renault, H. (1931), 'Etudes Théoriques des Graphiques de Carottage Electrique', *Proselec*, 1: 5–17.

Schlumberger versus Halliburton, (1939–1940), 20 Volumes, typescript, Court Records held at Schlumberger Museum, Crevecoeur-en-Auge.

Thomeer, J. H. M. A. (1937), 'The Application of Schlumberger Electrical Logs in Oilfield Operations', typescript attached to letter E. G. Leonardon to S.P.E., 11 June 1937, in Box USA.

ON VISUALISATION AS POWER

'Innocent stupidities': de-picturing (human) nature. On hopeful resistances and possible refusals: celebrating difference(s) – again

Philip Corrigan

Abstract

Meanings

Offering three texts-as-images (to illustrate photogrammar), a sketch is made of analogies between Foucault's *pastoral powers* and the grammar of the picturesque and the picturable as part of an investigation of the dialexis of Authority and Difference. Picturing, it is argued, works not only in the depicting but in the photogrammar of *what and whom is shown how*, they thus encourage ways of seeing and saying more general than any one re-presentation. Critique begins with the stress on these selecting and dividing practices but must then move to a study of orthogonality (who is projecting whom) as a particular form of Authority in relation to Difference. *Comme toujours*, distanciation that makes this feature of cartography clear begins with making strange what is obvious (hence innocence, *naiveté*) and being a little *gauche* (hence stupidity).

Memories

We forget, or at least I do. In close analogy with W. B. Yeats' poem for 'Unknown Instructors', I acknowledge here the influence of Jean Luc Godard and, in part through him, Ludwig Wittgenstein. Reviewing Godard's work, in a retrospective in Toronto (February–March, 1988) I was struck by the meanings and questions and methods I had taken from his work, especially from *Les Carabiniers* (1962) in the closing scene where these Rifle-*men* return with their booty: their postcards acting as the real; equally from the Godard-Gorin *Letter to Jane* (1972), how the struggle for new questions instead of old answers has to be a difference done differently. But, sentimentally, nothing surpasses (and

in this reviewing I wept again) *Alphaville* (1965) for its insight into
Authority as grammar, and as Terror. Thank you.

The project: To be able to converse, easily, about my/your Real.
The method: Doubt everything, but take everything Seriously.
The morals: Do not mis/take people as things.
The abstract: 'Once upon a time . . . somewhere, there lived a . . .
  who . . . and, then . . . soon after . . . finally . . . and *that's* the
  end of the story.' 'Really?'

1 Episodic imaginactions[1,2]

(a) Several days later Murray asked me about a tourist attraction
known as the most photographed barn in America. We drove 22
miles into the country around Farmington. There were meadows
and apple orchards. White fences trailed through the rolling fields.
Soon the signs started appearing. THE MOST PHOTOGRAPHED
BARN IN AMERICA. We counted five signs before we reached
the site. There were forty cars and a tour bus in the makeshift lot.
We walked along a cowpath to the slightly elevated spot set aside
for viewing and photographing. All the people had cameras; some
had tripods, telephoto lenses, filter kits. A man in a booth sold
postcards and slides – pictures of the barn taken from the elevated
spot. We stood near a grove of trees and watched the photographers. Murray maintained a prolonged silence, occasionally
scrawling some notes in a little book.

'No one sees the barn', he said finally.
A long silence followed.
  'Once you've seen the signs about the barn, it becomes
  impossible to see the barn'.
He fell silent once more. People with cameras left the elevated
site, replaced at once by others.
  'We're not here to capture an image, we're here to maintain
  one. Every photograph reinforces the aura. Can you feel it,
  Jack? An accumulation of nameless energies'.
There was an extended silence. The man in the booth sold
postcards and slides.
  'Being here is a kind of spiritual surrender. We see only what
  the others see. The thousands who were here in the past, those
  who will come in the future. We've agreed to be part of a
  collective perception. This literally colors our vision. A religious
  experience in a way, like all tourism'. (Delillo, 1985: 12)[3]

(b) . . . I was fascinated by this kind of relationship between me and my great grandmother . . . do you remember any of the stories . . . no I don't remember stories I just remember the feeling when she was telling me these kinds of things . . .

Yes. I suppose for a long time I forgot that feeling and when I could feel again this very strong relationship with the nature around me it was very important, because it's not only nature, it's a way a child looks at nature, which is really something with magic. I think if you have an experience like that when you're a child it signs you. It's something that stays in you for a long time, but you can't be a child anymore because you have to face society with all sorts of roles and for women there is so much pain in doing that. Of course you have to, not you have to – you forget. It's a part of you which stays inside. It needs something to get out again, something that can touch your body, so your body can change again and you can feel the same kind of magic feeling with nature and you can look at nature in the same way. It's not all nostalgic, it's just recovering something that's yours. It's very important because we take a lot of creativity from that point. There are conflicts also because it is not something easy to recognise. Going back is not easy because you have to face something, so there are a lot of conflicts in doing that. I think it's very important to remember the first feelings we had about the world, this very strong relationship, we have to recover something, we have to talk about it, we have to try to remember. Also try to remember what happened to make us forget, to make us enter roles that restricted us, took away space from us. (Nicolson, 1983: 83, orthography altered – see original.)[4]

(c) As a young boy, [Fritz] Peters spent several years at Gurdjieff's Institute for the Harmonious Development of Man at Fontainbleau, France. It seems that the master took the boy under his wing, giving him private 'lessons' for a time.

One day, during one of their sessions, Gurdjieff tells Peters to look out the window and describe what he sees.

'An oak tree', the child answers.
'Yes, an oak tree', his teacher agrees. 'And what do you see *on* the oak tree?'
'Acorns', Peters replies.
'How many acorns?' Gurdjieff demands.
The boy guesses, after much hesitation, 'Several thousand acorns?'

'How many of these acorns do you suppose will become trees?' the master asks.

Fritz Peters is stumped for an answer, but finally replies, 'Maybe five or six?'

'No,' retorts Gurdjieff. 'Only one will become a tree, perhaps none!'

He then launches into an explanation which is wonderful. He tells the boy that 'nature creates thousands of acorns, but the possibility for a tree to grow is very slight. It is the same with man. Many people are born, but few *grow*, the rest are just fertilizer! Nature depends on this fertilizer to create both trees and men. Eventually men go back into the earth, like thousands of acorns, to create the possibility for other men, other trees, to grow. 'Nature is always very giving', he explains, 'but it only gives *possibility*. It takes hard work and great effort to become a tree or a genuine man' (Miller, 1981: 35–7).[5]

2 Hoping, differently

I shall return to the three photograms (for that is how I would like them *viewed*) subsequently. Your viewing (strictly, importantly, a re-viewing: an aporia – if you were in/know 'the set-up' [what the seen scene seemed *like*] you cannot see the same photograph *once*!) is also a practice, importantly: a use. For over 150 years it has been known that use-values differ from exchange-values and, we have also known (differently) that whilst consumption–distribution realises surplus value, this can (a) disguise – even deny – use values (commodity fetishism, for example); (b) act as a displaced–condensation (yes, the terms are deliberate!) of surplus labour used (abused) in production; and, (c) shift our comprehension from the simultaneity of wider (e)valuations *and* multiple ways of seeing, making sensible, knowings (reification and idealization).

My work, here with regard to cultural production (which I locate, emphatically, with the *uses* of cultural products),[6] is a subset of a wider theme, taken from Marx (and others): doubt everything, but take everything seriously. Plus – from a different vector (older, more – if you like [and I do like] – more moral) – do not mis/take people for (as) things. Now, much in the manner of the programmed textbooks which flourished in the late 1960s and early 1970s (before computer-assisted[?] learning packages came our way), I want to say – go back, re-read (view), the three *photograms* above.

Foucault, in one of his last writings, speaks of *pastoral power*.[7] I want to keep that category in view but bend the light a little, just a little, toward what I want to call *picturesque power(s)*. Or rather, and this *is* only an essay, I want to indicate a genealogy from the picturesque to the pictur-esque, the picturable, the mindful pictures we already have/know *now* of – hence the three openers above – 'Nature'. But, equally, and at the same time, about what I also take to be Foucault's major contribution – that of *bodily refusal*, about a somatic knowing that is 'more than' *that* (precisely, psychoanalytically, an excess; a trace of that longed for bliss seen, and thus a pleasure, from a distant shore, to recall, fondly, a remark of Roland Barthes). Continued here, along with these themes, from other writings – deliberatively overwrought and timed – is that the project of critical realism (which once I called, and would defend, scientific utopianism and/or formalist romanticism)[8] involves *all ways* an undercoding, a timing, *and* a stretched (concertina is the image here) spacing that shows the situation through the stitchwork, through the knots *and* the dropped stitches, the garment (language) drapery, the wear of the weave, the tweeting of the woof. And, finally, in this telegrammar of A Very Large Project, that in the run of (to) the subject, in the threads we manage to catch up (and unravel *or* sew back up tight!), we have yet to find a discursive-regime, an image-repertoire – perhaps an anti-language – a *way* of truly celebrating difference(s).[9]

So, globalism put to one side, yet not too far out of reach, let me return to the pictures que-picturable genealogy.

One feature of the current 'fix' we (differently) are *in* (related to *The State of Things* as Wim Wenders called an important film that came out of his time in Hollywood with Zoetrope Studios and the 'Godfather' consequences – game of Francis. *Ford* Coppola)[10] is that, and again it is the simultaneity that is so significant, we (differently, to be sure) alternate between a 'from above' and 'from below' perspectival analysis (that is, the pictures we produce have that orthogonality) *and* we increasingly discover there is no comprehending social unity that 'works' like that of 'The Social' *but* we know that this is the product of a certain moment, simultaneously again. That is to say that 'the Social' is a rhetoric, an argument, of certain 'radical' white bourgeois heterosexual men which quickly, and it is perhaps one of the greatest victories of capitalism's cultural revolution that we know, moves (us) into an objectivist (scientist) methodology, a logic, a philosophy, a symbolic-cultural 'constitution' of (not only) *That* Is The Way The World Is, but *That* Is The Way The World *Has* To Be. Picturing (and the picturesque) is such a crucial part of this not, though, as (simply)[11] the victory of bourgeois perspectival, and perceptual, norms (plus values), but having as much to do with accountable pleasures. How we can give accounts of pleasure (which is, to recall, bliss seen from a distant shore) or, as I once wrote in a poem,

> not having done too badly,
> said with a smile, but
>   nonetheless sadly

This is survival language, and with it go survival practices, and *gross* dissatisfactions (plus dissati-fictions!), plus, more recently, and for a tiny minority of the world's population, the slogan 'No Pain, No Gain' (what a curious return on an ancient *orthodoxa* this is! Suffer to be Good, Suffer and Be Still, Think of England! . . .).

This has to be shifted (the perspectival organization of knowing, sensing, believing) to simultaneously (here is the point of critical refusal) deny that *as such* it really is (therefore The Real of) how people are constituted, positioned, identified, that is to say *live and love*; *and* yet not to disperse and deny this really being 'the case' through such excuses for theorising (with their varied masculinist pomposities of appearing to name, whilst actually claiming) billions 'below the level of critical consciousness'. That, in a, phrase, we (intellectuals, artists, academics) 'know better' because we are (edgily, to be sure) special kinds of persons. This stinks of an heroic (as also iconic) history of the sort indexed by 'with a single bound *he* was free' – the critic (marxist, structuralist, semiologist and, dare I add, feminist, socialist, anti-racist, anti-imperialist) *as better* hero/heroine/s! .To adapt a slogan-poem of my friend Pete Brown, 'Surely, we can do better than *that*!!'

That there is no such comprehensive other (alternative) 'site' to counterpose to 'The Social' is what has to be, through a developing praxis of difference (a pragmatics of cultural-love), seen as a magnificent resource. It enables us (differently) to evade the terrifying singularity of 'having to be' (Blake's 'Newton's one eyed vision') thus-ly, only *that*-sidedly, the enclosing imprisonment of correlatives: *because that* is the way the world is (has to be), *that* is the way 'I' have to be. The crisis of representation (in the dual meaning I shall discuss here) turns on(to) this, erratically but, in the end, all ways. There has always been that business of positing an other (real, valid, er, True) truth to the claimed distortionality of the *modus operandi* of bourgeois perceptual norms, values and forms. What this allows to slip through the mesh is that behind the characteristics of the ver*edictional* (and juris*dictional*) truths proffered for our conspicuous consumption (we do have to display back, in behaviours, more so than beliefs, that we are expressing 'These truths . . .') is a profound authority-claim: that there is a, single, axiological, *a priori* Truth! The victory of this is not around content, nor even the frequently erased context and connectivity of all social relations, but around *standpoint*[12] and around form. Hence the importance of picturing.

In the face of (facing up to) this ubiquity of the image-repertoire – that which can be pictured in the mind, in the media of mindfulness/distraction – we have to pan-back, *and* zoom-in, simultaneously. Panning-back alone suggests an alternative carto-graphic (re)presentational logic, and what post-structuralism/ modernism declaratively performs is the impossibility of any observations without observing *bodies* (who senses whom?). Zooming-in alone suggests that we can string together the particular(s) as if that semantic chain (*cora*) of the local instance was productive of a generalizable Truth. Reflect and review for one moment on your own historical construction of your social identity/subjectivities, the degree to which you have moved (and been moved by) the local, particular, specific, and – why are we afraid of this term – the unique? And also, but at the same time, by the global, abstract, generalised, and ordinary? Then, moving from this re-membering to the visual, think of how these *both* have been woven from the differential image-repertoires that you have viewed and reviewed, that have been constructed simultaneously (again) by both that magic mirror with a memory (photogrammar) and by that memory which is a magic mirror, your own re-membering, your somatic knowledge of what – if this can be forgiven – *feels good*.[13]

The 'Other' to the 'Social' is precisely multiple and contradic-tory, it is also intensively posed against those crucial distinctions of the cultural revolution that has defined our world differently and yet similarly: fact/value; is/ought; the same/different; the norm/ deviation. Authority (authorised) claims organise our possible *approved* ways of showing and knowing (they need not, as I have indicated, try to entrap our ways of sensing, believing, nor our somatic knowledges). How we have to dress and address our being in *that* world is what constitutes governance, our governmentality, where obedience is rendered up in return for promises (and evidence) of accomplished achievement.

For me it turns on (returns us to) our subjectivities, understood as all ways in/formation, be-coming. Out of the mess that constitutes the Enlightenment – whose dark sides we are only now becoming differently aware of – there is one hint that I wish to sentimentally conserve and nourish. It is that emphasis which can be found in Allen Ginsberg's *Sunflower Sutra*, when he declares (and it is, here, the grain of the voice which matters) and *we are not* old, tired, dusty locomotives; *we are not* our skin of grime, *we are all* sunflowers. . . . That is to say, we are not fixed and finally formed by any Laws (of God, the Father, of a socially-naturalised 'Social' that then can be naturalised again and further made cybernetic), nor by Tradition, nor by an Adamic moment of illustrious Genesis. Moreover, Now, 'History' does not end with this microcosmic achieved being (say, upper middle class white, heterosexual, men in the United States of 'America'), but might announce that suffering, oppression, denial, erasure, domination, exploitation, *has gone on long enough!*

Where *then* are the photography/photographs[14] in *all* of this? And so, by a necessary detour, to the picturesque-picturable, again. Photo*grammar*: (a) works like any language-game; (b) is intensively and extensively part of the projection (broadcasting *and* narrowcasting) of 'The Social'. Thus it needs to be traced through a double genealogy – in what ways was 'The Apparatus' caught up in force-Fields (and consensing-Wills) that predated its technological moment and 'development' *and* what did it steadily, edgily, but cumulatively, make *ab* normal, make difficult to depict, to show, to share, to 'say'. Barthes argues extensively that depictions that partake of photogrammar (by which I comprehend, for this text, also the filmic, the televisual, the designed-graphic, and the video) split into two (not quite parallel) series: Art/ Technology, *and* Professional/Private.[15] But this announces a problem, it does not provide either a solution (which is not to deny that Barthes did this elsewhere)[16] or a sufficient explanation of how people (that is, you and me) go on living differently despite the enormous euphoria of these powered depictions. It says nothing of the pragmatics (and thus a necessary ethnography) of use(s).[17]

Declaring difference(s) is, as I have indicated, central to all of *this*. For a long time difference has been held in the vice/vise of spectralization: that is, difference is measured and depicted against a norm (whether categorical, textualised, pictured, or not) and thus manifests that highly selective 'tradition' as actually valid and/or valuable. For example, there is 'Man' (later, 'men') and here is the contra-diction and -depiction, namely 'Woman' (or 'women'). Something 'peculiar' happens here – the Norm is further validated by what Barthes (referring to standard forms of criticism) calls 'supplementation' and what I want to call *decoration*. The Norm (Value) is adorned and *extended*, that is *this* claim (for the social form of cultural production, here photogrammar), and *this* naming (the modes of dress and address of the social identification being in/formed), does not disrupt – indeed, may not even make visible – the social algebra, that is to say the hieroglyphics of totalization and individuation which make up 'The Social' as 'The Normal' through a projected-regulated grammar of expressivity that *attempts* to order experience(s), to tell us how to behave, to inform our feelings, to reach inner-speech.

What has to be done here (and is, in fact, being done, that is lived, and, alas, more rarely, depicted and visualised) is to *refuse* the authorisation (which is very complex: authority-expertise, value(s) – reward(s), author-of-our-own-words/works, etc., etc.) on offer, as the only possible form of being (depicting, textualising, re-presenting). This refusal is in/formed from the body, from/by imaginactions based on practical, hopeful, possibilities. This is a far from easy task since all challenges (alternations to, supplementations of) against 'The Social' tend to 'stall' and 'dissipate' because they are claimed always along one axis. Thus, for example, where 'Authority' is seen, and organised against, as 'The Main Enemy' questions of socially significant difference tend to disappear or be deferred (like all *jouissance*) to some 'later moment' – that is 'Authority' becomes homogenised. In the contrary, where 'Difference' is established axiologically, then the ways that the 'figure in dominance'[18] entails, embodies 'Authority' is usually ignored. Both of these axes produce the chopping wounds typical of the instrument. I am not clear who (how many) are wounded proportionately by each.

A differential starting point (way of seeing and thence showing, sharing, changing) is to realise that 'Difference' is embodied by 'Authority'; just as there is no 'Authority' that is not a working out of 'Difference'. That is, to change the code, to realise that 'Difference(s)' cannot be, *as they are*, a starting-point since they

263

have been socially constructed through relations and structures of power: they are ordinal notations in a 'cultural-symbolic constitution' (as, e.g., *the* Body Politic', 'Nature', or 'Fashion(s)'). If to be differenced (to be rendered object and objective) results from 'Authority' (by which I shorthand, legalised power/power claimed to be legal, as also that which is neutral, natural, universal and Obvious) then what is remarkable about it? us? is that it is invalid and invalidating to start from there as though *that* (depiction, logic) was the site and sight of transformation.[19]

What is becoming clearer is that dominant, authorised, depictions (photogrammar) have a history (are social constructions) and have the same *SSN* pattern as all other 'institutionalizations' of 'The Social': *Systematization* – a claim that that *social form* (depiction, logic, agency, institution) is *all* that properly is comprised in the always-already more general historical experience of what the social form claims (names) to be 'the case', e.g. education *is* schooling (State regulated or provided), gendered and sexualised human beings *are* (have to be) like that, and that, and that . . . *Standardization* – a claim that not only is the general social form (named here as having a necessitarian logic of similarity) like *that* (or it is backward, inadequate, partial, incomplete, or – a KeyWord of that Cultural Revolution, (as yet) un- or underdeveloped); but that it has to be, and here we are addressing questions of inner form, a prismatic recognition of social difference(s), *regulated* either by that grand illusory community and collective *mis*representation of us all, called 'The State', or by that free-wheeling (and dealing) effectivity called 'The Market' (the mishmash miasma of these two producing that special space of wonderful signs called 'Culture'). Taken together *that* Trinity produces 'Official Politics', 'The Economy', and 'The Cultural-Ideological Level'. *Normalization* – recognition-practices that effect the two former modalities of 'Authority' to make the Normal *normal*, through rhetorics which effectively displace what the whole social constructivity is about, namely 'The Social', both through a media or realm which we can see as effectively replacing totalizing Religions, namely that of Reason and Rationality; and, to ensure that the totality of 'Les Autres' are discouraged, spending much attention to all border/lines and boundary-markers, to show the full range of the *sick, mad, bad* Trinities in discursive and pictorial splendor, sustained 'behind' the texts and images by techniques of social classification, technologies of power.

One such historical-social construction which is now being traced involves, precisely, the picturesque. Whether in studies of the social external 'Others' or the 'Aliens?' within (the national-populist cartograms of the territorial, geographical, cosmological, 'People'), what is now clear is that all dominant visual Traditions (*including* those of a marxist-socialist-communist character) are *Invented*.[20] But of course, in case we slip too simply into a 'Therefore the Problem is Difference(s)' mode of critical analysis, such 'inventions' embody 'Authority' (and all the cognate terms), not least of which are those of accountable pleasures and – yes – this too is no clean starting point, 'Feeling Good' (a man may feel very good, i.e. masculine, when he is beating to pulp a woman, for example; parents and teachers may feel very excellent persons when they are urging upon their children/students a replicative 'Model' of 'How To Be Good').

This might be another time to say (instruct) that you go back and re-view (again) the three illustrative photograms that open this paper. They are not there for decoration! You might surmise, as against the first, the history of agrarian radicalism (as in, say the CCF in Canada, or the Land Leagues in Ireland and Scotland);[21] as against the second, you could perhaps, dwell on Barbara Kruger's 'We won't play Nature to your Culture';[22] and, during the third, you could think of the paradigmatic Master–Servant/Slave dialexis entailed here.[23]

3 Picturing, similarly

The project of 'projecting' 'The Social' – which double-crosses the otherwise sustained dichotomy of the Private and *the* Public – is now become clearer to us. First, in the place of a 1970s theoretical fevered moment which tending to 'blame' 'The Apparatus' we can now trace how the different means of visual representation are caught up by (operate as) technologies of power.[24] Secondly, and correlatively, we can see that a typical technological determinism (and teleology) which makes the means into a social form (and provides a history of comprehensive technological 'breaks') is mystificatory; photography did not annihilate or end painting, no more did movies kill the 'live' theatre, nor visual means in general displace printing or publishing or reading. On the contrary, the codes and conventions (forms and norms) of former cultural practices[25] are taken up in complex ways in later means of production *and*, we can now trace, they operate within wider structured relations concerning, for example, audiences, 'providing institutions', directors and producers, and 'creators'. Third, and this is still largely un-developed, we can see how rapidly (and previous modes of theorising tended to add to this obscuring) *one* use, form 'nature' of each means of cultural production becomes associated with *what it is and has to be*.[26] The range of possibilities of all forms of camera (and transmission, as, for example, with television) quickly become (apart from a marginal 'high art' or 'technological/scientific' minority *alternative* practices) systematised, standardised, and normalised.

One of the most important complex 'carryings over' in terms of picturing concerns the picturesque; more so it concerns the rules of composing certain depictions (i.e. making images) that would declare (as their illocutionary force) that *that* was/is 'Otherness' (exotic, strange, *different* – including the abnormal: sick, mad, bad). First of all, I want to argue that the modes of this picturesque depicting were/are radically similar whether operating as a visual sociology in the heartlands of capitalism and imperialism, *Home*; or as a visual anthropology 'out there' in the colonies, *Abroad*. Second, I want to throw that project (of, to repeat, making 'The Social' visually *evident* since, to be sure, 'seeing is believing') into a deeper crisis than recent historiographical work[27] has done by linking into the crisis of documentary modes,[28] of what it is *to* document. I have been arguing, that crisis, too, is part of a general one, involving both an older liberalism and various forms of social-democracy and it entails both senses of the practice 'representation' (cultural and political).[29]

Here a photogrammar joins with (is revealed to be) cartography. 'The' world was and is mapped variously, but it was and is not done by those who live on the ground in question – or rarely so. To map, to depict, to conduct a survey or a census, to establish a system of law, or of schooling, or of medicine, is to simultaneously do a lot of *naming* and efface the orthogonality, the perspectival projection (intended both for depictions as pictures and as maps, which are also, of course, pictures) of who is declaring *that* view of somebody else's work to be *thus*. In the end we can see only what we are shown, on the screen, in the image, on the map, in the census. Even the rule-governed norms of the depicting form are not visible to us. Like one aspect of the Master Gurdjieff's diction to his pupil (a significant version of their being more to seeing than meets the eye!) or the Most Photographed Barn in America, Bernard Cohn quotes William Gilpin's rule for the picturesque:

In sketching a landscape gnarled trees should be placed on
either side, a Gothic ruin should be placed in the off-skip,
meadows inserted in the background . . . the foreground should
contain creepers, stumps of blasted trees, stony banks, and
rutted paths with shaggy animals and unkept (?unkempt – PC)
humans *to add the accurate touch of life*. (my emphasis, PC)[30]

The rapidity with which this creation of the Exotic Other (here
'Indians' in 'India') came to be 'the Real' is understood by Gholam
Husaid Khan, who reported in the 1780s how even an Indian of
great importance, who came to talk with an English (imperialist)
official, 'looks . . . (to the official) very much like a number of
pictures set up against the wall'.[31] Cohn provides illustrations of
these imperialist depictions at *work*; so that, by 1854, Fanny
Parkes, journeying up river, can note in her diary that not only is
the river 'picturesque' but its *effect* is 'greatly increased by the
native women, in their picturesque drapery'.[32] Crucial here, as
Cohn argues, is the creation and sustaining of distance through the
depiction of:

Indians as isolated, *decontextualised objects* whose meaning can
only be inferred from their special dress or the presence of the
tools of their trades, and displaying the *markers of the services*
which they were to provide to the sahibs and memsahibs. (my
emphases, PC)[33]

But of course, as Cohn details and illustrates, this has a larger,
longer history than that imperialization of 'India' – or rather, is
globally contemporaneous with it. Patrick Keiller traces the
picturesque formation of how we are encouraged to view the Dee
valley. His illustration (Richard Wilson, *The River Dee*, 1762?)
conforms to all that Gilpin ruled important. It is significant that
Keiller can begin by telling us the story of his recent re-viewing of
an episode of the television series *Z-Cars* (called, strikingly,
'People's Property' and originally broadcast 15th May 1962) in
which the two 'heroes' (Jock and Fancy, from police car Zed-
Victor-One) chased two 'delinquents' up a mountain, whereupon
– after the apprehending of the criminals is accomplished – they
turn and 'notice' the landscape in view.

The camera obliges with a slow pan over the view, during which not a word is spoken. An awesome spectacle of landscape, it seems, transcends even the most difficult predicament.[34]

Keiller goes on to make a number of connected arguments. The two that I want to select out involve, first, his emphasis upon how little of the (actual) English countryside counts *as* 'the English countryside':

> I suspect . . . that the hegemony of this type of view in the national imagination has more to do with the former appearance of Sussex than anything else, and reflects the class status of the home counties: their arcadia an imagined former rural identity now undermined by middle-distance commuting and suburbanisation.[35]

Secondly, I want to endorse his sense of a shift (which is what I intend with my notion of the move from the picturesque to the picturable) from 'seeing somewhere as somewhere else' to 'seeing somewhere in terms of a picture of somewhere else'.[36]

I think that by the late 1960s–early 1970s the principal source (textual and visual) of historical and geographical knowledge of 'Abroad' (for those 'at Home' in the dominant capitalist formations) comes from the activity of *promoting* tourism and travel. Aside from the specialist magazines (and, of course, travel brochures), and ignoring the always highly popular television series involving 'Travel', 'Exploration' and 'Nature', I am struck by what picturesque information is carried in the Travel *supplements* (and advertisements, of course, more generally) in the Newspapers. I have regularly read those in the *New York Times* (on Sundays) and in the *Toronto Star* (usually on Saturdays) since I came to Canada in the Fall of 1983. Apart from noticing a steady continuation of the project that Cohn, and others,[37] have traced, regarding an imperialized depicting of the Other(s) – *whether 'at Home' or 'Abroad'* – as exotic or terrifying 'decontextualised objects', there is also much currently that Keiller suggests also. This is not surprising, just as the formation of the picturesque (as a resource which also informs the technology of specular power) is concurrent *at Home* (likenesses being made of the lower orders, the aliens within, the folk, the rural idiots, the quaint and, of course, the mad, bad and sick) and *Abroad*; so these two forms of picturing-formation are still concurrent, still caught up in the same nexus of the same cultural revolution.[38] Sustained in this ubiquitous picturing of the world is both the 'hegemony of a type of view' *and* viewing which increasingly consists of 'seeing somewhere in terms of a picture of somewhere else'. Depictions of 'London' (as also of a certain 'Englishness'),[39] that I 'naturally' can more readily sense in their doubling mythification (*certain* views framed by *certain* rules for viewing), would be laughable did they not give me pause for thought as to how I think 'New York' (which I have visited) or 'Dallas' (which I have not);[40] or how I sense – even when 'I' *am* 'there' – a generalised 'Third World'.

When we say of a given scene (and that we declare a particular place or view as 'a scene' is not insignificant), whether we have seen it or not, that it is (we hear) 'as pretty as a picture (postcard)'[41] we are indicating ways in which we do not, as Murray puts it, *see the barn*, i.e. the scene. Hence views and scenes can be disappointing ('It was a nice ride but . . .(a) you couldn't see much once you were there; (b) it's not all that spectacular, really; (c) it was raining/foggy/misty') if they do not conform to *that* image-repertoire. The picturing I have traced here is now so ubiquitous that we are often tourists of our own times, of our own towns, of our own ground.[42]

But this is not all. To end here, with *all of that*, would be to remain fixated in a certain 'State of Things'. So, again, I ask you to review the three photograms with which I began.

4 Embodying, differently

Picturing (as part of more generalised image-repertoires), no more than discursive regimes, magnificent rituals, mundane routines or a generalised technological (powered) rationality, does not catch all of us up, all of our times. Exactly as the rules for depicting can be broken and transgressed (thus expanding the conventions of forms and norms), so too can rules for viewing. People can and do – to draw from the three photograms – (i) walk out back of the barn (out back of *that* Real) and view or photograph from there, some people might even go inside the barn, or stand with the barn to their back and look away; (ii) re-member, with a lot of 'trouble' and pain, why they forgot, and how what they forgot was also a way of going forward (living and loving) differently; and, (iii) tell the Master to cut the sexist crap and shift from a fertilising fatalism (a 'many are called, few are chosen' sort of heroism) to the realisation that possibilities are multiple, contradictory and restrained not by 'Nature' but by 'The Social'.

Much of this comes from other ways of viewing and knowing, that produces an active picturing which is at once historical and utopian; formalist – for example – in finding the orthogonality (what is being projected from where by whom at/of whom?), yet romantic in knowing there is more to seeing than that frame, that code, that picturing. To say this does not deny the 'hold' that *that* picturing has – it *has* made the world over – but it is to recall how the subjectivities thus encouraged, invited or harmfully imaged, are not thereby totally constituted, positioned or identified *that-sidedly*. One trace of being tactically 'obligated' to view that way is all semblance talk, e.g. when anyone says something *seems* that way there is a punctuation (possibly, anyway) in the perspectival and pictorial norms.

First, the project itself is riven with contradictions; central to which is a desire to hold what is extensively a *gone world* – a world of evaluation and worth which is catastrophically dispersed by other values (centrally, those of monetary worth and political power) associated with technological rationality, global capitalism and multi-national conglomerates producing-distributing-circulating-selling. Second, a tree is a tree is a tree; the mythologized 'Maple (Leaf)' or 'Oak' operates in a different sign system, one which has in fact not *signified*. Third, in the words of a valuable critical account, we live in a time when *The Empire Strikes Back*.[43] The rhetorics of both the scenic and the exotic, have new contexts and connections; this, I admit, splits two ways – centuries of picturesque fascism are not without their consequences, in new contexts they can operate as causal explanations. In fact, as I have argued before, monetarism with all its futurology is far better conceptualised within a rhetoric of Return (to the old verities, the old certainties, the basics); as Wilhelm Reich analysed the first fascisms in Europe, what we have is a mesmerism to do with 'The Past'. But that is not the only outcome of such splitting, there is also a recontextualization of those pictured as exotic as like us – once again the similar and the dissimilar can become re-arranged.

But, fourth, and most important, there are issues about resistance and refusal that need to be traced. What can be observed (about the barn), remembered (about stories), discovered (about pedagogy and oak trees) is evidentially there. These findings are affectual and bodily, finally communicated in textual and pictorial forms that sustain a sense of wonder that comes from that easiest of human activities, second-glancing and finding the frame or the form inadequate. Two examples. There is an exceptional essay, in Guy Davenport's *Geography of the Imagin-ation*[44] called 'Finding' about Sunday afternoons heading out 'to look for Indian arrows' in Georgia and South Carolina. It is so textured that quotation would be even more violent than usual, but since Davenport offers a reflective thought I shall use that:

> I know that my sense of place, of occasion, even of doing anything at all, was shaped by those afternoons. It took a while for me to realize that people can grow up without being taught to see, to search surfaces for all the details, to check out a whole landscape for what it has to offer. (p. 367)

This is not, as a *form* of finding (and then, perhaps, forgetting), unique.

The other, which links directly to the ending of Davenport's 'Findings' – 'They tell over the radio . . . that a bunch of Japanese airplanes have blowed up the whole island of Hawaii' (*ibid*) – is Dean Pitchford's 'A Father's Pictures'.[45] This begins:

> In all the time I was growing up, I never heard my father speak about what it was like to have been at Pearl Harbor on Dec. 7, 1941. He showed us photographs instead.[46]

The article continues with rare information about the *arranging* of persons and groups for the 'family snap' (this too has its rules):[47] 'In the photo that was finally picked we always looked like the perfect family, a perfect pose.' His father leaves, the day after he graduates from eighth grade, and for almost seventeen years there is no communication from his father beyond (unsigned) birthday cards and Christmas cards. He turns to the family album (whilst visiting his mother in Hawaii – mothers, note, are customarily the family archivists) and comes to a crucial orthoganal sense – his father's absence from the snapshots: 'He's the one we were all smiling for'. He begins to miss – in a crucial phrase –

> my father's peculiar way of snatching moments and preserving emotions. I missed the silent give-and-take that each picture implied. I missed him.

So he writes a long letter – there are seventeen years to talk about – and gradually communication (photographs and soon letters and then telephone calls and visits from his father) is re-established. His father, at first, continues as before, photographing him, his house, his street, but:

> I no longer want him looking at me with his photographer's eye, taking without giving back.

So he insists his father talks ('I get him to sit for me . . . ')

> He is, at last, the subject-revealing himself to me, providing the most indelible images of him I will ever have.

If it should be objected that what I am proffering here, as contra-picturing, is frail, personal, anecdotal, minor, private, nostalgic or – *even* (as if the word were like the huff and puff of the wolf) *romantic* – let me say 'Yes, yes, yes!' This *is* the micropolitics of a counter-power, a differencing picturing, in which the body and the emotions are never denied for the category, the concept, the definition, *or the pictured*. Involved here (and in the examples, some of them I have indicated previously could be multiplied) is a militant, if quiet, dispersed, prismatic to theoretical systems and political projects (narrowly defined), attention to *this-sidedness* as *against all of that*. This is not a refusal that ignores, can afford to not take seriously, the ways of the smart and powerful and vicious, but a refusal to believe, say, live and love as if *that* is all there is.

Although world-clocks, like world-images, tick and click, whirl and wheel, past us – and, of course, they govern us and catch us up *in part*, we remain. We are more than any sign system. Although cast, to play our parts, we are not puppets, nor yet cast in stone. Acting can be calculated for a given performance without any fully forming (handing over) of subjectivity: it is, I insist, the body (often absent) that resists and refuses, differently. It is the body that knows, re-members – both, as examples, the before-and-after of the 'perfect family scene' and the visit to a scene (pictured before as almost a 'shrine'). The body and signs of polyphony,[48] differencing which starts against (resistance, 1) the social forms of declarative rhetorical regulation (including picturing) by tearing at (resistance, 2) the limits of the means and media of those forms – that uncertain ethnography in which nobody knows (quite, fully, all the time) *What Works* (e.g. with the audience, the mugs, the masses. . . .) through a gentle apocalypse involving hopefulness, imaginactions, going beyond, unlearning to the point where Not Yet (resistance, 3) can be seen to be not there, not *that*, but this, and thus, and this, and then. . . . It is a texture, material and embodied, which is woven from (and thus unravels) the prohibiting Nots – yes, maybe (for there is also resistance, 4: *fear*) to retie them (and us) as Knots – but then that suture is known, and not accomplished whilst we are anaesthetised.

All of this entails and involves far more than the normal microsecond of the sociological glance; it means looking twice, the finding in (here, to return to the three photograms) not only that there is more to seeing than meets the eye, but that a picture is worth a lot *less* than a thousand words, or one walk in the woods, with the words of a great-grand-mother, or even a patriarch, ringing in the ears. The aura of the barn may not be metaphorical as Murray suggests, it may be that there are *signifieds* that come from 'barn' (as architecture in place; as storing plenty; as tracing multiple histories) which are remarkably absent (lost) for the many who drive there. *We see What/How we see.*

In all of this there is an issue about *observation*. Who is observing others observing others/'nature', and why, and for whom?[49] My weak, relatively content-less, contra-picturing makes no claims, utters no names. Today (September 1, 1987) I walked in the woods near the 'cottage' (as they are called in Ontario) where I have been living for three weeks. I was with a dog, called Train. As we walked (and talked) he and I (well, I suppose, mainly me) almost could 'tick off' the signs that we could be *taken for*. They are all true, valid, but *partial*; for he, in his way, and me, in mine, could by looking (he also by smelling), trace and be sensible of the extraordinarily complex world, we found, after the rain all night long. And, whilst he found sticks, I picked flowers and bright early fall leaves, for my lover, and thought about how I could not finish this article . . .[50] . . . convincingly, finally. So? 'The End'. Or, for John, *Imagine*, twice again!

Notes

Philip R. D. Corrigan is a Professor, and was Chairperson (1986–88), in the Department of Sociology in Education, Ontario Institute for Studies in Education, Toronto, Ontario, Canada; he was previously Lecturer, Department of Sociology of Education, Institute of Education, London, 1980–83, and Head, Cultural Studies Unit, London College of Printing, 1978–79. A librarian, and library-studies lecturer, from 1960–1971, he obtained his BA and Ph.D. from the University of Durham, England, and has an MA in Film and Television Studies (CNAA/ Polytechnic of Central London). 'Innocent stupidities' quotes Guy Davenport's 'Innocent stupidity' from his essay 'Ernst Mach Max Ernst' in *The Geography of the Imagination* (op. cit. 25 below, p. 375) like him, it *is* my sense that I am always telling a story. . . . (ibid., p. 376).

1 Like all writings, this is socially organised inter-textually in relation to certain
'amorous fits', obsessions of my own writings, which are twin-streamed: (a)
'Dichotomy is Contradiction' (1975); 'On Moral Regulation' (1981); and 'The
Body of Intellectuals' (1988), all in *Sociological Review*, for the years indicated;
together with numerous reviews in that journal, especially 'Into Textuality:
Timing our words' (1983) – a text that 'breaks out'; with Val Corrigan: 'State
formation and social policy before 1871' in N. Parry and others (eds), *Social
Work, Welfare and the State*, (Leeds, Arnold, 1970); the work with Derek Sayer:
'Class struggle, social relations, moral economy' *Radical Philosophy*, (12) 1975;
'Hindess and Hirst: A critique' *Socialist Register*, 1978; 'How the law rules' in B.
Fryer and others (eds) *Law, State, Society* (London, Croom Helm, 1981); our
chapter in T. Shanin (eds) *Late Marx* (London, Routledge & Kegan Paul; New
York, Monthly Review Press, 1983) and its fuller version, forthcoming,
*Dialectical Anthropology; The Great Arch: English State Formation as Cultural
Revolution* (Oxford, New York, Blackwell, 1985) 'Marxist Theory and Socialist
Construction in Historical Perspective' *Utafiti* Summer 1984; 'From "The Body
Politic" to the "National Interest"' Keynote Address, Mellon Symposium on
Historical Anthropology, Pasadena, Calif, 1987; and our joint editorship of
Journal of Historical Sociology (Oxford, New York, Blackwell, 1988–): plus –
our joint work with Harvie Ramsay: *Socialist construction and marxist theory*
(London, Macmillan; New York, Monthly Review Press, 1978); *For Mao*
(London, Macmillan; New Jersey, Humanities, 1979); 'Bolshevism and the
USSR' *New Left Review* (1981) and a paper originally presented at the British
Sociological Association Conference in 1977 – Ch. 1 in P. R. D. Corrigan (ed.)
Capitalism, State Formation, Marxist Theory (London, Quartet; New York,
Urizen, 1980) (b) with Paul Willis 'Cultural forms and class mediations' *Media,
Culture and Society*, 2, 1980; 'The Orders of Experience' *Social Text*, 7, 1983;
with Michèle Barrett, Annette Kuhn and Janet Wolff (eds) *Ideology and
Cultural Production* (London, Croom Helm, 1979); with Val Gillespie *Class
struggle, social literacy, idle time* (Brighton, John Noyce, 1978); with Paul
Willis, John Berger, Jean Mohr 'Dossier' *Screen Education* 32/33, 1979–80;
alone: '(Re)making it new' *Undercut* (1) 1981; 'Towards a celebration of
difference(s)' in D. Robbins (ed.) *Rethinking Social Inequality* (London, Gower
Press, 1982); 'What is the subject of (a) cultural production' *Undercut* (3/4)
1982: 'Towards a sociology of film audiences' Ch. 2 in J. Curran and V. Porter
(eds) *British Cinema History* (London, Weidenfeld and Nicholson, 1983);
'Doing mythologies' *Border/lines* (1) 1984; two reviews of R. Donegan
'Spadina' – of the exhibition, *Parachute* (37) 1984–5; of the book *Border/lines*
(6) 1986; 'In/formation' *Photocommuniqué*, Fall 1985 and 'Initial Eye
Photocommuniqué forthcoming; 'Did I hear bark?' *C Magazine*, December
1985; with Mark Nash 'Regarding Peter Fuller' *Art Monthly* (40) 1981; alone:
'Against biological aesthetics' *Banff Letters*, Spring 1983; 'Fuller's Earth'
Vanguard, Spring 1984; 'Playing, Contra/Diction . . .' *Teaching and
Curriculum*, 1988; 'Masculinity as Right' (forthcoming); 'Education for
Masculinity', paper presented ot the Gender Group Seminar, OISE-CIDE-
PIIE Cooperative Project, Santiago, March 1987; *X/S: For Roland*
(forthcoming, 1989). The 'educational' writings span this twin-streaming
somewhat: 'In/forming schooling' Ch. 1 and D. Livingstone (ed.) *Critical
Pedagogy and Cultural Power* (South Hadley, Mass., Bergin and Garvey;
Toronto, Garamond; London, Macmillan, 1986); with Bruce Curtis and Robert
Lanning 'The Political Space of Schooling' Ch. 1 in T. Wotherspoon (ed.)
Political Economy of Canadian Schooling (Toronto, New York, London,
Methuen, 1987); with Shmuel Shamai 'Moral Regulation and Statistical
Jurisdiction: The Canadian Census and Education' *Canadian Journal of Higher
Education*, Summer 1987; 'State formation and classroom practice' in G.
Milburn (ed.) *Qualitative Research in the Curriculum* (London, Ontario,

Althouse Press, 1988); 'Embodying ethnicity educationally' (and Roger Simon's response) in J. Young (ed.) *Breaking the Mosaic* (Toronto, Garamond, 1987); (ed.) *Education Now: Essays in Exploration* (forthcoming, 1989).

2 Apart from the material indicated at n. 1 above, it is particularly important that this paper be read as complementary to the one written contemporaneously 'A Day in Whose Life . . . Canada's IMAGE/nation' in G. McGregor (ed.) *Canadian Art and Contemporary Theory* (Toronto, University of Toronto Press, 1988).

3 Don Delillo *White Noise* (New York, Viking Penguin Inc. 1985). Who sees (for examples) (a) Big Ben; (b) L'Arc de Triomphe; (c) The Statue of Liberty? I remember (in 1952? perhaps) being *taken*, to a roadside, in London (appropriately, as I remember, it was Shooter's Hill) to see 'The Queen' – we waited, I think we were issued with flags, I was ten years old, and we waited, and then these big cars drove by and I could not see 'The Queen' but I waved and shouted and cheered. The first time (perhaps) when I was bodily caught up like that?

4 Annabel Nicolson 'In the Dark' *Undercut* (7/8), 1983; see also *Michigan Quarterly Review*, 26(1), 1987, issue theme 'Women and Memory', especially Esther Parada 'Women's Vision extends the Map of Memory'. I have learned much from the work of those who have made re-membering so crucial to their depiction work, notably: Jo Spence *Putting myself in the picture* (London, Camden Press, 1986) and her earlier work referenced in 'In/formation' *Photocommuniqué* cited in n. 1 above; Kathleen Rockhill *The Chaos of subjectivity* (OISE, Popular Feminism Series, 1986, forthcoming in a book from that series, 1988); Marian McMahon, cultural productions 1985–87, and MA thesis (OISE, 1987); Carolyn Steedman *Landscape for a good woman* (London, Virago, 1986); Valerie Walkerdine: 'Dreams of an ordinary childhood' in L. Heron (ed.) *Truth, dare or promise* (London, Virago, 1985), and 'Someday my prince will come' in A. McRobbie and M. Nava (eds) *Gender and Generation* (London, New York, Toronto, Macmillan, 1984; *Youth Questions* series). For very provisional attempts from my own body see 'My(?) Body, My Self(?): Trying to see with my masculine eyes' *Resources for Feminist Research*, 1983, and 'Masculinity as Right' op. cit. n. 1 above.

5 Henry Miller *Reflections*; edited by Twinka Thiebaud (Santa Barbara, Calif., Capra Press, 1981, from the chapter 'Gurdjieff'). This is also included for two other reasons: (a) a sentimental echo of so much 'Zen' story-ing, with their deeply 'master'/'man' (servant) talk through the 1960s and beyond; (b) for the otherness intended within a language of 'possibility' (or, better, *possibilities*) which is currently being illuminated for me in the work of Roger Simon, Magda Lewis and Donald Dippo; cf. their forthcoming book *Identities and Possibility*.

6 This theme runs through all the writings of twin-stream (b) in n. 1 above, especially 'What is the subject of (a) cultural production?'; 'Towards a sociology of film audiences' and, comprehensively in both 'Doing Mythologies' and 'In/formation'.

7 Michel Foucault 'The Subject and Power' *Critical Inquiry*, 8, 1982; but, see also his neglected 'Questions of Method', *Ideology and Consciousness* (8) 1981. The way I wish to take the sense of this is best displayed in the (b) stream writings in n. 1 above, but is also clear in both *The Great Arch* (with Derek Sayer) and the chapter by myself, Bruce Curtis and Bob Lanning, which forms part of the cultural production from The State Formation Project. For especially significant attention to the visual see the work of both Annette Kuhn (referenced in 'In/formation/ in n. 1 above; and her forthcoming monograph on Censorship in Film, Routledge, 1988) and Janet Wolff *The social production of art* (Macmillan, 1981). Photographically see the crucial journal *Ten-8*, 1980 onwards, along with *Camerawork*, *Screen Education*, *Aperture*, *Creative Camera*, *Undercut*, *Framework*, *Representations*, *JumpCut*, *Afterimage* (both

English and US editions), *Screen*, *Zones*, *Border/lines* and the work referenced in 'In/formation' n. 1 above, including Stephanie Bezcencenet and Philip Corrigan (eds) *Photographic Practices: Towards a Different Image* (London, Comedia, 1986).

8 'Towards a celebration of differences(s)' and 'The Body of the Intellectuals' cited in n. 1 above, plus the (unpublished) 'A look around the talent in the room' (Documentary Presentation to the Cultural Studies Network, 1979); and 'On not writing on the back of postage stamps' (Documentary Presentation to the History Workshop Conference, Oxford, 1978); or with Derek Sayer 'Overcoming the Obvious' (Presentation to the Centre for Contemporary Cultural Studies, University of Birmingham, 1978). But all my work, I can now see and sense, turns on a refusal to accept either the formalist (vanguard, avant-garde, scientific) or the romantic (withdrawal, utopian) 'options'. Instead I have been trying to rework the strategy/tactics contradictory unity (and yet, multiplying subjectivities) toward an expanded (and expansive non-exclusionary) *form* of politics. Regarding 'difference(s)' I shall have more to say later.

9 Since 1968 I have been troubled by all words that end in -y and the luxuriant -isms that flourish around them (e.g. hegemony, Gramscism; ideology, Althusserianism or Lacanism; semiology, Barthesism; Eco-ism; Cullerism . . .). They, catastrophically, miss the point: That of refusal/difference/multiplicity: How We Might/Differently Be More Than We Are Now (allowed, encouraged, coerced) Being; that is the project (open, a place of struggle as much as hope) of Becoming . . . living historically, so that we can love more fully. More later.

10 The triangular association of Wenders' three films – *The State of Things*, *Hammett*, and *Paris, Texas* – can be viewed and reviewed as the crisis of signifying (let alone, representing) 'the (socially) Real'. Avoiding the oh-my-gosh *enfant terrible* of both (e.g. Jean-Luc Godard, *and* the 'movie brats' hyped as 'taking over' Hollywood), Wim Wenders is the most consistently interesting *male* film-maker that I have viewed. In my own (only) idea for a film – SPLICE/ Formal Pleasures – I would try to follow where Wenders points, involving resources from Jean-Paul Sartre's scenario *In the Mesh* (1947) and Graham Greene's entertainment *Brighton Rock* – but who is going to fund that?

11 I suggested, during 'Overcoming the Obvious' (1978) that it might be efficacious for the 1970s to follow the labyrinth of Marx 'the poet' (*vs* the predominantly positive then, and residually powerful now, Marx 'the scientist'). For the 1980s I am suggesting the different slogan of 'It is not that simple'. As a slogan it is not that wondrous, perhaps, but it does effectively 'catch up' such connected phenomena as monetarist *mesmerism* (as Reich would have called it) as focused – especially – in official schooling in their slogan 'back to basics'. See, for a good 'refusal' of two best-sellers regarding 'The American Mind' P. Berman 'Cultural literacy' *Village Voice* September 8, 1987: 37.

12 There remains a sociology of 'standpoint' to be written. For a significant start to this project see the work of Dorothy Smith in her two volumes forthcoming (NorthEastern University Press, 1988; and *The Social Organization of Knowledge*, 1988) 'Standpoint' has to be differenced, for example in contrast to Schutz, Goffman, Garfinkel and so on (within) a phenomenological tradition, and almost anyone writing as a marxist (including most marxist-feminists). Neither can there be in such a sociology of 'standpoint' any establishment of cartographic devices like 'Woman'/'Women' – precisely as useless as 'Man'/ 'Men'. Standpoint is a crucial term of refusal since it counterpolitics both cartogrammar and the claimed wonders of the local, specific. It disturbs, exactly, the social algebra of re-presentation. It is a troubled, uneasy account. For example, see Ana Maria Alonso 'The effects of Truth' *Journal of Historical Sociology* 1(1) 1988; all of Dick Hebidge's writings referenced in my essay 'Playing, Contra/Diction . . .' *Teaching and Curriculum*, n. 1 above; and the

work of Derek Sayer: *Marx's Method* (rev. ed., Harvester/Humanities, 1983); *The Violence of abstraction* (London, New York, Blackwell, 1987).

13 Tears for Fears *Songs from The Big Chair* (1984); P. R. D. Corrigan 'The Politics of Feeling Good' forthcoming in R. Gruneau (ed.) *The Politics of Popular Cultures* (Toronto, Gramond, 1988).

14 The 'photograph/photographs' 're-arrangement' is central to my essay 'In/formation' cited in n. 1 above; but see also the two papers with Paul Willis also cited in that note.

15 The reference(s) for this distinction can be found in 'In/formation' cited in n. 1 above; a fuller investigation of Barthes is forthcoming as *X/S*, the central elements of which can be traced in 'Doing Mythologies' cited in n. 1 above, and 'All Ways a Third Way: Re-Reading Roland Barthes' presentation to the Graduate Department of French, University of Toronto, February 1984; see also 'The Body of Intellectuals' cited in n. 1 above. For a very different re-arrangement of these signs see 'BOOMista manifesto' *Shades* (Toronto), February 1984.

16 Particularly in 'Leçon' (his inaugural lecture at the Collége de France) translated in *Oxford Literary Review*, 1981; or his *Roland Barthes by Roland Barthes*. For one 'use' see 'Body of Intellectuals' cited in n. 1 above; for another see Magda Lewis and Roger Simon 'A Discourse not intended for Her' *Harvard Educational Review*, 1986.

17 Certain studies are never recognised as theoretically informative – a reading of Carolyn Steedman *The Tidy House* (London, Virago, 1982) and David Morley and Ken Worpole (eds) *The Republic of Letters* (London, Comedia, 1983) – thinking visually and as against, e.g. Terry Eagleton *Literary Theory* (Minneapolis, University of Minnesota Press, 1983) – would be incredibly transforming; as also Ken Brockington and Geoffrey White (eds) *Tales out of school* (London, Boston, Routledge & Kegan Paul, 1983). They can then be montaged with (what is now taken to be) Grand Theory (e.g. Wittgenstein, Volosoniv/Bakhtin) as also with (a) Ivan Illich 'Vernacular Values' in his book *Shadow Work* (London, Boyars, 1982); (b) Teodor Shanin 'Marxism and Vernacular Traditions' in same author (ed.) *Late Marx* (London, Routledge & Kegan Paul; New York, Monthly Review Press, 1983); (c) the closing chapters of both (and taken together) of Raymond Williams's *Country and the City* and Edward Thompson's *Making of the English Working Class*; and (d) those pervasive actualizations of counter-power, contra-hegemony, membered and overheard conversations, gossip, graffiti, and rumours in supermarket queues, transit line-ups, in response to the persisting invitations to 'Participate' in the face of antiDemocratic, engrossing centralization since the early 1970s.

18 This 'figure' (as much of grammar, including photogrammar, as physicality) is explored in 'Towards a celebration of difference(s)'; 'Masculinity as Right' and 'Re/Membering Modernity' cited in n. 1. For illustrative explorations see the Ph.D. theses of (i) Fiona Patterson, Edinburgh (Sociology), 1986; (ii) Lorna Weir, York (Social and Political Thought), 1986; and (iii) existing and forthcoming from the '1850–1950s' group of historical sociologists at OISE; Kari Dehli (1988); Debi Brock (1989); David Welch (1988); and Marion McMahon, Judith Millen; Robert Lanning; Judith Marshall; Magda Lewis; Ken Banks; Lindsay Manicom; Susan Heald; Cheryl Hudson; Donna Varga Heise and others. For significant work on 'embodiment' and 'voice' see the writings of Madeline Grumet (e.g. 'Body Reading' *Teachers College Record*, 1986) and Linda Brodkey (e.g. 'Writing Critical Ethnographic Narratives' *Education and Anthropology Quarterly*, 1987).

19 Apart from the material referenced in n. 18 above, see: Catherine MacKinnon *Feminism Unmodified* (Cambridge, Mass.; London, Harvard University Press, 1987, especially 'Introduction' and Ch. 2); Andrea Dworkin *Intercourse* (New York, Free Press, 1987); Trinh T. Minh-ha 'Difference: "A Special Third World

Women Issue"' *Feminist Review* (25) 1987; where Audre Lorde is quoted –
Survival *'is not an academic skill* . . . it is learning how to take our differences
and make them strengths. *For the master's tools will never dismantle the master's
house.* They may allow us temporarily to beat him at his own game, but they will
never allow us to bring about genuine change' (Minh-ha, p. 5, emphasis there).

20 E. J. Hobsbawm and T. Ranger (eds) *The Invention of tradition* (Cambridge,
New York, Cambridge University Press, 1983); T. Wilden: *The Imaginary
Canadian* (Vancouver, Pull Press, 1981); *The Rules are NO game* (London,
Boston, Routledge & Kegan Paul 1986); Jonathan Culler *Framing the sign*
(University of Oklahoma Press, 1983); D. Costrovano *The English Gentleman*
(New York, Ungar Press, 1987); Raymond Williams *Politics and Letters*
(London, Verso Press, 1978); plus *all the work* by John Berger and his co-
workers – see the *Screen Education* 'Dossier' cited in n. 1 and more especially
the connections between his book with Jean Mohr *Another Way of Telling*
(1982) and Berger's own *And our faces, my heart, brief as photos* (New York,
Pantheon, 1984).

21 For some highly provisional references to the rural counter-hegemonies see
P. R. D. Corrigan: 'China: Thought Reform for Intellectuals' *Journal of
Contemporary Asia*, 1974; 'Peasants and Politics: Response to E. J. Hobsbawm'
Journal of Peasant Studies, 1975; 'Feudal relics or capitalist monuments? Notes
on the sociology of unfree labour' *Sociology*, 11, 1977.

22 Cf. Laura Mulvey in *Creative Camera*, May 1984: 1377–82 and 1397.

23 Vincent Descombes *Modern French Philosophy* (Cambridge, New York,
Cambridge University Press, 1981); 'Masculinity as Right' and 'Playing, Contra/
Diction' cited in n. 1 above; M. Foucault 'The Subject and Power' cited in n. 7
above.

24 Apart from the references in 'In/formation' note especially *Ten-8*, (14) 1984
issue theme 'Consent and Control' and the articles there by John Tagg and by
Judith Williamson.

25 As Guy Davenport says 'How one art learns from another is a question better
asked as what one art learns from another', *The Geography of the Imagination*
(San Francisco, North Point Press, 1981: 375 from the essay 'Ernst Mach Max
Ernst', see also pp. 8, 311, 315). For examples see: Edward Lockspier *Music
and Painting* (London, Cassell, 1973); Raymond Williams chapter in Curran
and Porter, op. cit., n. 1 above; Gordon Fyfe 'Art and Reproduction: some
aspects of the relations between painters and engravers in London 1760–1850'
Media, Culture and Society, 7, 1985. One 'Carry-on' which has been disastrous,
in my view, is that of 'Reading' (as Reading a film, a picture, a dance, a scene) –
see 'In-formation' op. cit. in n. 1 above.

26 For the telephone see the Ph.D. thesis of Michèle Martin (Sociology, University
of Toronto, 1987); for broadcasting in Canada, the Ph.D. thesis of Jody Berland
(Social and Political Thought, York University, 1985); for television in
England, P. R. D. Corrigan 'The "moment" of English television' MA thesis,
School of Communication, Polytechnic of Central London, 1981. I hope to edit
a volume of studies *Things Could Be Different* – which will provide essays on all
such early multiple moments of cultural means and meanings before the
closures of SSN.

27 Apart from Hobsbawm and Ranger, op. cit., n. 20 above, in which the chapter
by David Cannadine on the Royal Family should be supplemented by John
Pearson *The selling of the Royal Family: the mystique of the British Monarchy*
(New York, Simon and Schuster, 1986, reviewed by David Cannadine as 'The
Merry Wives of Windsor' *New York Review of Books*, June 12, 1986: 15–17),
see the connected writings of Bernard Cohn (who also has a chapter –
'Representing Authority in Victorian India' – in Hobsbawm and Ranger);
particularly: *Law and the colonial state in India* (Bellagio, Italy, Werner-Gren
symposium no. 97 'Ethnohistorical models for the evolution of law in specific

societies', August 10–18, 1985; 'Language of Command and Command of Language', *Subaltern Studies* (6), 1986; and, 'The Peoples of India: from the picturesque to the Museum of Mankind' (forthcoming, as with many of his papers, in a collection, Delhi, Oxford University Press, 1988). For complementary analyses see David Green 'Classified subjects – photography and anthropology: the technology of power' and Roberta McGarth 'Medical Police' both in *Ten-8* (14), 1984; Michael Lesy *The Forbidden Zone* (New York, Farrar, Straus and Giroux, 1987) which needs to be read with Philippe Ariès *L'Homme devant mort* (Paris, Seuil, 1977) translated as *The Hour of our Death*, by Helen Weaver (New York, Vintage Books, 1981); and, Patrick Keiller 'Atmosphere, Palimpsest and Other Interpretations of Landscape' *Undercut* (7/8), 1983 – issue theme 'Landscape'; plus the work of Dick Hebdige listed in my article 'Playing, Contra/Diction . . .' cited in n. 1 above.

28 Again see references in n. 16 and in 'In/formation' cited in n. 1 above, especially B. Winston 'Documentary' *Sight & Sound* 48(1) 1978–9, plus Sylvia Harvey 'Who wants to know what and why? Some problems for Documentary in the 80s', *Ten-8* (23 1986, who refers to Derrick Price 'Photographing the Poor and the Working Class', *Framework* (22/23), 1983.

29 R. Barthes is clear on this in his *Mythologies*; and also *Great Arch* (op. cit. n. 1 above) Chs. 5–6–7. I would want to add to *that* sort of work, two others: (i) studies of how 'we' become (compulsorily) represented as 'Nation', 'State', 'People' or 'Place(d)': we need accounts like that of Colin Mercer 'Generating Consent' *Ten-8* (14) 1984 or J. Donald (ed.) *Formations of Nation and People* (London, Boston, Routledge & Kegan Paul) Conrad Swan, York Herald of Arms: *Canada: Symbols of Sovereignty* (Toronto, University of Toronto Press, 1977); (ii) we also need to understand how we have been *made* to dress: N. B. Harte 'State Control of Dress and Social Change in Pre-Industrial England' in D. C. Coleman and A. H. John (eds) *Trade, government and economy in pre-industrial England* (London, Weidenfeld and Nicholson, 1976); Bryan Turner *The Body in Society* (Oxford, New York, Blackwell, 1986), Francis Barker *The Tremulous Private Body: Essays on Subjection* (London, New York, Toronto, Methuen, 1984); Anne Buck 'Dress as a social record' *Folk Life* (14) 1976; Alison Lurie *The Language of Clothes* (New York, Vintage Books, 1983) plus references in 'In/formation'. But just as all semiotics need to be simultaneously historicised and differenced, so too with psychoanalytic categories and thus with Fantasies/Phantasies, for starts toward which see J. Donald (ed.) *Formations of Fantasy* (London, Boston, Routledge & Kegan Paul, 1986) and *New Formations* (1), 1987, the latter carries a review – Chris Turner and Erica Carter 'Political Somatics' – of Klaus Theweleit *Männerphantasien, 1: Frauen, Fluten, Körper, Geschichte* (Berlin, Stern, 1977) translated as *Male Fantasies, 1: women, floods, bodies, history*, by Stephen Conway in collaboration with Erica Carter and Chris Turner (Minneapolis, University of Minnesota Press, 1987); but note also Ernst Bloch *The Principle of Hope* (3 vols; Oxford, Blackwell, 1986) and Frigga Haug 'Daydreams' *New Left Review*, (162) 1987.

30 Cohn, 'Peoples of India' op. cit., n. 27 above, p. 7 of typescript. Hodges 'The Pass of Sicri Gully' (illus. 14) follows Gilpin's 'rules'.

31 Cohn, ibid., p. 8.

32 Cohn, ibid., p. 7.

33 Cohn, ibid., p. 8. In his writings Cohn is providing us with a means to study what a cultural revolution (here English, male, bourgeois and capitalist) *looks like*. It amounts to nothing less than a radical reformation of the 'cultural-symbolic constitution' which 'embraces such things as classificatory schema, assumptions about how things are, cosmologies, world views, ethical systems, legal codes, definitions of governmental units and social groups, ideologies, religious doctrines, myths, rituals, procedures and rules of etiquette' (Cohn, quoting Ronald Inden, in Hobsbawm and Ranger, p. 173). As a crucial

Philip Corrigan

complement to this see Roland Barthes *Mythologies* (1957) translated into English as *Mythologies* (London, Cape, 1972) and *The Eiffel Tower and the Mythologies* (New York, Hill and Wang, 1979) *as qualified by* his later work as I stress in 'Doing Mythologies' cited in n. 1 above.

34 Keiller, op. cit., n. 27 above, p. 126.

35 Ibid.; the major work (for me) here remains John Berger and others: *Ways of Seeing* (London, BBC/Penguin both videos, and book, 1972) and Berger's essays in, for example, *About Looking* (1980), but note also (i) Fred Inglis 'Nation and Community: A Landscape and its morality' *The Sociological Review*, (1977) vol. 25, no. 3; (ii) Francis Haskell 'The Manufacture of the Past in Nineteenth-Century Painting' and other chapters in: *Past and Present in Art and Taste* (New Haven, London, Yale University Press, 1987), (iii) issues of *Representations* especially on cartography; and (iv) Don Wayne *Penshurst: the Semiotics of Place and the Poetics of History* (Madison, Wis.; University of Wisconsin Press, 1984).

36 Ibid., p. 127. The same issue of *Undercut* contains Ian Jeffrey 'The culture of connotation, and after: Some notes on landscape photography in Britain since 1900' which shows how the picturesque began to become, photographically, the picturable. Recall that cheap(er) easier to use cameras became ubiquitous from the mid–late 1930s.

37 Of particular value are Roland Barthes analyses of 'Africa' in *Mythologies* (both translated volumes cited in n. 33 above) especially read with Berger and Mohr's *Seventh Man* or *Another Way of Telling*, (cited in n. 20 above). The advent of cheaper forms (web offset) of colour magazine production – even if only of front and back covers and centrefolds – and widespread colour television is very significant here.

38 A lot of the time, in fact, *Abroad* is mainly (only) known *at Home*. David Green's 'Classified subjects' (op. cit., n. 27 above) ends with two apposite illustrations, front covers of *The Oberver* magazine and *TV Times*. More recently the *New York Times Magazine* (July 13, 1987) ran – as a cover story by Vicki Goldberg 'The Unflinching Eye' – a study of a 'photojournalist' described as 'Resolutely apolitical . . . Mary Ellen Mark is our resident 35-millimeter anthropologist' (pp. 18, 20). The *whole article* is a major illustration of the themes of my argument. Likewise, Cohn's point about 'distance' is still being sustained. Ken Adachi writing in *The Toronto Star* (August 23, 1987: B1) explains that Anita Desai 'born in 1937 of a Bengalese father and German mother, is an exceptionally gifted novelist who, writing in English, can illuminate the Indian world that is probably closed and alien to most North American readers.' (Despite this she is likened to Chekhov in the next sentence!) Patriarchal blood will out!

39 Cf. R. Colls and P. Dodds (eds) *Englishness* (London, Croom Helm, 1986); Bob Morgan *Cultural Production of English studies* (Ph.D. Thesis, OISE, 1987); and – as one single example – the Travel section of *The Toronto Star* (March 7, 1987) which has front page stories with headlines: 'London's great free show' (Christie's: 'a fascinating fixture on the London art scene for more than 200 years'); 'The price is right at Commons, too, for drama, history' (The House of Commons: 'In a city of the world's best and most prolific theatre, Parliament remains its longest running show, now in its third century and playing to full houses'); and two photographs: one, of some sheep on a roadway with a hill in the background, is captioned 'The lakes are small and the mountains tiny but the Lake District near England's border with Scotland offers a tranquillity and beauty that visitors (and poets) [possibly policemen too?]) find breathtaking'; the other, of some men and women, formally dressed, eating from fold-out picnic tables and chairs under a rather large tree or two, is captioned 'A picnic on the lawn in full evening dress? It could only occur in Britain, where music lovers at Glyndebourne opera festival dine near pastured horses and cattle'.

Within the section – along with mythification in print and picture – there is one, let's, following Barthes, call it 'punctum' – beneath a photograph (p. H25) of people walking, away from the camera, on a path across relatively open country, is the caption 'Britain's parks like Exmoor in north Devon, were born out of working-class rebellion'. Well thanks for that. Meanwhile back to 'London', John Russell reviewing the exhibition, curated by Celina Fox, 'Londoners', at the London Museum (in the *New York Times*, July 23, 1987: Y20) explains how these images (prints, paintings and drawings) have brought 'home to its many foreign visitors not only *what they knew already* – that Londoners are a funny-looking lot – but that the Londoner has always been highly individualised.' Moreover, '*Peculiar themselves*, Londoners love peculiarity in others.' (my emphases – PC). Et cetera!!

40 I choose the USA deliberately – there's a lot being shown in *Dallas*, *Dynasty*, *Hill Street Blues* and *Miami Vice* by way of picturing as others have argued, but I had in mind 'another USA' – that brought to light by Vicki Goldberg (again) in her article 'An Eye for Ageless Beauty' (*New York Times Magazine*, January 19, 1986) which in/forms us that 'The Photographs of Laura Gilpin capture the enduring nature of the American Southwest'. For 'England' the steps of the 'gone-world' features of dominant televisual *cartovictory* picturing are traceable in *Coronation Street – Crossroads – EastEnders* (with the Channel Four serial *Brookside* providing a different *class* range). See Dorothy Hobson *Crossroads* (London, Methuen, 1982); Richard Dyer and others *Coronation Street* (London, BFI, 1983); and – especially – David Morley *Family Viewing* (London, Comedia, 1986).

41 For a different 'postcard' see Carol Schloss 'Algeria, conquered by Postcard' (*New York Times Book Review*, January 11, 1987: 24, especially last paragraph) reviewing Malek Alloula *The Colonial Harem* (Minneapolis, University of Minnesota Press, 1986).

42 One recent phenomenon – the version of 'Canada' being a major theme in my chapter mentioned in n. 2 above – is the series *A Day in the Life of. . . .* These are books of photographs taken on one day in one territory by different photographers. Thus far (with dates of publication) have appeared: 'Australia' (1981); 'Hawaii' (1983); 'Canada' (1984); 'Japan' (1985); 'America' (i.e. the USA) (1986) – the latter is reviewed by Alan Trachtenberg 'If it's Noon, it must be Phoenix' (*New York Times Book Review*, January 25,1987: 13–14); whilst the Canadian Broadcasting Company made a film about the making of the 'Canada' volume (broadcast on Canada Day – July 1 – 1985, 8:00 pm EDST).

43 Centre for Contemporary Cultural Studies (London, Hutchinson, 1983).

44 Op. cit. n. 25 above. In case of a misreading (of 'innocence' here) see the preceding essay, in the same collection, 'The Indian and his (sic!) Image'.

45 *New York Times Magazine*, July 12, 1987: 44 (in the 'About Men' series).

46 The silence (and silencing of 'the topic') around such issues is far from uncommon.

47 See the work of Jo Spence, cited in my 'In/formation' n. 1 and n. 4 above.

48 For discussions of this see Roger Simon, Magda Lewis and Donald Dippo op. cit., n. 5 above.

49 Valerie Walkerdine 'Video replay'in J. Donald (ed.) *Formations of Fantasy* (London, Boston, Routledge & Kegan Paul, 1986).

50 I would like to dedicate this article to the memory of my father, Stanley George Corrigan (1911–86) who loved walking in the country. I miss him a lot.